The Book of the
A1 and A2
PACIFICS

By Peter Coster

Irwell Press

ISBN 10-1-903266-84-X
ISBN 13 978-1-903266-84-7

First published in the United Kingdom in 2007
by Irwell Press Limited, 59A, High Street, Clophill,
Bedfordshire MK45 4BE
Printed by Newton Printing, London

The rather forbidding front view of 60131 OSPREY. The appearance of smoke deflectors varied somewhat, possibly due to the holding brackets working loose or being bent, or not having been correctly mounted in the first place. OSPREY has a rather asymmetrical look even allowing for parallax. That, coupled with the somewhat vandalised appearance of the electric lighting (perhaps it was under repair) gives the impression of the A1 having fallen on hard times during early diesel days. Even Neville Hill shed has by now been reduced to 55H.

PREAMBLE

In this book dealing with the principal steam express locomotives of the LNER and its nationalised successor, we consider the Pacifics that followed those of Sir Nigel Gresley, finishing with the last, and perhaps by post-war railway operational standards, the most successful steam design, the A1 Pacific of Arthur Peppercorn. The A1 was introduced not merely in the eleventh hour of the old 'Big Four', but almost in the last five minutes of that hour. In the mêlée of nationalisation, the new Railway Executive's mechanical engineering team, determined to create a new railway with the new standard locomotives, turned its back on the most successful large passenger designs. These were Gresley's A4 and Sir William's magnificent 'Duchess' Pacific, joined by Peppercorn's A1. The sequence of events that led to the A1 actually started with Gresley's Mikado of 1934, and it was the need to resolve the problems of these magnificent but flawed locomotives that led to the emergence firstly of the Pacifics of Edward Thompson, then secondly those of Arthur Peppercorn. With the relatively abrupt abandonment of steam in favour of diesel and electric traction, the working life of all post-war designs was truncated, and the engines' working life became shorter with the later designs.

Insofar as the last design is concerned, the Peppercorn A1, an outstandingly good, reliable and economical locomotive that bore the major part of ex-LNER express mileage in the post-war years of steam traction, the history is even shorter. There is not so much to say about a locomotive that performed its daily tasks with almost complete satisfaction but with relatively little spectacle. I have spent some while in the narrative examining the deficiency in Edward Thompson and Arthur Peppercorn's Pacifics – the poor riding that could be encountered. These things are relative, and particularly in the case of the A1, once the measures described later had been taken, the riding was no longer a difficulty.

The A1s were withdrawn having worked for less than half their natural lives, not because they had become inefficient, unreliable or costly in manpower and materials, but simply because they were merely steam engines. Dead money maybe, but in the certainty that dieselisation would cost far more than had been estimated, a graduated approach would have made more sense than putting underpowered or untried machines on the express services, replacing the best of BR's steam fleet rather than its worst. I remember my considerable anger and sadness at hearing of the withdrawal of FLAMBOYANT in the cull of Pacifics in December 1962, soon after it had been working regularly to Kings Cross, well cleaned and reliable. Like many others, I had realised the value of the roller bearing A1s, and their superiority as operating units, and this was an appalling waste. With hindsight I can see how BR missed a wonderful opportunity to invest in equipping more of the locomotives with roller bearings and so reducing the number of expensive failures on the road through overheating.

As mentioned before, to those brought up in the Second World War, with only the glories of the pre-war railways to mull over, the supremacy rested with Gresley's A4s. Yet when we watched the trains go by, the élite streamlined Pacifics rarely looked the part. It was hard to relate the neglected and run-down Gresley Pacifics with the great days and beautiful trains of pre-war years. But then new locomotives came from Doncaster and Darlington to claim our attention, and we could at least enjoy the sight of clean apple green locomotives again. After the Thompson Pacifics of the mid-1940s came more new locomotives, now more presentable, without names and with that businesslike little double chimney. Rumours assailed the youth of the school, for 'train-spotting' was de rigueur in my youth as are computer games now. There were tales of the LNER's plans to buy 32 main-line diesels, rumours of turbine locomotives powered by pulverised coal, and then there were the tales of the new A1s, which would sweep the Gresley Pacifics off the main line. When they appeared, in apple green, there was relief at the sight of handsome, capable Pacifics taking their place in the fleet. Unnamed locomotives were an oddity, as was the relative silence of their progress, and they created an impression of effortless power and speed. We took the stovepipe double chimney as sure proof that here was a Rolls and not a Ford.

All of this was a long while ago, and the railways have moved on since then, almost unrecognisably so. To describe the emergence of the A1 it is necessary to retreat back to 1934, and it is instructive to look at events of the time and their consequences from a general railway management viewpoint. This book is also an opportunity to show off some very fine photographs, as well as to explain and examine some of the things that happened long ago. Of course it no longer matters, for steam died as mainstream traction in the middle 1960s. We all have the benefit of hindsight now. It is, however, an opportunity to go back to a time when engineering judgement was learnt and practised and not defined by a set of rules, when mistakes were made or ingenuity rewarded without the threat of legal risk or sanction. We have some preserved examples of the magnificence of express steam, thanks to the National Railway Museum and the hard work of teams of dedicated enthusiasts, but it is no thanks to British Railways that the ultimate object of this book, the Peppercorn A1 Pacific, is unrepresented in preservation. Despite its excellent record of service, the class of 49 locomotives was swept away on the basis of a hurried and over-optimistic scheme based on a consultant's prejudice and pious hopes in favour of the new traction. Eventually of course, the change of traction succeeded, speeds were raised, and the railway moved on, but only after enormous sums of money had been spent. If only… However, when the A1 Project comes to fruition, we will see in 'Tornado' the recreation of one of our finest steam express designs, and Arthur Peppercorn's A1 will take its place amongst the fleet of preserved and famous locomotives.

As in the two previous books, I must acknowledge the invaluable assistance of those who were lucky enough to work at close quarters with the locomotives described in this book. Peter Townend and Malcolm Crawley both worked on and with the locomotives under construction, repair, and in service in a number of posts, and their recollections and advice are an essential part of the book. Peter Howe of the Darlington Dynamometer Car's Locomotive Testing Team has provided details of the 1955 braking trials, and the reports of the team have been used to describe earlier tests. The late J F (Freddie) Harrison patiently answered my many queries some years ago, as did M B Thomas at Liverpool Street even further into the past. My good friends George Carpenter and Dr.Geoffrey Hughes, together with Andy Robson, who worked on the A1s for many years, have provided advice and reminiscences. Canon Brian Bailey, John F Aylard and other good folk have allowed me to use their photographic work. It would not be possible to write such an account at this late stage without acknowledging the volume of information that exists already, especially in the RCTS LNER Locomotive Survey and the Gresley Observer. Many have written about these engines, but apart from those already mentioned, I acknowledge principally the late W B Yeadon whose remarkable and indispensable records have thrown light upon many a mystery in the ex-LNER locomotive world, eminent and knowledgeable enthusiasts Eric Neve and Ken Hoole, and also the monthly writings of C J Allen and O S Nock.

Peter J Coster
Pendoggett
Cornwall

The second Mikado, LNER No.2002 EARL MARISCHAL, stands in Ferryhill yard on May 26th 1936. The second P2 had piston valves, and the soft exhaust necessitated a second pair of smoke deflectors. In fact it might be argued that the first pair were not true deflectors, being simply extensions of the smokebox cladding. There is no doubt that No.2002 was a commanding sight, well shown in this view, and that her performance was as awesome as her appearance. No doubt when repairs were required, the removal of that great reversing rod was an equally awesome task! The tender is A3 non-corridor tender No.5575, which is fitted with tablet exchanging apparatus. (R J Buckley, Initial Photographics)

GENESIS

The reason for starting the history of the Thompson Pacifics with Gresley's Mikados is quite simple. Whilst there were many standard features common to all, it was the rebuilding of the Mikados which was the genesis of the four variations on the general theme initiated by Edward Thompson. The designs of the Mikados and their derivatives were separated by just under ten critical years during which there was a world war that changed the railway industry irrevocably in many crucial areas. Nevertheless, it was by their rebuilding that design started to move away from some of Gresley's firmly held principles, so as to cope better with wartime and post-war conditions.

The story of the Mikados is intriguing, despite its familiarity, and the controversy that arose with their rebuilding was quite probably the best known and most frequently discussed in the steam era. It is a complex story with a great deal of known information and a great less certain, plus speculation and exaggeration. It is perhaps that lack of clarity and the conflicting emotions and opinions that continues to fascinate railway enthusiasts and historians. Many engineers both eminent and experienced have cast their vote for or against the rebuilding, but it happened some 60 summers ago, and it has long ceased to matter beyond the world of steam traction history. In particular the

story of COCK O'THE NORTH is followed in detail, since it was one of only two large steam engines in Britain to be equipped with poppet valves. Nearly two decades later the DUKE OF GLOUCESTER became the second, curiously with a Doncaster man, J F Harrison, leading the design. COCK O'THE NORTH was also for many years the only large LNER locomotive to be sent for testing at a Testing Station, until in 1953 under BR auspices V2 No.60845 was sent to Swindon's Test Plant. More might be said about that but not here. Also, the story certainly bears looking at from the general railway management viewpoint.

The situation in Scotland was slightly unusual. One of the difficulties in this respect is that Scotland did not have a counterpart to Ken Hoole in the north-east or Eric Neve in the south, and we have a far less complete picture of locomotive operation as a result. Therefore while I have described the situation, I have had to make assumptions that may or may not be correct, and the description is not so completely accurate as I would have liked.

The story started with a request from the Scottish Area in 1931 for a more powerful locomotive to haul the 'Aberdonian' sleeping car service between Edinburgh and Aberdeen. In order to understand why, it is necessary to appreciate the position at the time. The NER had its own motive power establishment in Edinburgh prior to the

1922 Grouping, and as a result of that Act the NER and NBR amalgamated their resources. Until then, the NER had worked most of the traffic between Newcastle and Edinburgh, the NBR men only knowing the route as far as Berwick-on-Tweed. The Reid Atlantics were the principal express locomotives of the NBR, and they were largely deployed on the services to Carlisle and Aberdeen, also Perth and Glasgow. The increasing trainloads outstripped the haulage capacity of the Atlantics, and double heading was far more common in the 1920s. The C10s were allowed 345 tons, and the newer C11s with larger cylinders, 370 tons. They were strong locomotives, free steaming, and popular with the crews, but with two coupled axles there were limits on what they could haul over a difficult road.

The arrival of the five Gresley A1s at Haymarket from the North British Loco. Co. in 1924, Nos.2563-2567 actually did not alter the situation so much as one might think. The A1s did not work the route to Aberdeen, and they were used only on services to Newcastle and Glasgow at first. In 1927 WILLIAM WHITELAW worked a test train from Edinburgh to Carlisle and back. It was unsuccessful for a number of reasons, but in 1928 the run was repeated successfully with SHOTOVER, an A3. Three new A3s went to Carlisle Canal in 1928-29.

In 1928 the opportunity was taken to conduct clearance trials from Edinburgh to Kinnaber Junction with

The official record of No.2393.

No.2393 at New England.

HARVESTER, on loan from Gateshead for the 'Non-stop'. Presumably the Pacifics were allowed to work to Dundee, but it was a short if difficult 60 mile trip. The works on both the NBR and the LMSR route from Kinnaber into Aberdeen were not completed until 1930, by which time Haymarket had received three new A3s, Nos.2795-2797. They displaced three A1s from Haymarket to Dundee Tay Bridge, Nos.2565-2567 in 1930. The A3s appeared to spend much of their time working south, and two worked on the 'Non-stop' with distinction.

Ferryhill at Aberdeen was an ex-Caledonian LMSR shed with limited facilities, and Tay Bridge worked the route with Haymarket. Earlier the Ferryhill turntable was inadequate for the Caledonian 4-6-0s, which had to be split from the tender to turn, but at some time before 1930 a 70ft version must have replaced it. The important point was that the haulage capacity of the 180 psi A1s was 430 tons, later reduced to 400, only one coach more than the Atlantics. The A3s were allowed to take 480 tons north, but with the shorter but harder gradients going south, only 420 tons was allowed. Meanwhile the use of sleeping cars was extended to third class passengers in the winter 1928 timetable. This increased trainloads considerably, since sleeping cars were heavy vehicles. Services also carried enormously greater quantities of luggage, parcels and mails than today.

In the early 1930s the Aberdeen service was the LNER's route to Scotland and the Highlands, and was a

matter of prestige to the company. Also, this was a world in which the armed services were far more numerous and widely spread, and servicemen were normally moved by special trains. Even now, over seventy years later, the civilised if slower journey to Britain's oil capital still commands influential support. In the 1930s landed and wealthy families together with the Scottish aristocracy were regular patrons, people who could make their views known at Board level. The volume of holiday traffic was probably more significant to the local organisation than to the LNER as a company. It is curious to read so long afterwards of quite frenetic actions by railway companies to solicit traffic farther and farther into each neighbour's 'territory', or to safeguard what had been gained. Quite considerable sums of capital and revenue were expended on traffic which, on the face of it, might have been prestigious but in fact was often unremunerative, alarmingly so in more than a few cases.

The normal service from the south was the 'Aberdonian' sleeping car service, rather than the 'Flying Scotsman' or some similar day service that required an unnecessarily early start, or was very lengthy and wearying. Therefore the operation of the train was regarded as particularly important. It was a large train, and often exceeded the haulage allowance for the A1 or even the A3s starting south from Aberdeen. In summer it exceeded that loading for much of the period, and by a considerable amount. Not only did it

convey a rake of sleeping cars, first and third class, but it also conveyed catering vehicles for part of the journey, and a number of vans, for mail, parcels as well the cross that the railway companies bore stoically, that constant cause for complaint in later years, registered luggage. Patronage was growing, and in the Scottish Area, it was one of the principal services.

The Aberdeen road south to Edinburgh was difficult. The down road was easier in that although of course the line climbed to the same summits, it did so over a longer distance with easier gradients, and the allowed loading was heavier. The LMSR's old Caledonian route was used as far as Kinnaber Junction, a few miles north of Montrose, where the North British main line continued separately to Edinburgh. From the platform ends there was a climb of over seven miles up to Cove Bay on the coastal cliffs south of Aberdeen, a climb varying between, principally, 1 in 102-164. After six miles of broken grade, there was a descent into Stonehaven followed immediately by another four miles or so of climbing, largely 1 in 102, to Carmont, followed by two easier miles to the summit at Drumlithie.

The third climb started from Montrose, shorter at four miles, but the sharpest of the three so far with a curving mile and a half of 1 in 88½ from Montrose up to Usan signalbox. Montrose was an important call, serving a number of larger and important communities, and with the station perched on the bank of the Esk basin, there was no possibility of taking a run at the bank. The route over the Esk viaduct to Usan was and still is single and, while that did not affect the gradient it reduced the line capacity and made delay more likely for a service that was struggling or out of path. Many services had to slow down for the single line token working. In the difficult Dundee- Edinburgh section, the climb to Lochmuir was hard going, but the last climb of particular note was the sharp rise for nearly two miles at 1 in 70 from Inverkeithing to the Forth Bridge. Apart from these gradients, and the straight and level section along the banks of the Tay from Arbroath to Dundee, the going was generally heavily curved, sharply undulated, and liberally infested with speed restrictions for curvature and colliery workings. No doubt local difficulties further tried the officials. While a driver with an A3 in good condition might have accepted a heavier load on a good dry evening, it was less wise with a wet rail and winds on the exposed upper parts of the climbs. In those days the principal stations had a pilot engine around for much of the day, so banking assistance was available if required. At Montrose for example the small sub-shed housed a handful of elderly engines for the services to Brechin and Inverbervie, etc.

When the Locomotive and Traffic Committee met in January 1932 to discuss the 1932 Locomotive Building Programme, the draft contained five A3s for an unspecified purpose. These were deleted and provision was made for a single P2. There had been no Building Programme for 1931 nor was there one for 1933, but in the 1934 Programme four A3s were reinstated together with another five replacements for the Raven Pacifics, together with another five P2s.

DESIGN and DEVELOPMENT

Once remitted to deal with the problem, Gresley lost no time in preparing outline plans. Perhaps, informally, he had been advised in advance. He had, after all, ten years earlier mated an A1 boiler with a four coupled chassis to produce the P1 Mikado. The P1 was unfortunately way ahead of current freight operation. Its greater power was used on longer trains but the capacity of the main line, its loops and refuges, was inadequate. The 100 wagon trains were, frankly, more trouble than they were worth. One might think that it was a pity that the P1 was not used to raise the speed of existing freight loads, but I am equally sure that the contemporary rolling stock would not have stood up to the increased speeds. Axleboxes were tallow or grease lubricated in general, with oil axleboxes starting to become more common. Braking would have also been a problem. The realisation that freight trains required far better braking performance was a long way off, and hence fitted freight vehicles were not so plentiful in those days.

Now Gresley proposed to mate the A3 boiler with a four axle 6ft 2ins chassis. The enormous increase in adhesive weight thereby allowed an large increase in tractive effort – drawbar pull – that could used to haul heavier trains, or to increase the running speeds uphill of existing trainloads. As a member of the Technical Committee of the International Union of Railways (UIC), he was conversant with Continental practice and the general policy of building Mikados for faster mixed traffic duties. He would also have been aware of the work of André Chapelon in rebuilding and transforming the P-O Pacifics. The result was likely to be a very potent locomotive. There is not the slightest evidence to support the hypothesis, but I wonder whether Gresley saw that his P2 could be the forerunner of a more numerous class.

It seems inconceivable to me that the possibility of using a successful Mikado had not occurred to him. It would have been a valuable addition to the LNER locomotive fleet, ideal power for the heavy lower speed overnight services. He was also looking at the possibilities for an improved version of the K3, a debate that culminated in the V2 2-6-2 of 1936, but there is no doubt that the P2 was a far larger machine with roundly 80 tons adhesive weight.

Gresley had a number of considerations at the time, and one can see in the successive sketches how his concerns for smoke deflection, a larger grate, and such devices as the ACFI feed water heater and pump intended to improve efficiency, all came into consideration. The basic design was the tried and tested three cylinder drive on to the second coupled axle, allied to the

No.2394 with an up freight at Ganwick in the 1930s.

9

The first Mikado, COCK O'THE NORTH cruises into London with an express, past the site of the Vauxhall Sidings at Oakleigh Park. Considering the amount of new equipment on the locomotive, it is a remarkably clean and aesthetically pleasing locomotive.

A3 boiler, using the 2:1 conjugated valve gear. With the larger grate, the new boiler was given Diagram No.106. With four axles, Gresley could increase the cylinder diameter to 21 ins, with a rated tractive effort of 43,462 lbs, without jeopardising adhesion.

Experiments with an A1 and an A3 were in hand to assess the value of the ACFI pump and feed water heating equipment, and A3s CORONACH and HUMORIST were fitted with a variety of chimneys and smokebox shapes to improve smoke deflection. The W1 was also involved in the investigation with her unique smokebox front and deflectors. As the design hardened there were some hesitations and changes of direction: the cab was altered, first with a back sloping front and then with an angled vee-shape in plan similar to the shape used on the PLM railway in France. The larger grate became part of the design, together with the Kylchap double blastpipe and chimney. It was decided to alter the dome to a banjo shaped steam collector, also used on the last batch of A3s in 1934. It was also decided to incorporate an ACFI heater and pump by mid-1933, and shortly after the decision was made to use poppet valves. The poppet valves were rotary cam valves, not oscillating cam. A variety of fronts were tried with raked and vertical smoke deflectors, but wind tunnel testing of the smoke deflection arrangement pointed to the superiority of the vertical type. The exhaust was a fundamental part of the astonishing conversions in France by M Chapelon,

but had not been used in Britain before.

A novel development was the welded construction of the tender superstructure, carried out by MetroVick, which saved 2½ tons by comparison with the riveted tender and no less than 5 tons compared with the streamlined version. The MetroVick contract had to be paid for from revenue, but I would imagine not by Gresley but from the budget of A P Ross, the Chief Stores Superintendent. That expenditure could have been avoided by constructing the tender in-house, despite the economy in dead weight, but the idea no doubt went the way of many other good ideas for that reason. It was a great pity that the building cost of No.2001 was not credited with the saving due to out-sourcing the superstructure, as would have happened later.

The various stages of the design were set out in the RCTS 'Locomotives of the LNER' part 6B. The designs of the poppet valve gear and blastpipe were dealt with by the British office of Lentz Patents Ltd, now renamed the Associated Locomotive Equipment Co. (ALE). They were the agents for the design and manufacture of the Kylchap equipment as well as the Lentz poppet valve system. Gresley was keen to explore the benefits of poppet valves, and a number of successful rebuildings from 1925 onwards had encouraged him to equip 48 of the 76 D49 4-4-0s with Lentz rotary cam poppet valves. This had caused him to establish contacts with both ALE and Paxmans at

Colchester, through whom in 1927 he had met André Chapelon, Locomotive Development Engineer of the Paris-Orléans Railway working under the CME Maurice Lacoin. Bulleid had read a paper on the virtues of poppet valves to the Institution of Locomotive Engineers a year or so earlier. Gresley had wisely kept the experimental poppet valve conversions at depots where he could be confident that they would be properly maintained.

COCK O'THE NORTH was Gresley's largest locomotive to be equipped with poppet valves, and she was the first large engine in Britain to feature them. Unfortunately there was no great volume of experience on the LNER beyond the experimental rebuilding and the successful operation of the D49s, and even less elsewhere, to inform the design. The reasoning for using poppet valves was firstly that with a large diameter and a relatively short travel, the valve opened and closed much more quickly than a piston valve, and with a large opening gave less resistance to the passage of steam. Secondly, there was the promise of being able to control admission and exhaust independently, to maximise expansion in the cylinder. Another advantage was that the valves could be controlled while coasting so that admission was closed but exhaust remained open, with minimal back pressure, and the valve chests and cylinders were not cooled with air drawn in through the anti-vacuum valve. With piston valves the events are of course linked. Thirdly, there was the hope that the maintenance and setting of steam locomotive valves would begin to move into the automotive world with its standards of accuracy, relative cleanliness, and reliability. Also there is no doubt that the operation required less power than the relatively heavier components of Walschaerts valve gear with the 2:1 conjugated valve operation for the middle cylinder.

The drive for the valves came off the outside return cranks on the driving axle via two small gearboxes and a rotating shaft. The valves for the middle cylinder were operated by the outside drives. The 8 ins admission and 9 ins exhaust valves were operated by cross shafts, carrying scroll cams for each cylinder. The cut-off was altered by the translation of the cross shafts, moving the scroll cams to the required profile that adjusted the opening and closing to admission and exhaust. The design called for some very complex positioning of steam and exhaust passages, and it was decided to cast the cylinders and valve chambers for the three cylinders at Gorton Works as one massive 'monobloc' casting. No doubt it would later have been regarded later at general overhaul as something of a liability when worn, but as a demonstration of the foundryman's skill, it was superb. Gresley had evolved his famous 2:1

conjugated gear in 1918 in order to use three cylinders using concentrated drive on the middle axle. A decade or so later the successful use of poppet valves on smaller locomotives offered the promise of replacing the conjugated gear, which is why COCK O' THE NORTH was an important project in LNER locomotive development. However, the unfortunate consequence of the poppet valve design used was that the clearance volumes were substantially increased, and those of the middle cylinder were increased even more than the outside cylinders. Experienced engineers, on learning this, were not optimistic as to the engine's water and coal consumption.

No.2001 was named after a famous ancestor of the Duke of Gordon, and was completed at Doncaster on May 22nd 1934. It was massive, powerful, and bore the hallmark of Gresley's careful attention to the appearance of his locomotives. The name was lifted from the NBR Atlantic, No.9903, and was replaced by ABERDONIAN. To the LNER's small, new Publicity Office, it was manna from Heaven. André Chapelon, inspecting the Mikado at Vitry, was impressed by his friend's locomotive, and of the evident quality of workmanship that had been put into its construction. The Mikado was indeed a superb example of Doncaster's

workmanship, and while one might doubt the judgement that led to its creation, there was no doubt amongst those who saw COCK O' THE NORTH entering service.

TESTING and OPERATIONAL EXPERIENCE
The details of the development of the Mikados can be gathered from Part 6B of the RCTS LNER Locomotive Survey, and it is the troubles that arose from their work in service that led ultimately to their rebuilding. Gresley had produced a fine, handsome locomotive. While initially it seemed to be the answer to Scotland's problems, what might have been thought at first to be teething troubles began to have a more permanent look about them. As it was, it was not the answer to the haulage problems over a short, heavily curved and graded route where the operators were disinclined to make good use of the locomotives. The V2 2-6-2 emerged two years later and proved to be a far better answer despite having a lesser haulage capacity. That such a large locomotive could be designed and built without a careful study of the routes and diagrams proposed and a close consultation with the Area's engineers says a great deal about communications in the LNER and the culture of the

Locomotive exhibitions were very much a thing of the 1930s – when we had locomotives, that is – and here we see that held at Ilford on June 2nd 1934. Small boys of all ages are everywhere, even one on COCK O'THE NORTH. Where is the zealous official that would chase him off, and the perennial teenage groan, where are the girls? (H N James)

EARL MARISCHAL was a huge machine in appearance, especially with the second pair of deflectors, and the driver had to be quick with the brake as he backed on to the turntable at Ferryhill. Immortality in the messroom beckoned to those who were not quick enough! Derby turntable had a 'Knight's Road', where a Driver Knight, seeking to stable his engine in the dark, found that the road off wasn't quite where he insisted it should be!

1930s. The LNER seemed to work on the basis that Gresley decided what was necessary to meet the operators' requirements: if he did in fact discuss solutions there is little evidence of it. As most of his designs were successful, one can understand why.

The locomotive first went to Doncaster shed for running-in, and then in early June 1934 to Scotland where it was exhibited. On June 4th, she worked a demonstration train of 12 coaches to Aberdeen, returning the following day. No other work appears to have been done before it went south for testing, going to Kings Cross. It was worked to Peterborough and back with Driver Peachey in charge on a semi-fast with fairly heavy loads. Then came the first trial run on June 19th 1934 from Kings Cross to Barkston triangle, with 649 tons including the dynamometer car, giving the opportunity to see what No.2001 could do. Kings Cross top link driver Peachey was again in charge, and having become familiar with the P2, gave a very impressive performance. The departure from Kings Cross with an 18 coach train must have been astonishing, as No.2001 sailed through Finsbury Park in 6mins 6secs, unusual for an express of moderate weight, and unheard of with an 18 coach load. She continued to Peterborough North in an average time, running easily up to a maximum of 70 mph on the downhill and level sections, and flattening most of the rising gradients.

After a stop at Peterborough, No.2001 was given her head on Stoke Bank. The details are given in Appendix H. The cut-off was 15% at Essendine, lengthened to 20, 25 and finally 30% for the last four miles or so. Despite the load, 60mph was maintained, falling to 56.5mph at the summit. The drawbar pull measured rose from 4.1 tons to 6.1 at Corby Glen before falling slightly to 5.7 tons. The power measured at the drawbar rose with the cut-off to just over 2000 DBHP at the top of the 1 in 200 before Corby, and the final three miles were at 1920-35 DBHP apart from a transitory drop at MP.99. I am sure that the maximum IHP, briefly, was 2,500HP. It was a remarkable run considering the size of the load and the restrained approach to the speed before the start of harder climbing. The arrival of the A4 just over a year later brought a marginally more powerful locomotive into the field. While a single blast engine would have had a struggle, the double Kylchap quartet were capable of outrunning the Mikados with their greater speed. However as a demonstration of brute tractive power, this run was unique. Afterwards the P2 was handled by Bill Sparshatt, a notably hard runner, when speeds of 83 mph were noted. Interestingly, at no time in the early days at Kings Cross did anyone draw attention to the high coal consumption of COCK O' THE NORTH. With the novelty of a 50sq.ft.grate and a double Kylchap, the

Mikado would have left an enduring impression on the firemen to such as Bill Sparshatt!

The engine was returned to Doncaster for a series of dynamometer tests described in some detail in the RCTS LNER Locomotive Survey. The first test was between Doncaster and Grantham on June 27th returning to Doncaster, hauling 637 tons. It was uneventful apart from a brief burst of over 2000 EDBHP approaching Barkston. The crew were Driver F Elms and Fireman Walker. The train was stopped leaving Doncaster at Frenchgates signalbox and at Barnby Moor, and there was a 20 mph Temporary Speed Restriction (TSR) after Claypole. The down journey to Doncaster was more variable. Starting out of Grantham, the boiler pressure was no more than 170 psi and the steam temperature low at 365°F, and it was not before Newark that full boiler pressure was reached. The train was stopped at Muskham and No.2001 slipped on starting. Fireman Walker kept the pressure and temperature up from there to Doncaster. However, the boiler pressure had varied considerably which, in the light of post-war experience with Kylchap exhausts, seems curious.

The following week the tests extended to Kings Cross, now with an indicator shelter to enable cylinder pressures to be indicated. The train was the 11.04 from Doncaster, which usually weighed 420 tons. On the next test on July 2nd, the boiler pressure was low at the start but picked up by Rossington where the cut-off was 12%. At Bawtry the ACFI pump failed. After a 20 mph TSR south of Retford, the long climb to Markham caused the boiler pressure to drop to 180psi, although the temperature was much better. A cut-off of 12½% was enough for 75mph at Crow Park, but the TSR at Claypole was still in force. On the recovery to Stoke the pressure fell to 150 before recovering to 170-175psi at 20% cut-off. The minimum at Stoke was unremarkable, but the top speed down the bank was, 87½mph at Essendine on 12½% cut-off. After Peterborough the pressure varied from 180 to 210 psi, but the cut-off was generally 12½%, 15% on Abbotts Ripton bank, and 20% on the final few miles of Stevenage bank. The steaming of COCK O'THE NORTH was still inconsistent, and the fireman was clearly having trouble reaching and maintaining full pressure. At no time did the locomotive display the freedom in steaming that one saw in the Pacifics, and as soon as the regulator was partially closed for the downhill sections, the pressure dropped. As with all of Gresley's designs, he had endowed them with a fine turn of speed, but on hearing of the Mikado's descent of Stoke bank, he gave orders for the speed to be restrained.

The Kylchap exhaust was designed and patented by André Chapelon, as a result of his study of the various systems used to create higher smokebox vacuum and better draughting. A description of the design is given in Appendix C. One might observe that since time immemorial in steam traction design, a means of accelerating and intensifying the rate of combustion had been an imperative. As a result there were a plethora of devices designed to improve the efficacy of the exhaust steam flow in enhancing draughting. One senior engineer of my acquaintance felt sure that more hot air had been expended over exhaust systems rather than through them. Chapelon had studied many of them before selecting the optimum combination as he saw it. Two forms were designed, the 1K/1C or 1K/T, applicable to single or double blast, using the Bernouilli principles also applied in injector design. The 1K/1C assembly that was used on No.2001 consisted of a normal blastpipe with a separate interchangeable top, fitted at right angles with shaped and hardened tapered steel inserts, also interchangeable, known as vee-bars or barrettes.

On July 4th No.2001 was still fitted with a 5³/₁₆in exhaust top with 'No.3' barrettes (see Appendix B). The top was changed to 5½in retaining the No.3 barrette, but the following day's test was stopped at Kings Cross due to the overheating of the little end. There must have been continued steaming problems on the 5th, since the smaller No.1 set was fitted before testing resumed on July 10th. On July 11th a similar test run was made but again the steaming gave cause for concern. As soon as the regulator was eased the pressure fell, and the steam temperature was often low. Steaming problems persisted even when the engine was working hard, and from July 13th to the 19th, four combinations of exhaust top and barrettes were tested. They were respectively 5½in and No.1, 5¾in and no barrettes, 5¾in and No 3 restored, 5¾in and No 3. In the first three tests the intermediate petticoat was removed as well. The first and third combination was considered to be adequate for the Southern Area, and the fourth for the Scottish area.

COCK O'THE NORTH was sent to Scotland with the last combination on July 30th, and on August 1st and 2nd worked a huge 586 ton train to Aberdeen and back. That would have impressed. However, she returned to Doncaster on August 23rd for attention. Gresley had been concerned that the exhaust cam was not closing soon enough, giving insufficient compression, and new cams were to be fitted. On examination the cam and roller surfaces had become damaged with grooving, pitting and local flat spots, affecting the valve events as a result. After consultation it was decided to replace the continuously varying cams with stepped cams. No.2001 went back into traffic with a new set of new exhaust cams and repaired continuous cams. Within a fortnight she was back at Doncaster for a new piston. The stepped cams were fitted at the beginning of November before the locomotive was sent to Vitry Testing Station in France.

COCK O'THE NORTH had, as foreseen by those in the know, quickly

LORD PRESIDENT, magnificently clean, on shed – Tay Bridge, probably, in the period 1936-39. Of further interest is one of the O4s sent north to haul the Fife coal traffic, No.6582 of Dundee on the adjacent road.

The single blast Mikado, THANE OF FIFE, on the Haymarket turntable, turned and about to move off. (Transport Treasury)

established a reputation in Scotland for very heavy coal consumption, and no doubt in response to complaints from the Scottish Area, a senior member of the Drawing Office, E (Teddy) Windle was despatched from Doncaster. A test run was made on October 1st to Dundee and back, which ended prematurely at Dalmeny with an empty tender due mainly to a miscalculation as to the likely consumption of the Mikado, although the driver, despite the presence of an inspector, was known to be heavy handed. The test was repeated four days later with a heavy load in the 450-550tons range. The consumption was 103.75 lbs/mile, corrected for the coal used for non-traffic purposes, was an incredible 92lbs per mile. The engine had 6 ins blastpipe tops and No.0 barrettes at the time. Shortly after the engine returned to Doncaster. Chapelon and Gresley spoke on October 22nd, and in passing the latter mentioned that No.2001 was steaming adequately with 6 ins blastpipe tops and No.0 barrettes. Tests continued with the 6in tops, firstly with the No.0 set, and then with neither barrettes nor petticoats.

If Gresley's view has been accurately recorded, it has to be said that his view of the Mikados' coal consumption was distinctly optimistic. In a more deferential age, it would have been difficult for the Running Department representatives to speak frankly without risking their future prospects. Indeed one might wonder why Gresley was not drawn overmuch into the testing of No.2001, but at this time it has to be remembered that he was involved in the debate on accelerated passenger services. He was an important participant in those discussions, and was about to visit Maybach in connection with the

proposal to use a high-speed diesel unit on the East Coast main line. Then there was the need to consider the design of a large mixed traffic locomotive which emerged as the V2 2-6-2.

After modification to stepped cams, No.2001 operated from Doncaster for a week or so before travelling to Harwich and France. Gresley had arranged, probably through Chapelon, for the Mikado to be tested in France on the new OCEM locomotive testing establishment at Vitry-sur-Seine. Gresley had realised that a means of testing locomotives was vital to their design and development. The testing programme, the diary, and the results are set out in Appendix D. My copy of the report is now in old age, and I have therefore used the computer to copy it, making adjustments to the format as necessary. The written content has not been amended in any way but the tables of results have been omitted. The report must have been deeply disappointing not to say embarrassing to Gresley. On no less than nine occasions the locomotive ran hot, the exhaust beat was uneven, the poppet valves needed frequent attention, and the setting of the Kylchap was far from established. The engine had a worrying tendency to move laterally, but this seemed to be caused by a fault in the roller supports. On the whole the engine was the steadiest runner so far tested at Vitry. As the test runs to Orléans were trouble free, it confirmed advice from French engineers that the very robust foundations and lack of resilience in the test bank supports had caused overheating with French locomotives as well.

However each time the engine ran hot on the Plant, it had to be withdrawn from the test plant, towed to a nearby

depot, or in one case a more distant depot. After repairs, which were not necessarily straightforward, the locomotive was run-in and the process reversed, and if another engine was being tested, that had to be replaced. There was concern because during testing either there was excessive black smoke or the ejection of unburnt fuel, depending on the blastpipe top and barrettes used. The test runs on the main line produced useful information, but the engine's time in France had almost expired. Excellent figures were achieved for coal consumption and water evaporation, but only on one test, and moreover at something like a quarter of the engine's potential power output. As a result the testing programme previously arranged was largely ruined. Critically, the optimum setting for the exhaust had not been established during testing. The power outputs were often undistinguished, but on a 110 kph (68 mph) run at 35% cut-off, an average HP of 1910 was recorded. It was a rare glimpse of the engine's potential, although with full regulator and 35% one might expect something rather higher from a locomotive of such a size. Whether it was measured at the drawbar or calculated as the IHP is not stated. Bulleid, in retirement, was adamant that it was measured and the DBHP was 2,800, which would certainly be consistent with the working of the locomotive, but such an output was so far beyond the normal experience that the claim must be doubted. The decision to send No.2001 to France must have cost the LNER money, and it had received little by way of return. In September 1937 No.2001 entered Doncaster Works for overhaul, and as the poppet valves were replaced by conventional piston valves, presumably

Gorton's unique monobloc casting was scrapped.

The second Mikado, No.2002 EARL MARISCHAL, was completed at Doncaster in October 1934. Gresley had decided that the second locomotive should be the piston valve equivalent of COCK O'THE NORTH, and a sketch was produced that initially regressed to the first thoughts with a single chimney and no special front end shaping, before the double Kylchap was restored. The ACFI apparatus was omitted and a modified Diagram 94A boiler was used again. In fact the second engine was very much closer to the Pacifics from which the Mikados were developed. The

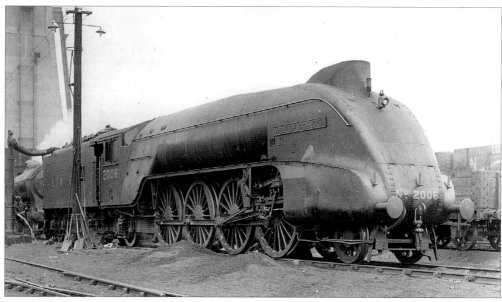

Haymarket shed, with WOLF OF BADENOCH taking water. The picture has a general air of dirt and untidiness that suggests to me that it might be during wartime.

new engine was allocated to Doncaster for running-in and testing. It was evident immediately that the exhaust was generally quieter and softer by comparison with No.2001, and smoke deflection was a problem unless the locomotive was working hard. This confirmed that the exhaust beats of COCK O'THE NORTH were more explosive due to the poppet valves. It was also evident that the steaming was quite unreliable, and that the blast was inadequate. The blastpipe top was $5^7/_8$in diameter, fitted with No.3 barrettes, but in January 1935 5¾ tops with No.3 barrettes were substituted. This reduced the net area by just over 2 sq in, but it was a better combination, sharpening the blast slightly, and the steaming was much improved. The P2 barrels were insulated with Alfol, a corrugated aluminium foil lagging that enabled the casing to be extended forward beyond the smokebox to form integral smoke deflectors. The difficulty with smoke deflection with EARL MARISCHAL was overcome after experiment at the wind tunnel of the City & Guilds College, by the addition of a second pair of smoke deflectors.

EXODUS

The two Mikados went to Scotland, and in 1936 four more were built and went to join them. By 1936 the A4 had been successfully introduced, and one of the best aspects of the design was the streamlined form that had been developed. Gresley applied the streamlined front casing to Nos.2003-2006, which solved completely any smoke deflection problems that remained. The first two engines were similarly converted. Of the four, one, No.2005 THANE OF FIFE, was built with a single chimney and fitted with a 6in blastpipe top. It gained the reputation of being the black sheep of the class, and in an attempt to improve

the steaming the locomotive was fitted with a jumper top blastpipe. The collar when lifted gave the equivalent of a 6¾in blastpipe. It was noticed that on starting, the exhaust beats of a P2, being heavier at long cut-offs, tended to lift the fire. In an attempt to give the driver some control over the smokebox vacuum, No.2004 MONS MEG was equipped with an exhaust bypass which took exhaust steam from the blastpipe base and, through a 5in pipe, exhausted through an additional orifice behind the double chimney. The device was operated by opening a plug valve. It was of course a source of constant trouble since the plug valve became jammed with carbonised lubricating oil, and a number of modifications were made. Drivers were reluctant to use the bypass since it detracted from the steaming when the locomotive was working hard. Bulleid suggested that the Vitry tests had shown the need for more firebox volume and a longer path from the firebed to the tubeplate. The last Mikado, WOLF OF BADENOCH, was fitted with a Diagram 108 boiler with a slightly different firebox extended to form a combustion chamber.

When the P2s were running normally, their coal consumption was reputedly heavier than it should have been, but there is no doubt that they could fulfil any operating requirements and haul anything hooked on behind the tender. C J Allen and O S Nock were the leading commentators on locomotive performance at the time, and although there is not a great deal of recorded information on Mikado performance, O S Nock rode on EARL MARISCHAL from Aberdeen to Dundee and COCK O THE NORTH from Dundee to Edinburgh. He recorded his experiences in an article, written for the 'Meccano Magazine' of the time. The engines had little trouble with 500 ton loads, and the steaming was fine while the

locomotive was being worked hard. It was noticeable that the top link Haymarket driver of No.2001 set the cut-off of the poppet valves and then drove on the regulator.

Footplate trips confirmed that the engine was not being worked unduly hard once the train was running at the speed the schedule demanded at the time, and on good track rode well enough. No doubt things were worse over the old NBR main line. There were persistent allegations about spreading the road, and although the road needed to be in less than robust health for that to happen, if it did, it was serious and potentially very expensive to correct. Gresley had left the P2s alone, but there was mounting evidence that some corrective modification was needed. One example of the chaos caused by a Mikado failure occurred when EARL MARISCHAL ran hot on a heavy up service at Montrose, having run only just over 40 miles from the start. The train eventually got under way with a NBR 0-6-0 assisted by the Inverbervie branch loco, an even older NBR 0-4-4 tank! Locomotive engineers were curiously reluctant to revisit designs to rectify mistakes: it was easier to let the Running department get on with things rather having to appeal to the Board for unspecified extra funds and explain why! Overheating was a constant problem, but the occasional fracture of the crank axle was clearly a far more serious matter, a symptom of a fundamental problem which required urgent attention. By the time that action was clearly necessary, war had been declared and constraints on the railways' freedom to deal with their own affairs had been imposed. Then came the death of Sir Nigel Gresley in April 1941.

60501 COCK O' THE NORTH pulls away from York with a motley collection of stock on July 6th 1957.

CHAPTER TWO
THE FIRST THOMPSON PACIFIC

REBUILDING

Sir Nigel Gresley's successor, Edward Thompson, was a man who had an aversion to some of his ideas, principally the 2:1 derived motion for the valves of the middle cylinder. With Gresley having declared his intention to continue during wartime to 70, Thompson might well have given up all hope of chief office. Now, contrary to all expectations, it was his. At a time when the armchair, pipe and slippers beckoned, he was appointed to head the CME department, struggling to keep going in a war of unprecedented fury.

It is to his credit that, despite approaching retirement, he threw himself into the fray. He changed direction radically, and concentrated on a much reduced range of designs as standard, rather than Gresley's more open approach. Gresley's engines were not designed for wartime conditions, and were consequently starved of the vital components to maintain them in good order. Thompson was determined to replace what he saw as a weakness, a view that was understandable in wartime, with the imperatives of the 2:1 gear now largely absent – regular and skilled maintenance together with essential components such as needle bearings. In wartime everything was used until it stopped, and repairs were minimal. Valve setting depended not only on the integrity of the gear itself, but also on the clearances present in the motion and axleboxes, and indeed possibly the state of the frames as well.

Although considerable progress was made, in some ways one wonders whether he was always aware of the wartime restrictions or content to abide by them. Quite where he expected all of the investment for some proposals to come from in wartime is difficult to imagine.

Thompson decided that the problems of the P2s should be addressed, but it rapidly emerged that rather than focussing on a solution to their shortcomings, rebuilding was intended. Moreover it was to be used as an opportunity to produce a new Pacific incorporating Thompson's ideas. The rebuilt W1 4-6-2-2 was sent to Scotland in 1942 for trials, to see whether a six-coupled locomotive with a similarly high tractive effort could replace the Mikados. By all accounts its work was quite satisfactory, opening the way to rebuilding the Mikados as Pacifics.

Certainly something needed to be done with the Mikados. Things could not continue as they were. Attempts were made by Teddy Windle and Robert Thom to persuade Thompson to replace the swing link pony truck with a truck with side spring control, but to no avail. At Edinburgh, Eric Trask tried hard to persuade Thompson not to rebuild, and raised such a clamour that Peppercorn was sent to restore order – but without success. In hindsight one can see that Thompson was probably right. A better pony truck would have provided a more positive guiding action, reducing but not eliminating the problems of the long fixed wheelbase. Some further modification of the latter would have been necessary to provide more lateral play. The Mikados had a limited radius of operation on the Edinburgh-Aberdeen-Perth-Glasgow routes, although Haymarket used theirs on Newcastle trains at times. Given the problems of running them on the above routes, together with the arrival of numbers of V2 2-6-2s, one would have thought it preferable to move them south where their greater haulage capacity would have been valuable, and a far better standard of repair prevailed than at Cowlairs. It would have surely been worth a trial.

So the first Thompson Pacific emerged in wartime, in January 1943. With stringent wartime restrictions, Thompson made use of as much existing material as possible. He was prepared to use divided drive in order to obtain room for the third set of valve gear and to use larger valves. The new Pacific design was achieved by removing one coupled axle, and replacing the pony truck with a bogie. Two options were considered, one with the bogie in the usual position beneath the outside cylinders, and one with the bogie moved forward of the outside cylinders. It was decided that the existing connecting rods could be reused, but the situation was not assisted by the comment, believed to be made by Robert Thom, that connecting rods should ideally be of equal length. It was a somewhat

2001 COCK O' THE NORTH after rebuilding. The locomotive is in wartime black livery with LNER reduced to NE on the welded tender superstructure. The date must fall between September 1944 and May 1946 when the engine was restored to apple green livery. The tablet exchanging apparatus was removed after 1949 when the class was transferred to England.

17

COCK O' THE NORTH, still with the old LNER number, immaculate in LNER apple green for the NBR Centenary exhibition at Waverley. She is seen here at Haymarket in June 1946.

academic observation that resonated with Edward Thompson. He accepted that the connecting rods should be of equal length, which ensured that valve events of the three cylinders – admission, cut-off and release – were as near identical as practically possible. Unfortunately, the Mikados, having a pony truck, had short connecting rods since the cylinders were just clear of the leading coupled wheels, driving on to the second coupled axles. Now used on a Pacific, still driving to the second (now middle) coupled axle, the position of the outside cylinders left no room for the rear bogie axle, and it had to be moved ahead by 2ft 5ins, giving the front end a peculiarly elongated shape. This was the option adopted; unfortunately, it must be said. Comparative dimensions of the different Pacific designs are given in Appendix E.

With different length rods the point of cut-off on the piston stroke varied slightly, depending on the difference in connecting rod length, and for example at top dead centre for each crank the piston and valve position would differ by a fraction of an inch. It is simple trigonometry. Fractions of an inch, in the world of valve setting, made a great deal of difference to running. However, experience would reveal that in the heat of battle in the Running Dept, in century-old running sheds, such academic considerations were less important. With three cylinders, equal length connecting rods and divided

drive, the middle cylinder was thrust well forward. Longer connecting rods, given the requirement for all three to be of the same length, would have allowed the bogie to be positioned normally, but would have made positioning the middle cylinder much worse.

This necessitated recalculation of the balancing on the coupled wheels. Although it left room for 10in piston valves, it meant that the layout of the steam passages was difficult to accommodate. In order to achieve a better live steam passage layout, the Diagram 106 boiler was shortened by just under 2ft, which gave the design an unusually long smokebox. No.2006 WOLF OF BADENOCH was built with a Diagram 108 boiler that included a larger firebox with a combustion chamber. The large smokebox was an advantage in that its greater volume cushioned the exhaust beats and reduced the entrainment of smaller coal particles when the engine was working hard. Ironically, the first rebuild was the single chimney THANE OF FIFE, and in the rebuilding she gained a double Kylchap exhaust, one similar to the pattern used on the A4s and not the P2s. Presumably the design service of ALE was no longer available in wartime, and interestingly, the new exhaust cross-sectional area was some 30% smaller than the Mikado Kylchaps. The rebuilds did not seem to be in any way incapacitated by this reduction and

indeed seemed to be more economical compared with the healthy appetites of the P2s. Thompson was well aware of the benefits of the Kylchap exhaust and used it on all of his Pacifics. The only other locomotives to be fitted with a double Kylchap without any special smoke deflectors were the W1 and A3 HUMORIST: small chimneyside deflectors were added in an attempt to cope with drifting exhaust. Similar deflectors, although longer, were added to THANE OF FIFE for the same reason.

The footplate was adapted to give a level floor, but this proved unpopular with footplate crews and the usual Gresley well was substituted. The rebuilt locomotives therefore had a distinctive look with their elongated front end boiler barrel and smoke deflectors. The Gresley Pacifics were fitted with vacuum cylinders on the engine and tender, but Thompson preferred to use steam braking. This necessitated the provision of a vacuum ejector for train braking and a proportional brake valve to blend the operation of the two systems. It was more immediate, and from the fitter's point of view, one 11in steam cylinder was a much more manageable proposition than the two large 18in vacuum cylinders.

THANE OF FIFE emerged from Doncaster Works in January 1943 and was run in and tested before returning to Scotland. It was over a year before the other five P2s were rebuilt, the last being LORD PRESIDENT in December 1944. Eventually classified A2, then A2/2, they were powerful locomotives, free steaming, and with large 10in piston valves they were free running. However, they suffered from four basic problems. The worst was adhesion. One of the best features of the P2s was that their adhesive weight was much greater, and despite having the highest rated tractive effort of any large-wheeled steam locomotive in the UK, their adhesive factor was 4.07. This was the adhesive weight divided by the tractive effort, both measured in the same units. The tractive effort of the rebuilt Pacific was not greatly diminished, but by removing one coupled axle the adhesive weight was reduced by 17%, bringing the adhesive factor down to 3.67. As one would expect therefore, the Pacifics were very light on their feet, a tendency unlikely to help performance in Scotland and ultimately the reason for their expulsion from there. One Haymarket top link driver was famously quoted as saying that they would even slip on Portobello sands.

While the new Pacific had fairly good if not perfect live steam passages, the layout of the exhaust steam passages was poor. From the centre of the valve chambers of the outside cylinders to the centre of the blastpipe was no less than 4ft 9in, and so the exhaust steam had to be carried forward from the outside cylinders in cast iron ducts. In an area where the different components were subject to different levels of heat and expansion, together with the vibration of the moving locomotive, it was not altogether surprising that the fixing bolts and ducts worked loose and fractured. War and post-war maintenance was no help either.

I have always suspected that the ducts were a last minute lash-up when it was realised that to convey the exhaust forward to the standpipe, the only alternative would have been to alter the casting design, and use curved external pipes, reminiscent of the GWR 'Castle'. Knowing that the CME had strong views over appearance and would almost certainly veto the suggestion, the ducts were an answer of sorts. I suspect that it was for that same reason he replaced the Gresley smokebox saddle with one which was roughly 12in narrower but longer, so that the live steam pipes could be straightened and brought inboard. However, when a locomotive, particularly one designed to run fast, encounters curved track at a speed in excess of the track design speed, since the chassis is hopefully restrained by the track, centrifugal force tends to throw the boiler barrel outwards. The barrel is normally carried between the saddle and the firebox end supports, with intermediate supports for the longer barrels. The connection at the rear is with sliding brackets to allow for the expansion of the barrel. Both connections need to contain uplift as the locomotive rolls at speed partly due to surging and partly due to variations in centrifugal force. It therefore follows that the saddle bolts must be sufficiently strong and tight to hold the engine together. With the load on the bolts thus increased 30% by the narrowness of the new saddle, the robustness of the fixing needed enhancing. Replacement of fixing bolts was a maintenance problem and vigilance was needed.

Thompson was said to be concerned over the appearance of his designs, and by common consent his B1, K1 and O1, even perhaps his largely unsuccessful L1, were all handsome and well-proportioned locomotives. So one might be surprised that he accepted the elongated front end in his Pacifics, and never sought to improve it. All of Thompson's Pacifics had the same layout, and while they were capable and powerful locomotives, they were always plagued by leaking to one degree or another, often badly, at the front end. The first rebuild, THANE OF FIFE, made numerous visits to Cowlairs Works with damaged exhaust steam ducts and pipes and loose cylinder blocks. The six locomotives were frequent visitors to shops for attention and general overhaul, and at one point five of the six engines were under repair.

It was said that they also suffered from poor riding as well. There was a great deal of prejudice against the engines from crews used to the excellent riding of Gresley's Pacifics, not without some reason. Whether crews used to harder or wilder-riding locomotives would have held them in the same disdain is an interesting question.

502 EARL MARISCHAL stands in Ferryhill shed yard at Aberdeen, resplendent in apple green livery. The numbering and livery of the Mikado rebuilds after the 1939-45 war is something of a minor science. Cowlairs was responsible for repainting and used larger, 12 inch cabside numerals, as can be seen here. (W G Boyden, Frank Hornby Collection)

Unlike Gresley's Pacifics which were fitted with D49 pattern bogies, the A2/2s were fitted with the B1 pattern. Gresley's A1 and 18 of his A3s were built with swing link bogie suspension, but it was later replaced by the D49 bogie. The latter took the imposed weight through a central bearing, which was transferred to the bearing springs. Horizontal springs provided a more positive control than swing links. The frames were set closer together than the main frames.

The bogie fitted to the A2/2s was a De Glehn type as used extensively in France and at Swindon, which had the frames set at main frame spacing and the weight was carried on spherical side bearings rather than a central bearing. Again the lateral control of the bogie was achieved by helical horizontal springs. The critical difference lay in the use of plate bearing springs rather than helical, for the dynamic performance of the two types was quite different. When the locomotive was static the two had similar deflection characteristics, but when moving the damping performance of plate springs was very much more random, relying entirely on friction between the leaves. With a moving locomotive the imposed loads fluctuated as it rolled and bounced, especially on poor track or on switches and crossings.

There was another comparatively minor problem in that, with the existing boiler, the 50sq.ft. grate remained. On lesser duties the combination of such a large grate and a double Kylchap caused unnecessarily high coal consumption. There were of course still far too many drivers who, consciously or not, were guided by the sound from the chimney in handling the locomotive. The Kylchap exhaust was much quieter, and in trying to make the engine bark as usual, a driver unfamiliar with such engines could give his fireman a wet shirt.

THE REBUILDS IN SERVICE

So the P2s were returned to Scotland as Pacifics. Thompson had been confronted with a serious maintenance problem, and it had been resolved. The consequences of an excessively long and inflexible wheelbase, overheated bearings and broken crank axles, had been eliminated. But now when Shedmasters were faced with a need to haul a heavy load, they needed to find two engines when previously a Mikado would have taken it in its stride. And when one of the new Pacifics was assigned to a driver, it was in the certainty that there would be a return visit from him afterwards.

Haulage capacity had been sacrificed in order to resolve a maintenance problem. One problem, however, had been dealt with at a stroke. The Kylchap exhaust of the Mikados, which had been fixed at the optimum setting with experience in service, had been replaced with the smaller design used on the four A4s in 1938, featuring twin 5in diameter exhaust orifices. Quite why this was done has been impossible to discover. I would like to think that it was the result of careful calculation, but in the war years it was rather more likely that the only available pattern for the standpipe was for a Gresley Pacific. One would have thought that the existing P2 fittings might have been usable in the rebuilds, entirely inappropriately as it happened, although the standpipe would need replacing. The only parameter affecting the exhaust design that had changed significantly was boiler tube length. But it was a change that was completely successful. The test figures show that the rebuilt Mikados were capable of quite modest coal consumption in contrast to their former existence.

In June 1943 on the other side of the country at Crewe, Stanier Pacific No.6245 CITY OF LONDON was completed with a double Kylchap exhaust as was Stanier's original intention in 1938 when he approved the modification. The dimensions of the Crewe-designed assembly were the same as that designed by ALE for the P2 in nearly every case, although the standpipe design left a great deal to be desired. It was subsequently removed at the first overhaul in wartime as a non-standard fitting, which was a great

MONS MEG, now with a lipped chimney, pauses at the platform end at Kings Cross before crossing to the station loco yard on February 21ˢᵗ 1960. (David Idle, Transport Treasury)

pity. LMSR engineers spoke of the strange rasping exhaust of No.6245. A year or so later the LNER could have given the LMSR five sets!

It is important to remember that wartime restrictions left very little choice: sophisticated devices such as needle or roller bearings and Zara trucks were unavailable. Resources for straightforward railway work were limited to overhauls and new building authorised by the Mechanical and Electrical Engineering Sub-Committee of the Railway Executive Committee. It was essential to eliminate the problems outlined above, but without reducing the haulage capacity of the engines if possible. Rebuilding as a Pacific achieved the first at the expense of the second, but to be realistic, there seems to have been little alternative in wartime other than finding a better use for the engines.

Returning to Scotland Nos.2001 and 2002, now Nos.501 and 502 under the LNER 1946 renumbering, went to Ferryhill and the remaining four to Haymarket. The traffic had changed, with most trains generally heavier and more numerous during wartime, although the heavy loads of pre-war days into and out of Aberdeen were less common. Most services were within the capacity of a V2 or Gresley Pacific. Engine changing at Dundee was discontinued during the war, and was reinstated on far fewer duties post-war. Crew changing had been introduced at a greater frequency during wartime in order to avoid men working long diagrams and being away from home and duties such as Air Raid and Fire Wardens. When the Haymarket engines moved on to express freight and parcels, they were handled by a much wider group of footplate crews from other depots. Gradually the number of appearances on the principal expresses decreased.

Whereas the Mikados were used between Edinburgh and Aberdeen, and occasionally to Newcastle and Glasgow, there appears to be no record of them going to Perth and certainly none of them working the Waverley route. The long and heavy gradients to Glenfarg, Falahill and Whitrope would not have troubled them. The rebuilds, however, were used much more widely, and most were seen on the Waverley route, despite their slippery reputation, working from Edinburgh or St. Margarets. The rebuilt Mikados, apart from requiring careful handling with a heavy load, frequently needed attention to the unconventional front end layout already referred to. Cylinder blocks loosened, bolts fractured, and exhaust ducts loosened and broke. The eccentric driving the middle cylinder valves seemed susceptible, although that may have been due to inadequate lubrication as well as design. The locomotives required roughly three times the number of works repairs needed by the Gresley Pacifics. A considerable number of visits were made to Cowlairs until the 1949 exodus to England, when Doncaster took over their maintenance. As mentioned, at one time five of the class were in Cowlairs for repairs. The Aberdeen engines were sent to Haymarket in September 1949, but within three months the six rebuilds were despatched south of the Border. Three, Nos.60501-60503, went to York, followed a few weeks later by the remainder, Nos.60504-60506 which went to New England.

It was hardly a vote of confidence, since these two sheds could hardly muster more than half a dozen express turns between them. I can remember, one Sunday morning in November 1949, a school friend rushing to tell me that he had seen COCK O' THE NORTH running into London. So far as we lads in the south were concerned, the six engines were only found in books and never in England, and even for those fortunate few who went over the Border, the rebuilds were not easy to track down. Therefore there was a considerable credibility gap to be bridged before we set off for London in pursuit. As we waited at New Southgate the 11.30 Glasgow appeared, headed by a filthy Pacific, turning main to slow for engineering work, and I must have gaped at the engine, WOLF OF BADENOCH. My overriding memory is of the old cliché, 'How are the mighty fallen'. Their work in service is described in Chapter 9.

P2 and A2/2: AN ASSESSMENT
A General View

Looking through the prism of railway management half a century later, one can see immediately that a number of things should have been considered and questioned. I am surprised that Wedgwood, an outstanding Chief General Manager, did not appear to question the proposal more closely: sixty years later a reply from the Chief General Manager would be couched in fairly brusque terms! It was simple to split the load, so that another engine could take an advance portion – indeed it was already established practice. However, there was more to it than that, which is why I have dealt at length with the position prior to 1934. Attaching a pilot to a Pacific was almost certainly prohibited then (though there is now no means of being absolutely certain) due to the excessive load on underline structures. In those days it was the practice to have cover in the shape of spare crews and locomotives, and there would have been a spare crew or two standing by and a pilot engine in Ferryhill shed yard, albeit on LMSR premises. The effect on operations would have been slight and the effect on operating costs imperceptible. If a path for a relief train did not exist, there is little doubt that it could have been provided, or 'forced' to use Southern Region jargon. Farther south, the 'Aberdonian' ran into Kings Cross at 7.25 with the Glasgow portion one block behind and a Q (Conditional) path behind that. It was known that Gresley had an aversion to piloting, and also the Company was concerned to contain operating costs by avoiding the practice. Nevertheless these views did not seem to have been communicated to the operators 'on the ground', who still used piloting when necessary in certain areas, Newcastle-Edinburgh for example.

A number of the practices of the old companies survived into nationalisation, giving some idea of the pre-war approach to loads and loading. Pre-war practice, I believe, very often amounted to non-passenger vehicles being allocated by user and not by traffic volume. It should have been quite possible to reduce the tare load without losing capacity. A great deal of coal was shovelled and burnt hauling often under-utilised empty stock up and down the East Coast. On the other hand, whether a more deferential culture of the day would have allowed the operators that authority with an important service one cannot tell now. It only needed a piece of luggage belonging to an influential passenger to go astray for a manager to be well and truly in the soup!

Finally, of course, there is the question of costs. The LNER used the former Caledonian route from Kinnaber to Aberdeen, and one suspects that the arrangement was not without financial implications. From the LMSR point of view it certainly ought not to have been. The cost of underline strengthening must have been shared with the LNER as it was carried out for their Pacifics at first. One must leave experts in detailed railway history to investigate this matter, but it was unlikely that the LMSR allowed their line to be used without at least sharing running costs. The arrangement was probably based on a sharing as defined by the timetable, but at least one possibility is that the LMSR allowed the use of their line on a per train basis, which would have encouraged the LNER to think in terms of eggs and baskets.

It says much for him that the LNER trusted Gresley to control costs, but it is strange that at a time of financial stringency the LNER Board was prepared to authorise a particularly expensive project. There was never any possibility that a 2-8-2 would come cheap. By the time innovation had been added to the project it was certainly going to be expensive. When viewed from a financial viewpoint six decades later, the whole proposition seems almost reckless. The country was beginning to recover from the recession of the 1930s, and the LNER, having suffered worst of the 'Big Four' in the loss of freight revenue, was very short of capital. To invest something like £50-60,000 in the 1932 and 1934 Building Programmes for six large locomotives to overcome a haulage problem with one train in particular (unless I have overlooked something) seems mistaken.

Of course one should not judge the past absolutely by later standards. As one regresses farther and farther back in railway history, increasingly one finds examples of what is best described as a sort of gung-ho attitude from which either triumph or disaster resulted. Whether it was a form of amateurism of the sort that pervaded sport – and I suspect, business – nearly a century ago, or whether it was landed wealth dabbling in matters far beyond their ability, is not within this book or for its author to judge. It is certainly something that, measured against more recent railway management practice, defies rational explanation. It was, however, an environment in which magnificent sweeps of Brunelian genius were possible, and we have a rich store of engineering achievement as a result. Just over a year after the first Mikado appeared, Wedgwood and Gresley produced the first truly High Speed Train – the 'Silver Jubilee' and its A4, a stroke of genius that, as a proposal, at first just might not have looked the stunning success that it became. However, it was also an environment in which triumphs and blunders were equally possible, and one has the feeling that the industry made some bad decisions as well as good, and this appears to be one of them. Engineering seemed to be a major influence on railway thinking and investment, possibly to the disbenefit of the operators. While in general, engineering had a record of success, the same could not be said of overall quality of railway management.

The Project
The Mikados were locomotives of such potential that their loss can only be described as a tragedy. The first Mikado (in retrospect, unfortunately) contained so much innovation that it was difficult to tell just what was the cause of the problems experienced. One suspects that Gresley was urged to include the various innovations, especially poppet valves, by his innovative assistant O V S Bulleid, who was keen to try them on a bigger engine. Looking farther ahead, the successful use of poppet valves would have made the 2:1 gear obsolete. The CME had produced a splendid locomotive, but once again poor communications within the Company come into the spotlight, for quite clearly no special attention had been paid to the particular requirements of the design for the routes over which it was intended to run. Likewise no hint of any special requirements had been volunteered from the Scottish Area, and no action had been taken to ensure efficient use

of the locomotives. As a result, the diagrams for what were very large locomotives for their time had long layover times, and the balancing turn to a heavy duty was usually much lighter and uneconomic.

When looked at from a general management viewpoint half a century later the whole project was an expensive failure, however it had originated. Harsh words maybe, but in response to the original request, that is the only possible view. However, there is much about this whole affair that simply does not add up. Wedgwood's failure to halt the proposal was completely untypical of him. The option of splitting the load must have been obvious at Area and District level, so why escalate the problem? The LNER Board did not comprise career railwaymen, but the directors were businessmen who had risen to pre-eminence in other fields. They were not fools, and wisely left the running of the railway to the professionals. Perhaps the clue lies in the ease with which this fairly outrageous proposal passed the scrutiny of the CGM and then the Board. We need to consider whether the dark art of railway politics has been involved here. It seems to me very probable that the initial suggestion did not come from District level at all, but from the Board. As mentioned already, a number of influential people used the Aberdeen service, not least the Royal Family. The Royal Train was a heavy load, and was about to become heavier with additional armour. The LNER Chairman was very well connected, especially in Scottish and North Country circles. In those days the views of an eminent passenger might carry a disproportionate influence at Board level. Knowing this, there would be little point in opposing something which was a Board proposal that, in effect, was already as good as authorised. It would also explain why the Mikados were confined principally to the Aberdeen-Edinburgh road, only with filling-in turns elsewhere. T C B Miller told me that he used the Mikados on heavy Edinburgh-Newcastle night services, knowing that use south of Edinburgh was prohibited, even in wartime. The reason for the prohibition was not known or explained. Later it emerged that the practice was less rare. There has not been a clear explanation of the P2 project, but this alternative has much about it that appeals. It rings true.

There is a curious similarity between the history of the P2s and their predecessors, the P1s. Both were considerably ahead of their time; the operators could have made better use of their potential, but Gresley seemed preoccupied with other designs. But it is necessary to go back more than sixty years to put both into perspective. Gresley was, in effect, the head of a very large engineering organisation, as were his three colleagues in the 'Big Four'.

He was a busy man with a huge responsibility. In the 1930s the steam locomotive fleet was vast and while in this book we have looked closely at six P2s, in the overall management of the locomotive fleet they were less important, despite their considerable cost, and there were many other issues and problems demanding Gresley's attention.

The Engines: General
While all six Mikados suffered from the problems outlined below, namely wheelbase, overlarge grate and exhaust, four of the six locomotives – five once No.2001 was converted to piston valve distribution – seemed to perform tolerably well. The sixth, THANE OF FIFE, was said to be the black sheep of the class, but since the exhaust design was similar to that of the Pacifics, it was unlikely to have been all that bad. Certainly the early results with No.2001 were desperately bad, and one wonders whether early results and impressions gave the class a bad reputation, not entirely deserved. No doubt they had a healthy appetite particularly if driven hard. With the driver using a long cut-off and partially opened regulator, a Kylchap exhaust, and with a grate nearly a fifth larger, being fired heavily, the sensation of great heat would be inevitable. The ACFI apparatus on COCK O' THE NORTH suffered from the same lack of close supervision in the sheds as that of the two Pacifics, THE WHITE KNIGHT and SHOTOVER, and was discontinued.

The Engines: Maintenance
Whilst the engines had been built and overhauled at Doncaster, the Scottish Area sent them to their main works at Cowlairs for casual or light repairs, presumably rather than send them south to Doncaster. This practice was later extended to include intermediate and heavy repairs, and even a general overhaul on LORD PRESIDENT. It should be explained that the extent of repairs needed determines their classification – light, intermediate, heavy or general, and casual repairs, the latter being usually the result of collision, derailment or some such. The standard of work at Cowlairs had declined badly before the war, and that decline had accelerated with the onset of war, with the shortage of skilled labour and materials. There were very serious problems with the management of the works that needed urgent action, and this reacted downwards to the quality of work on the shop floor. Bill Harvey gave the example of a K2 2-6-0, returned from Cowlairs after general overhaul, which was the subject of complaints by footplate crews. On investigation it was found that the internal dimensions of the two valve/cylinder castings were quite different, and one cylinder was

Whenever a relief to the 'Heart of Midlothian' ran, it was almost always worked by New England. The 13.45, comprising most of the oddments of coaching stock from Bounds Green, Hornsey and Holloway, headed by 60504 MONS MEG, passes the site of the future station at Welham Green, by Marshmoor signalbox on August 4th 1953.

either the wrong hand or from another class. Quite how the locomotive had functioned that far beggars belief. The position was sufficiently serious for a senior engineer, E D Trask, to go there and report back, by now to Edward Thompson. Clearly the P2s had troubles of their own, but visiting Cowlairs exacerbated them rather than cured them. When Trask's report was received by Thompson, no action was taken until the proposed rebuilding of the Mikados had been authorised.

The Engines: Wheelbase
The design itself suffered from four fundamental problems, most of which should have been foreseen. Firstly, the long rigid wheelbase needed lateral play in axleboxes and bearings to cope with the curvature, and possibly more vertical play since the number of pitfall Permanent Speed Restrictions (PSRs) in Fife might well have affected the road. The continual jolting and jerking round the curving routes would have caused pipe joints to open, leaks and possibly additional stress on the

staying of the boiler and firebox, all adding to the maintenance burden. The performance of the pony truck was inadequate, as was foreseen at the time. Yet elsewhere eight-coupled locomotives were running on curved track without the same problems. Motive power engineers reported that it was necessary to ease the lateral clearances, but in vain. The larger-wheeled eight coupled locomotives in France were provided with lateral play in the coupling rods and, as mentioned earlier, coped well with curving alignments through the Massif Central. Gresley had actually been asked in 1934 by Rupert Pennoyer, an enthusiast, why he had not used the Zara pony truck on No.2001. His reply was that there was quite enough innovation on the locomotive already and while he had considered it, he decided against. A pity.

The Engines: Grate
Secondly, the use of such a large grate was due to the prevailing view at the time that more power simply equalled

the ability to burn more coal. Anecdotal evidence from senior drivers attests to the great heat on the footplate. In truth, a 50sq.ft. grate required mechanical firing. Since grates that size or slightly larger were hand fired, the possibility seems not to have been considered. We are looking at a time when manual work was harder, but it made little sense to put more on the workforce. After the war, as we remember, young men voted with their feet, and this was as much the reason for the end of steam as anything else. Of course the purchase of six sets of mechanical stokers plus royalties would have fallen yet again on the Stores Superintendent, and one can understand his reluctance to meet the cost.

The rate of combustion was not such a simple matter, and Chapelon showed in 1929 and 1932 that the stronger draught stimulated by a more sophisticated exhaust forced a more rapid burning and release of energy. Power should not have been confused with tractive effort, for while the Mikados had the latter in abundance,

23

the need for high power was transitory at the sort of speeds permitted north of Edinburgh in 1934. With hindsight, for short bursts of power a smaller grate, certainly smaller even than that of the A3, would have been adequate. We need also to remember that No.2001 was the first large engine to have a sophisticated exhaust system, and firemen had no previous experience of firing to it. In most cases, apart from the few A1s and A3s, the firemen were used to grates half the size of the Mikado.

The Engines: Exhaust

Thirdly, the design of double Kylchap seems to have been wide of the mark, not only for the prototype, but to a lesser extent for the four piston valve engines. The diameter of the double blastpipe orifices seemed to be too large. The design would have been prepared by the Associated Locomotive equipment Co., as franchisees for Chapelon. The design itself would have been based on a specification of design criteria provided by the customer, the LNER, and if that specification had included information which was over-optimistic, inaccurate or plain wrong, I would suggest that neither party would realise it until much later. It was the first occasion that the design had been used in the UK. The early ALE exhaust designs for the P2s, A4s, the A3 HUMORIST and the W1 4-6-2-2, were all prepared with the central vane in each of the two branches of the standpipe. This was excluded and the barrettes were cast integrally after the 1939-45 war.

There were signs that all was not well with No.2001 right from the start, and before the Vitry testing, in a letter Chapelon expressed surprise at the size of the blastpipe compared with those of the generally more powerful locomotives in France. In his opinion it was too large and should have been replaced with a smaller one. He repeated this advice during the testing. The rebuilt engines seemed to function well enough on a blastpipe some two-thirds of the size of the original with most of the influential factors unaffected, which confirmed that Chapelon was correct. With the piston valve engines things seem to have been better but not entirely satisfactory. It may be that their coal consumption was not excessive, but the large grate would take more coal, and the reputation of the prototype probably coloured that of the class.

No.2001: Poppet Valves

Lastly, the decision to use poppet valves with the 2:1 conjugated gear as laid out in the design of the first Mikado was, again in hindsight, wrong. The unified drive forced the three poppet valve mechanisms into close proximity with the live and exhaust steam passages. The result was that temperature losses

In 1949 WOLF OF BADENOCH became No.60506, but retained her apple green livery. She is seen here at Haymarket.

occurred and the curious division of drives to the middle cylinder valves was forced on the design. Using a monobloc casting the necessary rigidity was obtained, but of course the very compactness of the design brought live and exhaust steam passages too close to avoid heat transfer away from the live steam. The design of poppet valves used also increased the clearance volumes considerably, and again the consequence of this was foreseen at the time. The five piston valve engines, of course, did not suffer from this problem. By carefully laying out the steam passages, it enabled a neat overall design, and one which allowed an aesthetically pleasing appearance. It was no small achievement: Gresley's care in producing a locomotive of impressive and clean appearance can be contrasted with Chapelon's magnificent 4-8-0, which appeared to have everything but the kitchen sink attached somewhere or other!

The type of poppet valve used, rotary cam (RC) instead of oscillating cam (OC) was also already known to cause excessive coal consumption when the locomotive was worked hard due to the heavy exhaust beats. The RC poppet valves enabled release to be delayed, using the steam more expansively and improving efficiency. As the engine was worked harder, however, the resulting increase in peak exhaust flow at release caused heavy exhaust beats that pulled at the fire. While cylinder efficiency was improved, it was at the cost of lessening the overall efficiency. With an over-large Kylchap exhaust, the effect on coal consumption was likely to be considerable. As an example, in France, the Alsace-Lorraine railway had introduced two modern, high pressure two cylinder class S16 Pacifics with Caprotti RC poppet valves with a double Kylchap exhaust. When the locomotives were tested, at low power they were very economical, but as the locomotive was worked harder, fuel consumption increased disproportionately. The adoption of OC

poppet valves instead of RC would not have been possible without a new monobloc casting, probably a case of throwing good money after bad.

The operation of the poppet valves now fitted with stepped cams seriously reduced the driver's options for handling the engine. The cut-offs available were 12, 18, 35, 45 and 75%, much the same as if the engine were fitted with lever reverse. With such a large and powerful engine it will be seen that in the normal working range of cut-offs, say 5 to 25%, there were only two options, where there needed to be at least five. There were no doubt constraints in the design of the valves that limited the space available to five cam positions in total. No doubt this forced drivers to use the regulator far more to control speed. The rapid wear of the continuous cams, together with that of the stepped cams discovered at Vitry, indicates difficulty in maintaining lubrication. It also suggests that the components had not been sufficiently well case-hardened for the temperatures and abrasion in the high temperatures at which they had to function, although this seems difficult to believe. On return to the UK, No.2001 was fitted with a circulatory system whereby the oil was pumped out of the camboxes to radiators in order to lower its temperature. The success or otherwise of the system is not recorded, and it was scrapped with the poppet valves.

Another Option

With the luxury of hindsight we can see that perhaps it is from French locomotive practice that the best alternative option emerged. In 1929 André Chapelon rebuilt a Class 3500 compound Pacific of the Paris-Orléans Railway into a locomotive of barely recognisable power and efficiency. In 1932 using the same basic principles he rebuilt the older and smaller-wheeled Pacific No.4521 into a 4-8-0 with even more astonishing results. Whereas in 1929 No.3566 was capable of 60-70% greater power, the output of No.4521 was virtually *doubled* to 4,000 IHP.

It was unfortunate that Gresley, a member of the Technical Committee of the UIC and a friend of Chapelon, did not investigate the design of the 4-8-0 in more detail in 1932. Perhaps it was the fact that No.4521 was a compound, bearing in mind the failure to employ compounding successfully in the UK with large designs, especially his experiment with No.10000. Some of the ideas were used of course, but it would have been instructive to learn what precautions had been taken to ensure that a four-coupled wheelbase could run sweetly over a heavily curved route.

The possibility of Doncaster producing a simple 4-8-0, if it had been considered at all, must have been dismissed fairly quickly as well. The association of a four coupled axle high power locomotive with his preferred three cylinders, unified drive, conjugated valve gear, pony truck with swing link control and a trailing axle would have appealed as a neat and practicable basis for development. It had been used before in the P1. All of Gresley's locomotives wagged their tails if there was no carrying axle; being powerful locomotives, they became quite vigorous riders when run down. The lessons of 1925, when PENDENNIS CASTLE had started heavy loads away without fuss from all the awkward starts on the GN main line, were forgotten.

With hindsight, I have no doubt that a three cylinder 6ft 2ins 4-8-0, based on the chassis of the French rebuild, would have been a better answer to Scotland's operational problems. The bogie would have guided the locomotive into curves more positively, and an ample provision of lateral play and knuckled connecting rods should have eased if not cured the problems of the long wheelbase. Had Gresley ever considered the idea at length, the lack of a suitable boiler would have been a major obstacle. The LNER had no modern taper boiler allied to the use of a relatively large but narrow grate, similar to the King or rebuilt Royal Scot boiler. Gresley preferred his faithful servant, the large Doncaster taper boiler, with a wide firebox, with a trailing axle. Without doubt the conjugated gear would have been used with poppet valves in a monobloc casting. Of course the 4-8-0 would have suffered from heat transfer as a result, as did No.2001. Had Gresley followed Chapelon further and used Lentz oscillating cam poppet valves rather than rotary cam, a great deal of trouble and disillusionment would have been avoided. In Chapelon's Pacifics and 4-8-0s the oscillating camshaft was driven by conventional Walschaerts valve gear and the heavy wear, inflexible cut-off settings and explosive exhaust beats when working hard would have been avoided. A design using these features would have been as free-running as the French Pacifics and 4-8-0s, although some of the early teething troubles with deformed and leaking poppet valves would have still been difficult. Even in France, poppet valve technology was not perfected in 1934. However with a grate only 60-70% of a Mikado, the coal consumption would doubtless have been much less.

However, the 4-8-0 would have required Gresley to break with several of his firmly held principles – independent instead of conjugated valve gear, divided instead of unified drive, no pony and trailing trucks, and a new firebox married to the Doncaster taper barrel. It was never likely to have been contemplated. Nevertheless, a three cylinder 4-8-0 designed for a sinuous road, with independent valve gear driving 10in piston valves, about 35sq ft grate area, and a double Kylchap would have been quite something.

But it was all a long time ago.

506 WOLF OF BADENOCH at Haymarket in 1948. (J T Rutherford, Transport Treasury)

60507 HIGHLAND CHIEFTAIN about to depart from Edinburgh Waverley on August 2ⁿᵈ 1950. (F W Goudie, Transport Treasury)

No.511 AIRBORNE at an unspecified and unrecognised location, during 1946-48.

CHAPTER THREE
EDWARD THOMPSON'S A2/1 and A2/3 PACIFICS

The A2/1 Pacifics

When THANE OF FIFE emerged from Doncaster Works in January 1943, there were already 165 large 2-6-2s of Class V2 in operation alongside the 113 Pacifics and the W1. In fact many of the 165 were fairly new locomotives, Gresley's 'Green Arrows', and they were the mainstay of the locomotive fleet. As mentioned already, many LNER motive power men spoke of them as 'the engines that won the war'. The V2 originated as the design intended to replace the K3 2-6-0s on faster work, especially as the LNER sought to exploit the growing market for faster freight. With its surprisingly good turn of speed, the ability of the class to deputise for Pacifics led to a widespread use on express passenger duties. With the onset of war in 1939, a considerable number of the enormous passenger trains operated by the LNER were powered by newly built 'Green Arrows'. The heaviest on record was hauled by a new V2.

On February 19th 1941 the last batch of 25 V2 2-6-2s was authorised at an Emergency Board meeting for construction at Darlington Works, numbered 3675-3699. At a further meeting on July 27th 1943, following a memorandum from the Chief General Manager reflecting Thompson's views, it was agreed to construct the last four of the batch as Pacifics with three sets of independent valve gears replacing the 2:1 conjugated valve gear. Authority was issued in August 1943, seven months after the appearance of the first rebuilt Mikado THANE OF FIFE, for the last four V2s to be constructed as Pacifics. It was claimed that this was decided in order to gain experience with a larger and more powerful mixed traffic engine to succeed the V2.

The majority of the V2s were fairly new locomotives, and the class was limited as much as the Pacifics in its radius of operation. With 113 Pacifics and 184 of the V2 2-6-2s already in service, one wonders quite what operational need Thompson's new heavy mixed traffic locomotive was supposed to meet. It was unlikely that the new design would be less than RA9. More to the point just what did he have in mind for the nearly-new V2s thus displaced? If a wholesale rebuilding of 184 V2s on the lines of the new Pacific was contemplated once war ceased, one also wondered where the cash-strapped LNER would find the necessary funds, and on quite what work it would use 184 extra Pacifics. The initial purpose of the V2 was an advance on the existing K3 and B16 mixed traffic classes, and not as a supplement to the Pacific fleet.

60509 WAVERLEY just fresh from Doncaster Works on June 4th 1950. It is a shed visit by the look of the two delighted occupants of the cab. The illustration shows clearly the rear bogie axle that was originally intended to carry a dynamo. She originally had a B1 tender but in October 1946 an eight wheel A2/3 non-corridor tender No.706 was built (after the first two had been coupled to 500 and 511) and fitted in its place. (B K B Green, Initial Photographics)

LNER No.3697 with GREAT NORTHERN behind, at Top Shed by the look of it. The A2/1 is as built, showing an almost identical appearance with the rebuilt Mikados. The A2/1 has the V2 tender that eventually was attached to Hitchin's B1 No.61105.

No.60509 WAVERLEY just after general overhaul in her new dark green livery on June 4th 1950 at Doncaster. Both HIGHLAND CHIEFTAIN and WAVERLEY seem to have been popular engines at Haymarket, having been used on express work to Newcastle as well as their frequent haunt, the Waverley route. (Transport Treasury)

The four A2/1s were completed at Darlington between May 1944 and January 1945 as Nos.3696-3699, the first Pacifics to be built there by the LNER since Raven's, Nos.2400-2404. No.3696 was, however, more than a V2 with an elongated front end. It was clearly a larger and more powerful locomotive and, on paper, it should have been a fine machine. The wheelbase was the same as the A2/2 rebuild except for the smaller grate allowing the trailing axle to be 3in closer to the coupled axles. The coupled wheelbase was quite different from the V2 being 2ft 6in shorter. The Diagram 109 V2 boiler was fitted with a rocking grate and a hopper ashpan, valuable aids to depot servicing. The design of the rocking grate allowed each half to be agitated separately, so the fire could be cleaned and ash and clinker dropped in each half without dropping the whole fire. The hopper ashpan allowed the contents to be dropped into the disposal pit rather than have to be raked out by disposal staff.

Thompson persisted with his belief that cab floors should be level, and replaced the Gresley screw reverser and pull-out regulator on the grounds that they were stiff and difficult to use, which was often true. No.3696 was fitted with a steam reverser similar to the former NER pattern and a GCR type transverse regulator. The arrangement was unpopular and the four A2/1s reverted to the conventional Gresley arrangement at the first general overhaul. Steam brakes were fitted as the new standard. Thompson also sought to improve the locomotives operationally by providing electric lighting and white discs as used on the GE section to denote train classification. Although the axle-driven generator on the rear bogie axle proved fragile and demonstrated that further development was essential, the ideas were good and the two innovations would have greatly facilitated train operation. A conservative operating department (and most were) was unlikely to adopt any new idea readily, still less from outside the department, and certainly not one from the CME!

At the leading end was the lengthy smokebox of the A2/2, with a double Kylchap exhaust, surmounted with the small chimneyside deflectors used on HUMORIST and the A2/2s. The latter were replaced by large smoke deflectors after a year of running, similar to those introduced on the A2/3s. In place of the monobloc casting with 9in piston valves and 18.5x26in cylinders, separate castings were used giving 10in piston valves and 19x26in cylinders. Unfortunately, the steam passage layout of the A2/2 was used once again with the poor layout of the exhaust passages using extended ducts. However, despite the innovations and deficiencies of the new Pacifics, clearly they had greater potential than the V2

from which they were developed. With slightly larger cylinders and significantly larger valves, they could develop and sustain a greater pull, but the major improvement was the provision of a double Kylchap. Again based on the A4 design, it raised evaporation and lowered back pressure, increasing power output by some 400 IHP at full power.

As the A2/1s were built in place of V2s, they were coupled to Group Standard tenders intended for the V2s that carried 4,200 gallons of water and 7½ tons of coal (nominally). This restricted their operation. An adequate supply of coal and water was necessary to meet all traffic requirements, and while on a good day with a skilled fireman one might have reached Newcastle from London, it was not a good idea to run the railway on the basis of frequently having to empty the tender completely. The Motive Power Department requested 5,000 gallon Pacific tenders, and the tender off the withdrawn No.4469 was repaired, renumbered and coupled to No.3696. The other three engines were attached to new tenders as and when the latter were built, in 1946 (3698) and 1949 (3697/3699).

In January 1945 the new No.3697 was tested with A2/2 LORD PRESIDENT in comparison with A4 SILVER FOX in coal consumption trials on heavy expresses and fast freight. Difficulties were experienced with the three Pacifics, and the weather was impossibly difficult with fog and snow. It is perhaps surprising that such an exercise should have been considered in wartime, with an overall speed limit of 60mph in force. The locomotives worked the 10.30 from Kings Cross to Leeds throughout, returning with the 7.50 from Leeds the following day, and the 9.40 Kings Cross-Newcastle as far as Grantham returning with the up Ripon express leaving Grantham at 15.17. The freight trains were the 00.35 from Kings Cross Goods to New England and the 04.50 from New England to East Goods at Finsbury Park. They were classified as fast freight and normally ran as Class D. All were heavy trains, although the schedules were undemanding, and probably well within the compass of a K3 2-6-0.

It must have been a difficult task to present the results to Thompson, who was known not take bad news easily or quietly. The coal consumption of the A2/2 was 70.8lbs per mile, for the A2/1 69lbs, compared with the A4 at 52.3lbs. It is clear that the poor weather had affected the trials, and with semaphore signalling without AWS it was essential to reduce speed to be sure of sighting the signals. Bearing in mind that crews were changed more frequently in wartime, and that what little experience existed in the south with Kylchap locomotives was at Doncaster,

the figures achieved suggest that the driving and firing left a great deal to be desired.

The tests were repeated after Easter in 1945. The arrangements were changed so that one footplate crew worked the three engines throughout the trials. The freight turn remained the same, but the engine on the 10.30 to Leeds came off at Grantham and returned with the 15.17 Ripon express. Each engine spent a week on passenger and then freight. The coal consumption of the A2/2 progressively reduced from 51.94lbs to 42.73 over five days while the A4 reduced similarly from 41.79 to 38lbs. The A2/1 figure dropped from 43.22 to 41.69lbs but then rose unaccountably to 44.39lbs. On the freight turn the figures were more variable, 56.17 down to 40.85lbs for the A2/2 and 42.38 down to 36.75lbs for the A2/1, and 46.50 down to 42.32lbs for the A4. Clearly the crew were improving in their handling in the six weeks, but it is hardly surprising that the A4 should show up less well on work for which it was not designed.

The Report attributed a great deal to causes that should have been perfectly obvious to a locomotive engineer. The A4's superiority in coal consumption on express passenger work was attributed to its greater driving wheel diameter, although that argument fell flat on its face when the reverse was the case on fast freight. With hindsight we can understand that the potential and the steaming of the newer Pacifics would have been impressive. The acceleration of the 6ft 2in locomotives was judged to be greater than the A4, due to the smaller coupled wheel diameter. The greater tractive effort would have been the reason rather than wheel diameter. The Report tactfully refers to the need for care in starting to avoid wheelslip. The Scottish crews would have been more explicit. The Locomotive Running Superintendent dealt with the running aspects of the engines, criticising the steam reverser but praising the rocking grate and ashpan. Attention was also drawn again to the inadequacy of the 4,200 gallon tender and the lack of the 5,000 gallon tender requested.

The quartet had emerged in the days of black livery, and two, 3696 and 3699, remained black until BR dark green was applied in late 1949. Ironically, it was not until the first year of national ownership that 3697 and 3698 were painted green, but it was LNER lined apple green and not the dark green that appeared at the next overhaul. The dark green suited them reasonably well, although often DUKE OF ROTHESAY might as well have remained in unlined black for all that could be seen of her paintwork.

The four locomotives were allocated to Darlington for running-in before moving to Heaton. Darlington had little express work, but Heaton had much

LNER No.510 stands at Waverley's platform 12 in 1946-48. The A2/1 is in original condition with small deflectors, dynamo and Group standard tender. The first coach is an antique, fine to look at but one feels for the passengers of those days! (Transport Treasury)

more express and heavy freight work. The bulk of the last batch of V2s, of which the A2/1s were originally a part, was shared between the North Eastern and Scottish Areas, only two going further south. However by early 1945 the first two A2/1s had moved to Kings Cross, and the second two to Haymarket where they remained for the most of the fifteen years of their existence. At the end of 1946 large deflectors were added, and the four Pacifics were given splendid names, HIGHLAND CHIEFTAIN, DUKE OF ROTHESAY, WAVERLEY and ROBERT THE BRUCE. No.3697 spent a few weeks at Gorton during the coal trials in spring 1945, and the two Scottish engines spent three weeks at Ferryhill in autumn 1949. In the latter case presumably the arrival of the first A1 at Haymarket begged the question as to the use of the A2/1s to strengthen motive power further north. Their factor of adhesion was better at 4.06 instead of 3.67 for the A2/2s, and perhaps they were sent north in the hope that they would not be so prone to wheelslip. With the A2/2s about to emigrate southwards, more of what looked very much the same must have been unlikely to appeal at Aberdeen. Gresley's engines were coping with Scotland's problems, shortly to be reinforced by the arrival of 10 further Peppercorn A2s in addition to Haymarket's No.529 PEARL DIVER. In late 1949 a considerable reallocation of Pacifics happened. One of the Kings Cross pair, HIGHLAND CHIEFTAIN, moved to Haymarket. Then, as already mentioned, the six A2/2s were

transferred to York and New England. Quite why the fourth engine, DUKE OF ROTHESAY, was not also sent is inexplicable, as six months later she was offloaded to New England where she remained until withdrawal.

THE A2/3 PACIFIC

During wartime, all new building had to be approved by the Railway Executive Committee. In 1944 the Committee approved the LNER's proposed 1945 Locomotive Construction Programme, which was authorised at an Emergency Board meeting at April 27th 1944. Despite the LNER fleet already containing 123 Pacifics, the W1 and 184 V2s, no less than 30 new 6ft 2in engines were contemplated, and in the 1946 Programme another 13 6ft 2in and 16 6ft 8in engines were planned. Again one wonders quite what process of reasoning – or desperation – led to such a decision, which left the LNER and its successors with large budgetary commitment and a surplus of larger engines. In the short term, with the reliability of the Gresley engines leaving much to be desired and the steaming of the single blast locos no longer reliable with inferior coal, the new locomotives were a valued transfusion. But in the longer term the Gresley Pacifics steadily recovered, and the former LNER was unable to make effective use of its whole fleet of 'big engines'. The sight of under-utilised Pacifics and V2s became a familiar one.

The new engines were to be Class A2, based on the rebuilt Mikados but with the boiler pressure raised to 250psi

and the cylinder diameter reduced to 19in. The rebuilt P2s, hitherto Class A2, were reclassified A2/2, whilst the four A2/1s remained unchanged. In June 1944 the Programme was promulgated with orders for firstly ten A2s, then a further five. The Diagram 117 boilers, a new variant of the large Doncaster taper boiler, were built at Darlington and sent to Doncaster. They were very similar to the Diagram 106A of the rebuilt Mikados, except that the firebox had a small combustion chamber, and the banjo dome was replaced with a simple dome as directed by Thompson. The dome enclosed a double-beat regulator, and it was now located at the joint between the tapered and parallel sections of the boiler, several feet farther ahead of the location of the banjo dome on the Gresley boilers. Surprisingly the rocking grate introduced with the Class A2/1 Pacifics was discarded in favour of the Gresley design with a drop grate, although a hopper ashpan was fitted. Rocking grates were fitted during repairs at a later stage. No spare boilers were built, and the Peppercorn Diagram 118 boiler was later agreed for use with the A2/3s.

Thompson had apparently given up trying impose his ideas for the cab on the Running Department, and it had reverted to the familiar Gresley pattern with a well for the fireman, pull-out regulator handles, and a vertical screw reverser. Steam brakes was again fitted. Steam sanding was supplied ahead of the leading coupled wheels and both sides of the driving axle. BTH speed indicators were fitted but then removed. As a result of a BTC decision following an accident, Stone electric speedometers were fitted from 1960 onwards. Thompson disliked the angled cab front introduced on COCK O' THE NORTH, and it was discarded in favour of that of the original GNR A1. The small chimneyside deflectors were considered, but eventually large deflectors were fitted, and the general arrangement drawing shows large deflectors.

A significant change was made to Drawing Office practice in that general arrangement drawings were no longer produced for the large designs, and the side elevation was only available as a 'Pipe & Rod Plan'. The detailed information formerly on the one large master drawing, somewhat impenetrable to the untutored gaze, and indeed a masterpiece of draughtsmanship and a skill now all but lost, was now produced on individual drawings. The drawing no longer carried a title block carrying the author's initials as well as those of the tracer and the senior engineer certifying the drawing. The A2/3 plan was signed by K Kingsley, but the certifying engineer would have been Chief Draughtsman Teddy Windle.

The first to be completed in May 1946 carried the new LNER number, 500, and was named EDWARD THOMPSON in honour of the CME who was to retired a month later. The new Pacific was fitted with an electric lighting set and long lamp irons, but this was later removed, probably when the Operating Department refused to accept electric headlamps in lieu of the oil-lit lamps used hitherto. In a flurry of publicity, No.500 was presented as the 2000th locomotive to be built at Doncaster. Ten LMSR 2-8-0s were omitted from the list in order to contrive the happy but artificial conjunction. As it happened, ten works numbers were unused in 1923, so in a roundabout way, No.500's works number *was* correct.

The following fourteen locomotives were all named after racehorses in accord with LNER practice, and allocated to all three Areas, five to the Southern Area, one to the Scottish Area, and the remaining nine to the North Eastern Area. Again, one might question the wisdom of keeping a solitary representative of the class on one operating region, and much the same argument about the A2/1, DUKE OF ROTHESAY applies with equal force to the A2/3, HONEYWAY. On the other hand Haymarket used their solitary A2/3 to far greater effect than did New England with their A2/1 – or indeed any of their Pacifics – running twice the annual mileage for much of the time.

Early experience with the prototype was somewhat mixed: Thompson instructed that the A2/3 should be fitted with a welded drawbar and side buffers on the leading end of the tender frame. These had been discarded by Gresley in favour of a robust drawgear and coupling drawbar, but Thompson was seeking to restrain the swaying of the locomotive. This proved quite unsuccessful and the normal arrangement was substituted. The second engine, AIRBORNE, was fitted with a stub axle extension for a generator, but none was fitted. The forward position of the dome and regulator meant that the engines were susceptible to priming, a tendency exacerbated by heavy-handed steam braking causing the water to shoot forward. Although palliative measures were taken to keep water out of the steam manifold, ejectors, etc, the locomotives retained an endearing ability to shower unsuspecting passers-by with dirty water once the vacuum ejector or the blower were operated!

The truth, of which I daresay nobody felt able to remind Thompson, was that all of his 26 Pacifics contained far more of Gresley's work than his own. It was known that he could be exceedingly difficult, and even on the LMSR Stanier (later Sir William) cautioned E S Cox

No.60512 STEADY AIM is south end pilot at York on March 28th 1959. (N Skinner)

60513 DANTE in New England shops in the early 1960s, undergoing attention to the left-hand motion and cylinders. (B Richardson, Transport Treasury)

that all was not well at Doncaster. It may well have been that senior staff were reluctant to make a bad situation even worse, and there was ample evidence that it was not beneficial to one's career to be the bearer of bad tidings. Chief Engineers of whatever department possessed enormous powers of patronage or sponsorship in earlier days, rightly or wrongly. Contrary to what one might think, it was either an ill-advised General Manager, or an extremely wise and clever one, who took on a Chief Engineer.

The few but critical changes made by Thompson improved matters in some respects and detracted slightly in others from the considerable potential of all of the A2 variants. The independent valve gears and divided drive were well laid out and gave the considerable advantage of allowing large piston valves and, by implication, larger ports. Although they were generally satisfactory in running, they gave a little cause for concern as regards the lubrication of the inside eccentrics. However the biggest problem was their riding and the need to keep the front end tight, and not their performance. It was curious that as each A2 variant succeeded the previous one, Thompson saw no need to improve a design that very clearly needed further development. One can understand the reluctance of subordinates to precipitate a dialogue that could

become, at the best, tense, but the Running Department was farther removed from retribution and could speak with greater freedom. No doubt Thompson was busy planning the re-ordering of the LNER locomotive fleet, producing the excellent B1 4-6-0 and O1 2-8-0, and developing the K1 2-6-0. However, one would have thought that he would have been anxious to discover the success or otherwise of his changes, and take steps to improve his designs.

One cannot imagine at this distance how difficult wartime conditions were and what could or could not have been done, but it seems strange that an excellent drawing office team could not produce a better steam passage layout than they did. Maybe personal feelings entered into it. It seems odd that the simple adjustment of the middle connecting rod length was left to Arthur Peppercorn. As referred to earlier, the rebuilding of the Mikados was influenced by Edward Thompson's promise to retain as much of the original locomotives as possible. There was no logical reason for perpetuating the expediency, but it was carried forward in the designs of the 20 locomotives that followed.

Edward Thompson retired in June 1946, succeeded by Arthur Peppercorn. One of the latter's first actions was to send an instruction on August 7th to the Mechanical Engineer, Darlington, ordering comparative tests between an

A2/3 and a V2 2-6-2 to establish comparative fuel consumptions and capacities. The V2 was known already to be a remarkably economical locomotive in service. Originally the dynamometer car and the counter-pressure locomotive No.1699 were to be used, but it was later decided to work service trains. There was some difficulty noted in the Report in getting suitable diagrams that were run in daylight to aid the necessary observations. The services concerned were the 9.45 from Newcastle to Leeds via Sunderland, Stockton, Ripon and Harrogate, and the 13.50 return via York and Darlington. In theory neither route, schedule nor loading were demanding for either locomotive. The A2/3 was No.500 EDWARD THOMPSON and the V2 was No.959 of Gateshead depot, later to go to Haymarket. No.500 worked the 9.45 from Newcastle and 13.50 return on November 5th, 6th and 7th, the run on the 8th having been abandoned due to a hot axlebox. The loading was the normal service loading varying around 350 tons, but for the following week from the 12th to 15th, it was increased to 14 coaches, averaging 460 tons. From November 19th to 22nd, No.959 was tested on the heavy loading, and then with the normal loading from 26th to the 29th. The loading of the 13.50 varied more than the up service.

The dynamometer car had not been used since 1938/39, and I assume the

60513 DANTE at Top Shed, Kings Cross, on the turntable in the early 1960s. (E D Bruton)

60514 CHAMOSSAIRE waits for release from her train on the freight loops at New England, around 1961-63. In the close-up of the Thompson front end one can see the difficulty in getting a good layout for the steam passages from the superheater header to the blastpipe, with the outside cylinder blocks positioned so far back. (B Richardson, Transport Treasury)

No.60517 OCEAN SWELL pulls away from York with an up express in the early 1950s.

testing team too, together with new members, had served elsewhere, and it would be understandable if everyone was short of 'match practice'. The train weight was carefully recorded in the report, but as sometimes happened, it seemed to overlook the 15-25 tons additional weight of the passengers for whom the service was operating! The trials were 'weighed on and off' using bagged coal, identifying fuel separately for lighting-up and standby, and by measuring water consumption before and after stops and water troughs. In retrospect, the four weeks' testing ought to have been more successful. It had been decided not to disturb the drivers' rostering, unfortunately, presumably due to growing trade union militancy.

As all who have been in the rail industry know well, Murphy's Law of Perversity is ever-present, and there was a great deal about in the autumn of 1946. The result was firstly that the crews on the Pacific were unfamiliar with their steed and their handling left something to be desired; secondly, the weather was often unhelpful, and the coal supplied was of poor and quite variable quality. In fact the coal was so poor on one test run with the normal loading that by the time the fire of No.959 had been cleaned and the pressure raised, departure was 23 minutes late. The boiler pressure fell and the brakes dragged on north of Darlington, almost stopping the train. The result of different crews handling the Pacific in particular was a variety of differing figures for coal and water consumption, superimposed on the variations in loading, weather, coal and

the rates of firing. The trials were adversely affected by a number of what were once dryly referred to as 'operational perturbations'. Apart from the attitude of crews to time recovery varying from one set to another, faulty brakes dragging on the train and an error in measurement rendered some tests with the A2/3 ineffective, while the V2 was hampered by wrong line working in emergency from Marshall Meadows to Burnmouth, and being held at Acklington for 40 minutes! Train heating could not be measured and had to be estimated.

When the detailed conclusions are read against the number of interruptions and adverse influences, the clear conclusions were that the A2/3 was a more powerful locomotive, and the blastpipe and chimney combination of the A2/3 was much superior to that of the V2. Certainly one has the luxury of hindsight nearly six decades later, but I would be surprised if there were not many in the CM&EE's department who could have written those conclusions before the trials were held. In view of subsequent deployment of some of the Thompson Pacifics, the comments to the effect that the use of the A2/3s in place of V2s on light duties was wasteful of coal, water and engine power, while their use on heavier loads would make better use of their greater capacity and probably lead to economy in coal and water, make salutary reading. It is a pity that the advice was not communicated to the Motive Power departments on BR.

THE THOMPSON A2 CLASSES IN SERVICE

To avoid repetition, the work of all of the Thompson A2 variants is described together. After the frequent movements between depots between building and 1951, when the position stabilised, the allocations were as follows:-

New England
60504, 60505, 60506 (A2/2)
60508 (A2/1)
60500, 60513, 60514, 60520, 60523 (A2/3)
Total 9

York
60501, 60502, 60503 (A2/2)
60522, 60524 (A2/3)
Total 5, later 7*

Gateshead
60516, 60518, 60521 (A2/3)
Total 3

Heaton
60511, 60512*, 60515*, 60517 (A2/3)
Total 4, later 2*

Haymarket
60507, 60509, 60510 (A2/1)
60519 (A2/3)
Total 4

*60512, 60515 moved from Heaton to York in 1952.

It will be seen that New England had by far the largest number of the classes, which was illogical since the depot, for much of time, had little main line work that would have embarrassed a 'Green Arrow', of which it had a fleet of 30 or more. Each was usually balanced with a 'parley' (passenger all stations) to Kings Cross which would not normally have taxed a B1 4-6-0 or even a big 2-6-0. This was exactly the sort of deployment vetoed in the 500-959 Test Report of 1946. One suspects that the main line passenger work was allocated to maintain route knowledge at New England, and what existed was the result of trade union lobbying as much as anything else. In fact New England was used as a reservoir of motive power, and their locomotives seemed to be borrowed with or without the Shedmaster's knowledge or consent. On summer Saturdays their fleet would be very much in evidence, and probably the service in the south would have been inoperable without it. Of course crews were not to know what they were getting at times, and there always seemed to be a New England V2, struggling with self-cleaning screens, losing time with an up service some time in the afternoon!

New England had a moment of glory in September 1956 when the Pacific off the up 'Aberdonian' was diagrammed to work the down 'Flying Scotsman', returning home light from Grantham. It had lost the 10.10 to Glasgow, re-timed to 11.00, to Gateshead, whose engine and men had worked the up 'Talisman' the previous evening. This was rightly stopped with the next timetable in May 1957, but it had the incredible effect of getting New England, for the first time in living memory, to clean their Pacifics. They had a good

shot at running the flagship service, too, and the sight of such as EDWARD THOMPSON or a sister A2 variant being driven hard through the suburbs, leaking steam often surrounding the cylinders, was good to see.

The Pacifics worked the up 'Aberdonian', its second part, and the 8.00 from Newcastle up to Kings Cross, and the 1.00 and 10.10 Glasgow (until 9/56) back. The 'Aberdonian' and the 10.10 were the only express pairing, each of other turns being paired with a 'parley' or parcels. In summer a number of turns were added to cover the extra traffic. Northbound, the 1.00 Edinburgh was worked on to Newcastle, the Pacific returning, I believe, on an overnight parcels. New England had a number of fast freight turns both north and south, but they were invariably worked by V2s: the sight of a Pacific on fast freight – for which they would have been excellent – was less than common in the south.

York worked to Kings Cross overnight, returning with the morning semi-fast leaving at various times after 8.00 and also, for a time, the 9.15 from York and 15.50 return. York also had six new A1s which dominated the passenger turns, while the two or three freight turns were handled by V2s and the occasional B16. The 6ft 2in Pacifics were used on a variety of duties usually within the NE Region; express, semi-fast and parcels on and off the main line, with much more involvement in cross-country traffic. In the same way as New England, York seemed to have far more Pacifics and V2s than were necessary and as a result their Pacifics appeared on other depots' diagrams and extras quite often.

The Newcastle and Haymarket engines were more integrated into the Pacific fleets and were more commonly seen on the principal turns, although the few Scottish Thompson Pacifics were less often used to Dundee and even less often beyond.

Class A2/2

The New England A2/2s were regular visitors to the capital along with the other Peterborough residents. A New England A2/2 pounding north with the Glasgow, with steam invariably leaking profusely around the rear of the smokebox, was quite a common sight. Sometimes the escaping steam assumed such proportions that the driver's view seemed to be obscured. Holloway bank on a wet morning could be impressive. They were powerful locomotives, and once the slipping had been contained, they could pull a good load, and with 10in piston valves, they could fly – provided the crew were prepared for the rolling and hunting at speed.

The line from Dundee along the Tay estuary towards Arbroath is straight and level, and although it appears suitable for fairly high speeds, the line speed limit ensured that fast running was neither experienced nor encouraged. Except once, when a driver had a rush of blood. Driver Duncan of Tay Bridge with an A2/2 on an Aberdeen-bound express with a good load, opened out the engine and worked it up to 85½ mph, a speed way in excess of the limit allowed. Experience of railways and staff suggests to me that there was a wager involved: I hope Driver Duncan's fireman was suitably rewarded!

The valve gear and front end of OCEAN SWELL. (J Robertson, Transport Treasury)

Farther south on the easier roads south of Darlington where the engines could show their paces, 70-75 mph seemed as fast as crews were prepared to push them as a rule. On two recorded occasions, EARL MARISCHAL was let go between York and Darlington on a light express of 220 tons with spectacular results, averaging 71.2 and 74.1mph start to stop. COCK O' THE NORTH herself, with 355 tons averaged 66.95 mph. The New England A2/2s took their part in the various New England diagrams, but the schedules were undemanding and again the speeds normally were not often in excess of 75mph. The loads of the expresses were 400-500 tons, which called for care if not imagination in climbing out of Kings Cross to Holloway.

The York A2/2s were comparatively infrequent visitors on diagrammed turns southbound, sometimes working the morning semi-fast referred to above, but never, as I recall, the 9.15 from York. They did appear on the main line with reliefs and unbalanced duties, and were often borrowed by other depots. They also worked northwards and on cross-country turns to Leeds and Middlesbrough. I cannot recall their use very much on heavy, fast freight, however. As with New England's Pacifics, that large grate would have not endeared itself to firemen weaned on Green Arrows, and their mates would not have relished slower running and frequent stops with a heavy load and a slippery engine.

The A2/2s remained much as they were rebuilt until scrapped, with two exceptions. The stovepipe double chimney was modified with a small half-round beading once the A2/2s were overhauled at Doncaster, except for No.60504. Then cast lipped chimneys were substituted for all except No.60506. The six engines retained their truncated boilers, although the solitary Diagram 108A was scrapped in 1946 and the spare Diagram 106A substituted. The A2/2s had to wait in the works for their boilers to be repaired, and in 1948 authority was given to use the slightly heavier and longer Diagram 118 Peppercorn Pacific boiler. Four engines, Nos.60501, 60502, 60505 and 60506 were altered, and No.60504 was fitted with the slightly heavier Diagram 117 Thompson Pacific boiler. Both the 117 and 118 boilers were operated at 225psi. Due to the different position of the safety valves, the meeting point of the angled cab fronts had to be cut short as on the Peppercorn Pacifics. No revised diagram showing the altered weight distribution was issued. Their outward appearance changed little. The inadequate small deflector plates remained, and the smokebox suffered small changes as numberplates were introduced, and then they were lowered to fit on the top hinge of the door. They led an undistinguished career, and as

the first diesels appeared and the steam fleet reduced, they were among the first casualties, in late 1959. The last was EARL MARISCHAL, arguably the most frequent performer on the principal expresses, and seemingly the best of the bunch, in July 1961. So much seemed possible at their introduction in 1934, and indeed could have been possible, were they modified successfully or used farther south. As it was they were overtaken by war conditions and ultimately met their unlamented end at the same time as Gresley's original Pacifics were enjoying their Indian summer.

Class A2/1

DUKE OF ROTHESAY had a moribund existence at New England along with the other varieties of A2 there. As mentioned with the rebuilt Mikados, the depot had a little express work. The annual accumulated mileage must have been about half that of the Scottish engines. DUKE OF ROTHESAY appeared on most of the East Coast expresses over the years, often hauling one of the overnight Anglo-Scottish expresses from Peterborough to Kings Cross. On July 17th 1948 she was on the 19.50 from Edinburgh, having taken over at Grantham, a Kings Cross turn for most of the post-war period. Passing through Barnet Tunnel at 60 mph or so, towards the south end the rear axle of the bogie derailed and turned the engine on its side. Remarkably the engine continued southwards on its side some way and remained a strange sight for local schoolboys and photographers for a few days, for many our first acquaintance with the underside and innards of a steam locomotive. The driver was Bill Hoole, later to become well-known to many enthusiasts. Years later he told me that he followed the advice of an old driver – 'Stick with her, boy; she'll stand a good bump!' The fireman didn't, and was killed. Bill hung on and emerged, very shaken but unharmed. The cause was defective track: in days when track was maintained by hand, a smaller size of ballast was used in tunnels, and staff were not always as attentive to maintenance in such difficult and dangerous places.

The three at Haymarket were used on express work alongside the other Pacifics, although never displacing the A4s, A3s and A1s from the senior links for long. They were generally kept in far cleaner and better condition than their English counterparts, and the figures show that their mileages were far better. HIGHLAND CHIEFTAIN, WAVERLEY and ROBERT THE BRUCE were very popular at Haymarket, and deputised for an A4 quite often. They were often used on the difficult Waverley route on the principal duties, and were a fairly common sight on the principal expresses, their greater steaming capacity and tractive effort

compensating for the need to anticipate wheelslip. They were used on freight and parcels diagrams quite often, where their greater power was not often put to effective use. The steam brake would have been valuable for freight work.

When the end came for the Mikado rebuilds, it was unlikely that the rest of Thompson's Pacifics would survive for long, and the four engines were withdrawn in 1960/61 at less than half life. Their running appeared to be much the same as the other Thompson A2s, fast running being the exception rather than the rule due to poor riding. This small class only reached the articles of Messrs Allen and Nock twice, as can be seen in the appendices.

Class A2/3

By the time LNER No.500 EDWARD THOMPSON entered service, there were 11 of Thompson's Pacifics in operation, the six rebuilt Mikados, four A2/1s and GREAT NORTHERN. With the Mikados regarded as a poor design not greatly improved, and the storm over the inelegant rebuilding of Gresley's prototype in full fury, expectations were not high. On the railway the Motive Power department was grateful for the arrival of powerful and free-steaming locomotives, and the new engines were put to work on heavy services straightaway. In the enthusiast world, Gresley's Pacifics were regarded very fondly, and the received wisdom was that the new Pacifics were heap bad medicine and so was the designer.

When Edward Thompson retired in June 1946 he was succeeded by Arthur Peppercorn. It was the latter's A2s that displaced the rebuilt Mikados, and it was his A1s, ironically envisaged by Thompson, that swept the A2/3s aside. They were moved from Kings Cross, Grantham, Doncaster and Copley Hill. Occasionally one or two came to Grantham or Doncaster for a short period or moved between Gateshead, Heaton and York but the distribution of the class seemed settled. By September 1951, when L P Parker's policy of more frequent engine changing and regular manning came into force, the three varieties of Thompson A2 were concentrated on New England, and York with a few at Newcastle and Haymarket as listed above. Now with no less than 202 Pacifics and the W1, the A2/3s reverted to a general purpose role on the East Coast main line.

In the south, the work of New England's Pacifics has been described earlier. If HONEYWAY and DUKE OF ROTHESAY could have been exchanged it would have tidied up at least the maintenance of the locomotives. Haymarket looked after their engines well, and so produced much higher mileages with them. Their one A2/3 achieved the highest mileage for the class, and probably saw more express work than her sisters. Both York and Peterborough had to provide main line pilots, which justified the allocation of a number of Pacifics in addition, although Peterborough provided V2s since the station turntable would not turn a Pacific. It seems to have been a deliberate policy to provide large allocations at New England and York as referred to above, not only of Pacifics but of V2s as well, in order to provide a reservoir from which other depots could borrow when necessary. Even if that was not the intention, that seemed to be how it worked, and both depots' varieties of A2 were familiar visitors on reliefs or other depots' turns of duty. They were often on expresses working from other depots or reliefs, and occasionally one would show the power and speed that must have been within their ability. HERRINGBONE, for example, with 380 tons, was driven hard from York to Darlington, and with an astonishing turn of speed averaged 72.6mph over the 44.15 miles.

Peter Townend told me of the occasion when, with the large allocation of Pacifics at Kings Cross requiring inspection, repair and washing-out, he had arranged with his colleague to borrow OWEN TUDOR from New England. He was assured that No.60520 was in good condition. No doubt the exterior looked unpromising before the cleaners got at her, and Fred

Dines, the top link man for the 'Yorkshire Pullman' was reluctant, to put it mildly. As Fred's regular A4 was the excellent WALTER K WHIGHAM (which was unavailable) one could understand his point of view. An accommodation was reached whereby, provided he took the A2/3 on one trip, he could have another A4 as a replacement afterwards. On his return he said that No.60520 was a good engine and he was happy to keep her for the week.

There is no doubt in my mind that the south end of the East Coast main line always had a more generous allocation of Pacifics by comparison with the NE and Scottish Regions, making allowance for the varying levels of traffic requiring Pacific haulage over different sections of the route. As a result those allocated to the old Eastern Region did not accrue such good mileages as farther north, and the Thompson Pacifics were not used overmuch other than on reliefs and extra summer services, together with their handful of express diagrams. With the summer timetable a considerable number of additional services were operated, which often involved the A2/3s. On the old NE Region, the A2/3s were used rather more widely, and between Newcastle and Edinburgh the five Tyneside engines and Haymarket's solitary HONEYWAY were a more

common sight on express and fast freight work.

Late in their careers York's Nos.60512, 60522 and 60524 went to Scotland in exchange for that Region's Nos.60519, 60531 and 60536, one of those pointless exchanges dictated by accounting rather than engineering reason. There was a time when in the south the lineside youth would have thought that their prayers had been answered, but the ex-Scottish trio were immediately withdrawn since presumably the NE had not withdrawn enough of its own locomotives. The three York A2/3s prospered in Scotland along with three or four Peppercorn A2s as a sort of ad hoc supplement and later replacement for the Stanier Pacifics, sadly withdrawn, abruptly and prematurely, in 1964. The Thompson engines were appreciated by the crews that used them, as powerful and free steaming, if a little light on their feet, and a considerable improvement on the 4-6-0 alternative.

No.60518 TEHRAN neatly posed at Haymarket on February 1st 1953. (J Robertson, Transport Treasury)

60502 EARL MARISCHAL stands at York in LNER apple green livery with the larger Cowlairs numerals, but bereft of the main steam pipe insulation and cladding. I would estimate the period as 1949-50. (Transport Treasury)

CHAPTER FOUR
A SUMMARY OF THE THOMPSON PACIFICS

There is no doubt that Edward Thompson has had a bad image for decades. Like many others my introduction to railways was strongly Gresley-coloured, and the received wisdom was that Thompson's Pacifics were not a patch on the master's work. Gresley was one of the triumvirate of great CMEs, with Churchward and Stanier, but even the great engineers made their mistakes. To the west of London one needs to remind people that even Churchward built THE GREAT BEAR. Looking at Thompson's career, one gains the impression of an engineer who tended towards the academic. Personal relationships are not in the scope of this book, but most of the anecdotal evidence points to an unhappy and sometimes stormy five years on the LNER. One cannot think of him getting his hands dirty, although in his youth he must have done. There is no doubt that his specifications for his designs were absolutely sound and in some respects an advance on Gresley's designs – think of that for GREAT NORTHERN for example. His B1 and K1 were excellent responses to the needs of the motive power department, although he seems to have found it difficult to acquire that 'feel' for practical day-to-day running.

Although it was a difficult time at Doncaster, there is no doubt that Thompson's engines were much the better for the skilled design team that he inherited from Gresley.

All of which makes me wonder whether the Thompson Pacifics were quite as bad as they were painted. Their riding was not so smooth as the Gresley engines, which didn't please the drivers, and the 50 sq.ft. grate was not regarded fondly by the firemen. Whether the extended front end reduced the stability of the locomotives at speed, and how, has exercised many minds. Whether the geometry of the locomotive affected the slides of the Cortazzi axleboxes, and whether their lubrication was as effective as it should have been, are questions that might have yielded interesting answers. Certainly the riding was not so smooth and drivers seem to have been disinclined to press beyond 75mph. However, the Pacifics would pull, and when on occasions they were required to stand in for diesel traction, such as on the (at times) extremely heavy Northfleet-Oxwellmains bulk cement train, their performances were impressive. The middle cylinder eccentric was said to be vulnerable over long runs, but in that knowledge careful attention would

ensure freedom from overheating. They were never allocated away from the main line, where it was obvious that they were not needed and, I am sure, not wanted by some.

Otherwise the locomotives could usefully have been diverted to the Leeds-Carlisle-Glasgow service where their considerable power and free steaming would have been an asset, although adhesion might have been a problem for some of them. Alternatively, with the unrebuilt Bulleid Pacifics posing maintenance problems (which led to their rebuilding) they would have brought a burst of the conventional to steam traction on the troubled South Western. That is of course, always provided that the CME could get them past the CCE, since the Southern Region was not so robustly constructed, very generally, when compared with the others of the 'Big Four', and the secondary routes abounded with weight restrictions. In theory they were a more powerful machine than the Merchant Navy, certainly heavier and more economical and reliable than the original design and might well have served the Southern well. Such a move had become far more complex with nationalisation, especially on the old LNER, now split

Even rebuilt MONS MEG looks splendid in freshly painted apple green livery. It would be March 1948, and the Pacific is on her way back north, probably at Darlington. (Paul Chancellor Collection)

into three autonomous Regions. One indeed, the Scottish, was jointly controlled with the old LMSR. In theory the BTC could have intervened as they did later in Ron Jarvis' excellent redesign of the Merchant Navy Pacifics. The ability of the BTC to overrule Regional management declined through the 1950s as General Managers and their management teams gained in authority, and by the 1970s it had almost disappeared.

I think one has to accept that Edward Thompson's Pacifics were better than we thought, although there was room for improvement. There is no doubt in my mind that the old LNER built far too many Pacifics, and the blame for that must rest with Thompson, who argued a gullible Board into authorising 83 more Pacifics that were not delivered until after the war. Whether it was intended to replace the oldest Gresley Pacifics was never revealed, but I cannot help feeling that it must at least have crossed the mind of Edward Thompson. Of course in the short term the new engines were invaluable, but in the longer term they were left to work services that could easily have been worked by other depots, or secondary duties. That they were sidelined early on says something about their unpopularity. However, given the load and a determined crew, there was no doubt about their power and freedom in steaming. It was a great pity that Peppercorn did not rebuild Thompson's Pacifics with his own front end design to conform with his own A2s and A1s.

THE SUCCESSION

The succession in 1941 has been debated at length. First of all the relationship between Gresley and Thompson as CMEs, and the personal aspects of Edward Thompson's stewardship are old ground and it is not my intention to plough it up again. Over sixty years later it no longer matters. I have concentrated on his work as the CME of the LNER, in particular that concerning the Mikados and Pacifics.

The LNER Board was taken by surprise by Gresley's death, clearly. It may be argued that even in wartime they should have been more circumspect with older senior staff, making provision for the need to replace key personnel at short notice. Gresley had indicated that he intended to work until he was 70, at which time both Thompson and Peppercorn would have been too old, and Harrison would have taken over. Despite Gresley's failing health, the warning signs were ignored. In the enveloping wartime context, the ability of senior staff to keep going was more, not less important.

While in other circumstances they would have looked for a younger successor to Gresley, there was no practicable alternative in 1941 other than the appointment of his deputy,

Edward Thompson, despite his 60 years of age. His claim was by far the strongest; indeed the LNER Board would have needed extremely good grounds to reject his candidature. The fact that he and Gresley did not see eye to eye was probably unknown to some of the Board and even if known, not a concern to them. He had proved himself an able but academic engineer with very good organising skills, who was familiar with the LNER's M&EE and Motive Power departments. However, he could be a difficult man by all accounts, perhaps troubled, and certainly most accounts of working for him during his stewardship emphasised the need for tact and care. In fairness it must be said that he could be as charming and courteous as he could be difficult. The loyalty of Gresley's staff that he inherited to their old chief and his ideas could well have irritated him further.

Digressing for a moment. it is an interesting insight into management practice in the 1930s that Gresley, despite his prestige and authority, was prepared to accept and tolerate as a senior assistant a man who was quite

out of step with his own thinking. Of course there may well have been other issues and personal relationships that were in play at the time. Gresley was not always a master of tact and patience and also, significantly, Thompson appeared to be fairly well connected. As a rule, the situation would not have been allowed half a century later. Career planning was far from perfect in later years but it should have worked, hopefully to the benefit of both men, channelling Edward Thompson's evident abilities more productively. One wonders why Gresley did not move to correct the situation. Planning one's own eventual replacement is difficult but an imperative. It was accepted then that seniority was a prime, if not the main consideration, and 'dead men's shoes' was an accepted practice of the 1930s. A vacancy was *normally* filled by the principal assistant – not always, as the appointment of Gresley himself showed – but very often. The consequence of that unsatisfactory situation, overtaken by hostilities, was that the LNER Board had no other realistic choice. Looking back, there can be no doubt that,

unusually for a man in his sixties, Edward Thompson was not lacking in drive and energy. He did not like the conjugated gear, and preferred divided drive, and many locomotive engineers agreed with him, then and subsequently. These were the two Gresley design principles that Thompson rejected. It was significant that there were some with which he agreed, notably the double Kylchap exhaust, without which his locomotives would have been far less potent. It may not be a popular view even now, but while some of his designs and rebuildings could have been better, his output of worthwhile designs in just five years was very creditable. Of course his record with smaller designs looks much better. The most pressing need on the LNER was not big engines but a good, simple, versatile 4-6-0 to replace the large numbers of the obsolescent pre-Grouping designs that Gresley had perforce kept in the fleet, but which were now at the end of their working lives. His B1 4-6-0 was as good as any other 4-6-0 in the UK and probably the cheapest to build and most economical overall. The B1 was simply a two cylinder Sandringham with smaller coupled wheels – no doubt a point better not made in senior circles at the time! He laid the foundation for the A1 Pacific, the splendid K1 2-6-0, also built by his successor, and his O1 2-8-0 was an excellent design.

While we have a considerable store of personal anecdote illustrating the views of those who worked with Thompson, we have little that illustrates his own views and opinions beyond his vision for the future. He was too easily angered as the proponents of the nickname 'Bongo' for his B1s found out. Privately, he must have been very disappointed with his rebuilt Mikados, and one wonders why some improvement was not made to the A2/1 or A2/3 designs. An intelligent man, he must have realised that they needed improvement. Even in retirement nothing emerged from him that would have thrown light on his short period of leadership.

In summary, Edward Thompson's appointment resulted, in five hard years, in the B1, O1, later the K1 and eventually, the A1, together with a new Pacific design that solved some of the problems of the P2s but brought its own. Although some of his ideas were unpopular and less successful, many CMEs would be pleased with such a number of good designs produced in five years. His record can hardly be condemned.

An immaculate 60507 HIGHLAND CHIEFTAIN pulls away from Waverley with the 10.27 departure to Leeds, which conveyed TPO vehicles (Travelling Post Office). The A2/1 has the A4 non-corridor tender No.5675, off the 'lost' A4 No.4469, with the stainless steel trim now painted over. Under a renumbering scheme introduced by Edward Thompson it became No.703. The date is probably in the early 1950s. (J Robertson, Transport Treasury)

No.525 A H PEPPERCORN, with an up Grimsby express in 1949. This may well be the 8.50 to Kings Cross that was turned over to Immingham B1s in March 1950. (D C Ovenden)

CHAPTER FIVE
ARTHUR PEPPERCORN'S A2 PACIFIC

The 1945 Locomotive Construction Programme contained 30 6ft 2in A2 Pacifics. One might wonder just what for, in the long term. Nevertheless, the 1946 Programme contained a further 13, together with 16 6ft 8in express locomotives. However, the LNER's big engines had been bearing the brunt of the wartime traffic and were in a poor state, and so the new engines were welcomed. Edward Thompson retired on June 30th 1946, a month after his first A2/3 was completed. Arthur Peppercorn, the Assistant CME at Doncaster, was appointed as his successor. At some stage before Thompson's retirement, the succession having been decided, it was decided that before the Works Orders for the second 15 A2/3s – or the further 13 – could be implemented, the design needed revision. Quite how the decision was taken to start a new plan without the CME's authority is an interesting question. Somewhere between Harrison, Spencer and Windle, however, the decision was taken to revise the A2/3 design and Peppercorn's tacit approval must have been given in order for it to be implemented. Bernard ('Barney') Symes commenced the new drawing, starting at the cab end. The drawing was rolled and kept under the drawing board dust sheet when Thompson made one of his rare excursions into the Drawing Office. Again, one wonders what he would have made of it had he seen it. Was it passed off as the new A1, for example? The Peppercorn cab featured the sloping cab faces which Thompson disliked but the Running Department had requested, and that detail was added after June. On the other hand, Thompson may have been too close to retirement to care, although it seems uncharacteristic of the man. Be that as it may, the plan appeared in August 1946. The principal change was the return of the front bogie to its normal position under the outside cylinders, the centreline now being 2ft 7in nearer the leading coupled axle.

The boiler was designed by November 1946, and was to be manufactured from nickel steel with a rocking grate and hopper ashpan, and a 'banjo dome' steam collector. Being sufficiently different from the Diagram 117, it was classified as 118, and was actually 0.35 of a ton lighter, the two sections being rolled of $\frac{1}{8}$in thinner plate. It was decided to retain divided drive and three independent sets of Walschaerts valve gear rather than reinstate the conjugated gear, even though that required the use of longer outside connecting rods. The A3 and A4 cab sidesheets were 8ft 2in apart, but the A2 cab sidesheets were 8ft 6in up to window sill height, then tapering in to 8ft 4¾in at roof height, constrained by the loading gauge. It was also necessary to vary the shape of the cabside glasses. At the front, a step was welded to the smokebox door. The provision later on of numberplates required the top lamp irons to be raised; when headboards were carried, they projected above the smokebox crown, causing the exhaust to be sucked down behind the board. So, despite the presence of smoke deflectors, drivers often had to contend with the annoyance of drifting exhaust, although the problem was not as serious as with the small chimneyside deflectors.

A curiosity was the reversion to single blast in early 1947, despite Sir Nigel Gresley's directive that all future construction should feature the Kylchap double exhaust. A number of explanations have been ventured for this aberration, for it was certainly a serious misjudgement on what otherwise was an excellent design. The single chimney exhaust limited the steaming capacity of the engines, often seriously so. The report of the trials with the A2/3 had drawn attention to the inadequacy of its large smoke deflectors with a soft exhaust, and remembering the similar troubles with HUMORIST, it was decided to revert to single blast. Perhaps also Peppercorn was trying to return to a balanced and handsome

No.60526 SUGAR PALM, as dirty as she normally was, stands as York South End Pilot in the early 1950s. (J W Hague, Transport Treasury).

No.60527 SUN CHARIOT at Ferryhill Shed in April 1963. (Leslie Sandler)

appearance, but it was not very successful since, by comparison with double chimney, the single chimney appeared undersized and gave the engines a puny appearance, misleadingly.

In fact the middle cylinder of the A2/3 required very little alteration for the A2, and the distance from the front tubeplate to the vertical central axis of the middle cylinder was almost exactly the same. However the dimensions of the casting needed to be slightly different since the centreline of the 5¼in diameter exhaust had moved 9in closer to the front tubeplate. The casting provided the base for the exhaust standpipe. The A2 smokebox was 16⅝in shorter than its predecessor, leaving insufficient room for the proposed self-cleaning screens and a double Kylchap, unlike the A2/3. It would not have been possible to lengthen the smokebox without seriously compromising the appearance of the A2, not to mention endangering shed and footplate staff when opening the smokebox door. I think Peppercorn opted for single blast since it avoided potential problems with drifting exhaust and allowed him to fit the screens as well.

I questioned J F Harrison about the reversion to single blast, and he confirmed that the middle cylinder pattern already in existence then would not allow the fitting of a double blastpipe (known as a breeches pipe)

to the A2, with self-cleaning screens in place. Presumably this was the one used for the A2/3, but as already explained the longer smokebox of that design could accommodate a double Kylchap whereas the A2 could not. This had been raised with Peppercorn, who was unwilling to spend money making a new pattern for the middle cylinder casting. Arthur Peppercorn was a very popular chief in the Gresley tradition, very well liked, and he had been Mechanical Engineer, Darlington. Clearly he did not realise the value of the double Kylchap, although an engineer of his seniority certainly should have done. One might wonder where he was in July 1938.

The last Thompson A2/3, HERRINGBONE, emerged from Doncaster on September 26th 1947, and the first Peppercorn A2 was completed on Christmas Eve that year, a week before the LNER disappeared. Construction continued in 1948, but it was already apparent that the steaming of the A2s was not good when the engine was being driven hard. On May 6th 1948, Peppercorn, under pressure from his new Assistant CME J F Harrison and others, directed that future A2s and the forthcoming A1s should be equipped with double Kylchaps. This required the preparation of a drawing and then a new pattern for a middle cylinder casting which would take a breeches pipe.

The first A2 to feature the new double exhaust was in fact the last,

BRONZINO, which was completed three weeks after the first A1 on August 27th 1948. This engine spent its working life at Heaton, where it was highly regarded. In a much-quoted incident during Peppercorn's periodic visits to the Works, in the New Erecting Shop he came upon the new No.60539, and was surprised to see a new type of middle cylinder and a double Kylchap being fitted. On enquiring why, the foreman told him that 'Mr Harrison had given instructions to do it'. Back at the office, Harrison was sent for, and sharply reminded that AHP was the CME, and not him! When the CME was reminded that he had actually issued the instruction, he withdrew in good humour: 'Ah yes, now I remember!'

It was Thompson's intention to build 43 A2/3s but under Peppercorn that became 15, with 15 of his own A2s in addition. The order for a further 13, now plus a further 7, was cancelled by a Railway Executive intent upon using the investment on its own designs. This was not unreasonable since it could well be argued that the varieties of A2, powerful and in the main, free steaming engines, were already surplus to the requirements of the East Coast Route. The 15 A2 Pacifics were completed between late December 1947 and August 1948, five going to the Eastern Region, nine to the North Eastern, and as now seemed usual, only one to the Scottish Region. As with the A2/3s, the first locomotive was named after the

CME, and the following 14 were named after racehorses in the Doncaster tradition. No doubt as with the A3s, the names seemed odd to those whose favours lay elsewhere, and there were certainly some odd ones.

Patience in Scotland with the rebuilt Mikados finally expired, and after little more than a year, two of Gateshead's A2s, SUN CHARIOT and TUDOR MINSTREL, went in June 1949 to Dundee Tay Bridge, a strange transfer since Ferryhill and Haymarket were the principal depots for the route. BAHRAM went north from Gateshead, plus two New England engines, A H PEPPERCORN and BACHELORS BUTTON in July and August 1949 to Ferryhill. At the end of the year, SAYAJIRAO, BLUE PETER, IRISH ELEGANCE, HORNET'S BEAUTY and TRIMBUSH joined PEARL DIVER at Haymarket. So within two years one was left on the Eastern Region at New England, and three on the North Eastern at York, Gateshead and Heaton. On the GN section reminiscences were somewhat brief since the A2s moved away shortly after arriving, but the engines were found to be strong. Schedules were not challenging and the steaming problems were not insuperable, but the abiding memory was of wild riding at speed. It was significant that already, some were finding their way to New England. The depot had little express work for its stud of Pacifics, as made clear earlier, but they seemed to find their way on to expresses working from other depots.

In April and May 1948 the newly nationalised Railway Executive held the Locomotive Exchanges in which the old LNER was represented by three A4s. The A4 was the most economical of the express locomotives, notwithstanding the fact that their drivers made no attempt to rein them in and used expansive working with full regulator. With the engines running hot three times there were, however, questions as to their reliability. One feels that the overheating was a very welcome excuse to dismiss a design that had the unacceptable 2:1 gear. Many – indeed the majority, it seemed – were uncomfortable with the idea. As the A2 and A1 were unable to take part in the Exchanges, it was considered important to test the A2 and A1 so that comparison could be made with the A4 figures. These trials, which were held in May 1949, are dealt with in the description of the A1s.

Further trials were arranged in late 1949 with an A2 on express freight, and No.60533 HAPPY KNIGHT, by then the only Eastern Region A2, was loaned to Copley Hill for the duration. The trains were 1343 up, the 20.00 from Leeds to East Goods, Finsbury Park, and 1224 down, the 18.55 departure from Kings Cross Goods. This train was later the Copley Hill freight lodging turn, and ran to Leeds. In 1950 it ran to York. No report was issued, but the RCTS LNER Locomotive Survey relates two examples. With 1224 down the load was 616½ tons, 60 wagons, and with a bracing climb to Potters Bar, HAPPY KNIGHT recorded a peak DBHP of 1,615. Both services suffered slow and goods road diversions and signal checks, but given a clear road, East Coast Route express freights could keep pace with most expresses of the day, as witness 69 mph at Biggleswade. On April 27th 1950 the load was heavier at 701 tons, 70 wagons, but the speed was limited to 55mph. The maximum DBHP of 1,540 was recorded on the rise to St. Neots.

It was noted that the train rode badly at speed on occasions, so much that the rough riding was transmitted to the dynamometer car. I am not surprised, for however great the drawbar pull, speed is an essential component in order to achieve a reasonable HP. The former LNER had an enviable reputation for the speed of its fast freight services, and I do not doubt that HAPPY KNIGHT and her crew gave the test car a good shaking. The short wheelbase wagon (or van) with leaf spring suspension could be a notoriously rough rider despite being in good physical condition, and with the advent of CWR Continuous Welded Rail) was the cause of innumerable derailments. The reason for the locomotive's rough riding at speed, usually hunting, I am sure, was insufficient stiffness in the horizontal control springs in the front bogie, coupled with a similar lack of control in the Cortazzi rear axle. The A2 was a

PEARL DIVER, after the introduction of the later BR totem; there is no other indication as to location or date.

Ferryhill's BLUE PETER well cleaned and coaled ready for an up service in the period 1951-57.

powerful locomotive, and with divided drive the middle cylinder was placed forward by comparison with a Gresley Pacific. The De Glehn bogie as used on all post-Gresley Pacifics gave an inferior ride generally by comparison with an A4, although it is difficult to understand why. The higher the speed, the more kinetic energy was consumed in hunting. The Pacifics were not widely used on freight on the southern end of the main line until October 1956, and then it was the A1s and rarely one of the varieties of A2. The bulk of freight mileage remained in the capable hands of the V2s, which had a smaller appetite for coal, and rode superbly even when run down.

Doncaster was directed in June 1949 to equip five locomotives with MLS multiple valve regulators and tangential steam dryers, as these were being considered for use in the new BR standard locomotives. SUGAR PALM, PEARL DIVER, BLUE PETER, HAPPY KNIGHT and VELOCITY were modified between September and December 1949. The experiment did not specify the provision of double Kylchaps, but the opportunity was taken to fit them and remove the self-cleaning screens. The regulator itself was placed transversely ahead of the superheater header, and controlled the flow of superheated rather than 'wet' steam. As a result the superheater elements were constantly under steam, reducing the tendency to burn. It protruded above the smokebox wrapper, but as it rendered the anti-vacuum valve ('snifter') redundant that was removed. The tangential steam dryer was fitted in the banjo dome where the regulator would be normally. Its purpose was to prevent scale-forming impurities

leaving the boiler and affecting components that were difficult to descale. The regulator consisted of five valves, one a pilot, and they were opened by a camshaft running transversely. The regulator handles in the cab were attached to a cross shaft mounted on the boiler backhead as on all big Gresley engines, and the camshaft was operated by external rodding on the fireman's side of the cab with a compensator halfway along the boiler. It allowed the driver 17 options as the regulator was opened. The equipment remained with the five A2s for the rest of their working life, and one, BLUE PETER, survived into preservation.

The six double chimney engines were built with the stub stovepipe chimney with a small beading around the rim. When lipped chimneys of the pattern first seen on HUMORIST in 1938 were reintroduced commencing with A1 ABERDONIAN, they received new chimneys. The problem of exhaust turbulence with headboards referred to earlier was made worse by the rimmed chimney, and often headboards were carried on the lower central lamp iron.

The Diagram 117 and 118 boilers were interchangeable, with 118 used on A2/2s and A2/3s, and 117 used on A2s. One, No.60536, having been fitted with a 117 boiler, kept it thereafter. Again, BTH speedometers were fitted, later being replaced by the BR standard Stone fitting. The locomotives were also fitted with electric lighting, together with generating equipment. Despite the provision of a single chimney, smoke deflectors were fitted, mercifully smaller than the elephantine pattern used on the A2/3s. In mitigation, the omission of smoke deflectors would have left the A2 at a slight visual

disadvantage, aesthetically, having a rather foreshortened look, in comparison with the elegant Gresley A3.

With 11 of the class working in Scotland it seemed that their considerable tractive powers would be used to advantage. Nos.60525, 60531 and 60537 were at Ferryhill, Nos.60527 and 60528 at Tay Bridge, and the remaining six, Nos.60529, 60530, 60532, 60534, 60535 and 60536 at Haymarket. None was fitted with tablet-catching apparatus for the single line section from Usan to Montrose. The LNER designs were having trouble with the self-cleaning screens, largely due to being blinded by small char and ash, the smokebox vacuum and hence the steaming being reduced. The V2s suffered quite badly, and whereas the A2s could have displaced them on the heaviest turns, they suffered as well. G H K Lund at Aberdeen complained vigorously, especially over No.60537, which seemed to be the statutory 'dud'. One of Haymarket's double Kylchap A2s, No.60532 BLUE PETER, was sent in exchange in January 1951 to Ferryhill, and in investigating the unfortunate No.60537 BACHELOR'S BUTTON, the exhaust was found to be incorrectly assembled. The fault was corrected by machining the blastpipe and cap, and the performance of the A2 was restored. Apparently Haymarket 'forgot' to fit a replacement and when the locomotive went for general repairs, the balloon went up! District staff were not allowed to alter designs – the fact that they had improved it didn't seem to matter!

BLUE PETER was an instant success at Ferryhill, and the Assistant Motive Power Superintendent Geoff Lund, an outstanding Gresley man, went to great pains to ensure that the drivers understood why. She would lift any load out of General station up the hard climb to Cove Bay, or up to Carmont, or out of Montrose to Usan for that matter. As a demonstration of the engine's potential with a double Kylchap, hauling the 16 coach 'Aberdonian', 575 tons gross, BLUE PETER was opened out, with remarkable effect. The hard climb to Cove Bay was tackled in a manner reminiscent of the Mikados, the A2 maintaining 2,300-2,500IHP, and the following speeds were high despite the load. The climax came on the dash down over the Esk viaduct at Craigo, where the A2 reached approximately 100mph. Arrival at Montrose was 14 minutes BT! One may argue about the precise maximum, but it was an amazing sprint on the main line north of Edinburgh where speeds were normally much lower. Of course it impressed Higher Authority not a bit. The single blast A2s were also powerful machines at lower speeds within their evaporative capacity.

In March 1951, the problem of poor steaming on the Scottish Region was referred to Doncaster. One might think that the answer was simple, but there seemed to be a dogged determination at Doncaster to do anything but fit a double Kylchap. One would have thought that a high proportion of the senior staff were very well aware of the achievements just over ten years ago, even if those at the Railway Executive were not. In fact there was a prejudice at Marylebone and Derby against double chimneys – almost fanatical at times – and at the BTC as it had now become. Even in 1953 there was an authoritative report from the CME's department stating categorically that double chimneys gave no significant improvement over single blast. I suspect the hand of Stewart Cox was not very far from the final draft! MALLARD? DUCHESS OF ABERCORN?

Therefore, to retain the self-cleaning screens, experiment with various single blastpipes was the only course of action open to the engineers. Since the B1 4-6-0 steamed well despite the fitting of self-cleaning screens, it was decided to try a B1 blastpipe, which had a nozzle diameter of $5^1/_8$in and had a shorter standpipe with a longer chimney liner. The fact that the A2 was a completely different locomotive, potentially twice as powerful as a B1 seemed not to have been considered! Five A2s were modified, Nos.60525, 60530, 60531, 60535 and 60537, and the two Ferryhill Pacifics were found to steam a little better as a result. The coal consumption when measured, however, had increased by more than 10%, and the water used had increased by 5-7%, which would suggest that the back pressure had increased and the driver was having to work the locomotive harder. The blastpipe orifice diameter

had been slightly reduced from 5¼in. So much for the science of sophisticated exhaust design!

In 1953, flushed with success after restoring the steaming capacity of V2 No.60845, which had been roughly halved by the insertion of self-cleaning screens, the British Transport Commission agreed to look at the A2 problem. Two A2s were selected, Nos.60527 and 60531, but after a long delay Nos.60525 and 60530 were converted instead. The dimensions of the exhaust are not known, but the nozzle diameter is believed to have been 5½in. Edinburgh reported that no complaints about bad steaming had been received regarding No.60530, but Ferryhill were adamant that their No.60525 was no better and her coal consumption had increased further. Comparative tests, locally undertaken, showed a clear superiority with the double Kylchap, but apart from reporting this and recommending conversion to double blast, it was concluded that Doncaster was immovable and there was no point in persisting. Nos.60527, 60528, 60534 and 60536 were additionally modified to the BTC proportions, now with a 5¼in nozzle, whilst Nos.60531, 60535 and 60537 retained their B1 exhausts. When one remembers that the four English A2s were all double Kylchap machines of significantly greater potential, and that they led a rather mixed existence – indeed to be frank they were badly under-utilised – there was a cast iron case for sending them to Scotland. In January 1957 the BTC drew a line under the experiment since there seemed to be little to favour either exhaust arrangement. This was one of a number of problems that the BTC dropped quietly, one imagines, thankfully, filing it under 'Too Difficult' on the promise of imminent diesel traction under the Modernisation Plan. Ironically, at the same time the Eastern Region General Manager had instructed the CMEE to convert all of the single blast Gresley Pacifics to double Kylchap!

The A2s had the reputation of being strong but extremely rough, indeed wild riding engines. One always has to remember the innate conservatism of drivers who were used to the comparative armchair comfort of the Gresley Pacifics and V2s, and perhaps the A2s were not so bad as all that. The springing was the same as the A2/3 except for the bogie, which had helical springs rather than leaf. In fact the last A2/3 also had helical springs in place of leaf as well. In service the springing was a cause for concern, and longer springs with a greater deflection were tried experimentally. There was no conclusion formed from this, and no further action was taken. As the last A2 and the first A1 were built together, it was not a surprise when each had the other's bogie, although the designs were

the same but for the lightening slots, one for the A2 and two for the A1.

HAPPY KNIGHT spent most of her life at New England, and the Thompson Pacifics there seemed to be preferred to her. Perhaps she was borrowed by other depots. Five coach Parleys were not an efficient use of a potentially 3,000IHP locomotive. In September 1951 the 17.52 Kings Cross to Cambridge and Peterborough, a heavy train for basically a suburban service, 10 coaches, was re-diagrammed for a New England Pacific. The 17.20 'Yorkshire Pullman' was a heavy train, hauled by a top link A4, followed by a Grantham A1 with a similar load on the 17.35 Newcastle, then the 17.39 outer suburban to Royston with an L1 2-6-4 tank and the 17.52 followed behind. With the Hadley Wood 'bottleneck' still in place, stopping services had to be slotted in between the expresses. It was an attempt to accelerate the exit of a crucial service in the rush hour, which had a number of services following. As presumably HAPPY KNIGHT was elsewhere, York's SUGAR PALM was borrowed for three weeks, driven in very spirited fashion. The 17.52 fairly rocketed out of London at unprecedented speeds. The regular New England A2 took over, but clearly there were problems emerging, firstly at Hitchin where the train split and also, judging from the speed achieved climbing out of London, from the disturbance and delay to other evening services. In response the working was changed again so that the GN main line had the unusual sight – intentionally – of a double headed train, New England and Cambridge each providing an engine as far as Hitchin. Quite often, the New England engine was a Pacific, which was then piloted. On at least one occasion GREAT NORTHERN appeared piloted by B17 DARLINGTON, a very Thompsonian pairing.

York's SUGAR PALM spent much of her time playing second fiddle to five A1s at a shed with comparatively little express work, but often got used by other depots. Late in its existence, she was used on the 9.15 from York and Hull alongside the A1s, and for once she was cleaned and ran well. It was just such an occasion when Copley Hill, strangely for a depot not without A1 Pacifics, borrowed her for a return trip to London on the 'West Riding' in 1961. Of course the rostered A1 may well have had, say, an injector failure at the last moment and the A2 was on hand. York had taken to cleaning some of its bigger engines, but SUGAR PALM was often as black as the ace of spades and usually looked neglected. One can imagine the feelings of the crew – the signs were not good. The train had shrunk from its 14 coach load to 9, so the A2 was not overtaxed. The driver must have been an intrepid soul, as he put the A2 to it in great style, and the top speed down Stoke was a

No.60533 HAPPY KNIGHT at New England in typical condition. The date would be about 1959-60 I think. One of the shed's stalwart 'Green Arrows', No.60866, is in the background. (B Richardson, Transport Treasury)

remarkable 101mph. One might suppose that the A2 was in splendid condition, but Arthur Cook, an engineer and enthusiast who recorded the run, spoke of his surprise that an engine in such a poor condition, off beat and filthy, should be capable of such running. It speaks volumes about the determination of the crew not to be deterred by a little thing like a rough riding.

Of the two Newcastle engines, VELOCITY, at Gateshead, again had a considerable stud of A1s to compete with, but was used much more on freight. BRONZINO at Heaton was more regularly used on express work, and was well liked. The Scottish A2s worked passenger and freight alike, but the senior men at Haymarket would only take them if their regular A4 or A1 was unavailable. As speeds were necessarily lower, rough riding was not so much of a problem. One has to remember that although the principal services north of Newcastle were loaded to 10-11 coaches, many others were lighter and slower. The routes were generally more heavily curved and graded and trains called at more frequent stops. Very often it was not the sustained power of a Pacific that was called for, nor capacity for high speed, so much as the greater tractive power, in short bursts, that justified their use.

The Scottish A2s, despite having been sent north specifically to replace the rebuilt Mikados, led a mixed existence. With 11 powerful Pacifics replacing 6 rebuilds, it was inevitable that they were not always fully or economically used since there was only so much mileage in the timetable. The single chimney engines were, as described, not the freest of steamers, but strong and reliable. It was the two Kylchap A2s that were the stars of the Scottish fleet, PEARL DIVER and BLUE PETER. They were very strong locomotives, and with care would manage Mikado-sized loads. When the work of the two Scottish Kylchap A2s with 550 tons is compared with the English counterparts, the rationale of locomotive allocation is impossible to fathom. The late John Bellwood, Chief Mechanical Engineer at the NRM, regarded the A2s as the best Pacifics in the UK in terms of potential and economy.

At Ferryhill, BLUE PETER was undoubtedly the star, with single blast sisters A H PEPPERCORN and BAHRAM as often on fast freight as on passenger. The A2 was a mixed traffic locomotive, after all. In the last years of steam they worked on the 15.30 'Postal' from Aberdeen to the south, a very heavy train as far as Perth. Here it divided and the train engine ran south with the postal coaches, while a 4-6-0

followed to Buchanan Street with the passenger portion. The two at Dundee Tay Bridge, SUN CHARIOT and TUDOR MINSTREL again seemed to lead a humdrum existence, working in either direction on expresses or fast freight. At the time there were a number of fast fish services from the busy East Coast ports such as Aberdeen, two, three or four bound for London in the early 1950s. The six at Haymarket worked to Newcastle, Carlisle, Glasgow and Perth as well as northwards to Dundee and Aberdeen. Although Dundee was only about 60 miles north, the road was not easy and infested with colliery speed restrictions to protect the workings below. While engine changing at Dundee was wasteful, it avoided a delay for taking water, and not every locomotive worked through. Once again, there was fast freight work as well as passenger. It was noticeable however, that provided the load was not too heavy, a V2 2-6-2 was often preferred, with its smaller grate, better adhesion and more comfortable ride.

The end came for the A2s at the turn of the 1960s with the arrival at Haymarket of a batch of English Electric Type 4 2,000HP 1-Co-Co-1 diesel electrics. Although underpowered for the southbound traffic from Edinburgh, the Type 4s were comfortably masters of the Aberdeen road and all others. Loads were falling and often a 4-6-0 was used on the Aberdeen-Glasgow services. With higher availability, a much reduced need for servicing, abundant power and unimaginably cleaner, the new diesels swept steam off the main duties, leaving the Pacifics, the A2s among them, to the reliefs and the fast freight. There were the humorous moments in the changeover, and I recall with some fondness two items in the notice case at Haymarket. One required shed crews to desist from trying to tow-start reluctant diesels (!) and the second reminded drivers of the likely and inflammable consequences of parking diesel locomotives over the ashpits!

Fortunately we have BLUE PETER to remind us of Arthur Peppercorn's A2, a fine, sturdy and strong locomotive, fortunately in its double Kylchap condition. Those of us who, as youngsters, followed the railway scene at the London end remember them as the successors to the Mikados. They were very rarely seen, and then only by the grace of the Doncaster Shedmaster, running in from general overhaul, usually late at night. The Scottish, and perhaps the Newcastle A2s as well, joined that elite and elusive group of locomotives remembered in the inscriptions on the close boarded fences alongside the railway - 'Died waiting for .....' followed by the name of a rare visitor such as SIR VISTO, SILVER KING, or in this case BAHRAM or TUDOR MINSTREL.

The cab of BLUE PETER, the distinctive Peppercorn profile caught by the sunlight. (J Robertson, Transport Treasury).

GREAT NORTHERN on exhibition at Edinburgh Waverley on 19-20th June 1946, following completion of her overhaul in December 1945, with the old LNER number 4470. The exhibition celebrated the opening of the NBR, and while the inclusion of a manifestly English locomotive in a Scottish celebration was a touch insensitive, Edward Thompson was still CME (just) and No.4470 was one of the few locomotives in good external condition and not in wartime black livery. She is in the unique dark blue livery, with her 1930 A3 non-corridor tender No.5582. (Transport Treasury)

GREAT NORTHERN at Kings Cross on May 12th 1946. (E R Wethersett)

CHAPTER SIX
EDWARD THOMPSON'S A1 PACIFIC

If we retrace our steps to the start of Edward Thompson's period of office, we would find him faced with two problems. The Gresley conjugated valve gear was not performing at all well in wartime conditions, denied the proper levels of skill and materials on which it was dependent for reliable service. Also the replacement of the 180psi Diagram 94 boilers with the 220psi 94A version was in full swing, and 18 A1 Pacifics were not yet committed to rebuilding. Thompson strongly disliked the conjugated gear, and sought the support of Stanier before approaching the LNER Board with his plans for its removal. William Stanier was a good friend of Gresley, and the families were on very cordial terms, and he reluctantly deputed E S Cox from his staff to report to Thompson. Cox's report was good, and he identified the cause of the problem, which was not the 2:1 gear but the design of the middle big end. So Thompson received the report, which fell a long way short of condemning the 2:1 gear as he had hoped. However, it did not stop him subsequently offering Cox a post as Mechanical Engineer (Commercial), a curious idea for 1944, but perhaps it was intended to enhance the CMEE's budget in order to afford Thompson's grand ideas! Quite what the Chief Commercial Manager would have made of the CME's excursion into

his area of responsibility, I shudder to think. In fact Cox was prevented from accepting, which deprived the LNER of someone who was an outstanding engineer but who later proved unfortunately to be somewhat dogmatic.

Thompson had initially proposed various schemes for the removal of the 2:1 gear, which in wartime conditions were out of the question. This was no time to indulge personal preferences. After the rebuilding of the Mikados, the construction of the last four V2s as Pacifics, plus the rebuilding of smaller engines such as the B2s, K1/1 and K5, he concentrated on his new A2 and A1. The A2 became the A2/3, very much on the lines initially used on the Mikados with divided drive, equal length connecting rods, independent valve gears, large piston valves and bogie displaced forward.

The decision was taken to build a prototype A1, and two options had been considered, the first being a Gresley type Pacific but with divided drive and independent valve gear, and the bogie in the conventional position. The second had the bogie ahead of the outside cylinders as in the varieties of A2 Pacifics. New construction was not an option, even if Edward Thompson had deployed the charm and articulacy of a Bulleid – which he could at times. He

was within sight of retirement, and time was not on his side. It was the second option which prevailed, and it is interesting that the first option was ultimately the basis for Peppercorn's two Pacific designs. It was a pity that Thompson was dissuaded. He was still of a mind to insist that the connecting rods should be of an equal length, despite the repositioned bogie, external steam ducts *et al*.

Thompson's choice of the A4 Diagram 107 boiler allied to the use of a double Kylchap exhaust as a basis was faultless. On the four A4s so fitted it had proved an inexhaustible steam raiser, and in service it had proved economical to maintain. Gresley understood the value of the Kylchap in his time, but until 1941 its use involved the payment of a sizeable sum, some £500, in royalties and design and manufacture by the Associated Locomotive Equipment Company. Before his death he had issued an instruction that all future new large locomotives should be fitted with double Kylchaps. Edward Thompson used it on all his Pacifics, the need to pay royalties having expired. The firegrate area was unchanged at 41.25sq.ft., rather than increasing the size. The use of three cylinders with divided drive and independent valve gear was, again, absolutely right:

No.4470 GREAT NORTHERN with a down express at Ganwick, approaching Potters Bar Tunnel. (H C Casserley, courtesy R M Casserley)

unified drive was no longer imperative and in wartime there was no case for using conjugated gear. Large 10in diameter piston valves were, again, an improvement. A hopper ashpan was fitted, which was appreciated by the Running Department, but it was usually associated with a rocking grate, whereas the Gresley drop grate was retained, which limited the effectiveness of the former.

On paper the credentials of the new A1 were impeccable. It was the post-war version of MALLARD and her three sisters, the three cylinders in line with conjugated gear having been replaced with divided drive and independent valve gears. Freed from the constraints of the Gresley design, the cylinders and their piston valves could be enlarged to give greater power. It is not within the scope of this book to debate the conduct of Edward Thompson and his attitude to his predecessor, despite the strongly held views by those involved. Enough has been said elsewhere. Accounts suggest that he had little time for discussion or persuasion when his mind was clear on the way forward, in many ways a good trait provided history proves that one was right. Under wartime restrictions, the building of express locomotives was not allowed. So an existing locomotive had to be rebuilt. The choice was Thompson's, and it was very unfortunate that the choice should fall on GREAT NORTHERN, Gresley's 1922 prototype. With this rebuilding, the remaining 17 A1s became A10s.

In those days enthusiasts would have had greater regard for the prototype Pacific and its place in steam locomotive history. Nor did it help that the emerging rebuild in September 1945 looked a mess compared with Gresley's A1. As a result there was great anger among enthusiasts and railwaymen that dogged the locomotive to one extent or another throughout its existence. Thompson, who for personal reasons had what would later be described as a bad image among his staff, was widely anathematised by railwaymen and enthusiasts, and this decision 'put the cap on it'. J F Harrison knew him well, and came to the conclusion that he had severe problems insofar as his predecessor was concerned. Senior staff had attempted to change the decision, knowing what the result would be, but the CME was adamant. It would have been far more sensible to choose a less well-known A1. O S Nock, a professional engineer, enthusiast and railway writer, was well connected with the Gresley regime, and was taken into Thompson's confidence. His comment was 'Why, oh why did he have to choose that one?'

When looked at from Thompson's point of view, there would have been a slight justification for his choice. This was the new Pacific, the improvement on Gresley's A3 and A4, the machine for the post-war era. This would carry forward the continuing development at Doncaster, and where better to start than by using the prototype? A touch of arrogance maybe. We must remember

that Edward Thompson was not trying to ruin a good locomotive, rather that he was convinced that his A1 was an improvement and a worthy successor. In many respects he was right, but appearance was not one of the improvements. There is no doubt that the rebuild looked awful, compared with the Gresley A1, a fine looking locomotive. Thompson's was probably nearly 1,000 HP more powerful but didn't look at all fine. It could hardly fail with an A4 boiler and Kylchap exhaust, and in fact, potentially, it was an advance on the A4 with larger cylinders and piston valves. GREAT NORTHERN, one suspects, was famous in April 1922, but had gradually faded into the background, especially once FLYING SCOTSMAN became the standard bearer. She was a Doncaster engine for many years, but not one of the famous ones such as LEMBERG, SOLARIO and FELSTEAD. Only a few performances by the prototype have been published, and first-hand experiences of her at the time were quite unimpressive: perhaps she was showing her age. Insofar as it mattered, very little of the GN Pacific survived into the rebuild, since a new A4 boiler and frames were provided, and the front end layout was entirely different. Even the nameplates were different. The components replaced were consumed in repairing other A3s.

Thompson had persisted with his fixed ideas regarding the cab and controls. The traditional flat fronted cab that he preferred was retained. A

GREAT NORTHERN at York shed in preparation for the return trip with the GN Centenary special train on 16 July 1950. The BR blue livery is more evident in this view of the engine. In the pre-automatic half-barrier age, manned level crossings always had an element of unreliability about them in that the crossing keeper/signalman either was less than vigilant, or the signalman in the rear offered a bell signal with insufficient time to clear the crossing gates. Sometimes the driver assumed, wrongly, that the signals would clear as he drew near. A number of crossing gates were nearly always in pristine condition as a result of collisions, such as at Walton crossing, near Peterborough. Even at a very low speed with the brakes hard on, the gates never looked quite the same after being bumped by several hundred tons of locomotive and train! On this occasion GREAT NORTHERN demolished the gates at Balne, and arrived at Kings Cross sporting white painted timber as a trophy!

flat cab floor made its appearance again, but raised by 6¼in to a higher level than the original locomotive, and the cab side sheets were reduced to resemble a sort of B1 cab. There were misgivings about the cab before leaving the Works, principally because it was inadequately braced, allowing it to sway disconcertingly at speed. The locomotive was fitted with steam brakes. A GC type regulator was tried once again, but was replaced with the conventional Doncaster pull-out regulator in 1947. The steam reverser that had been introduced in place of the screw reverser on the first A2/1 was reintroduced in the design with more robust support, and then removed. A pity, for excellent though the screw reverser was when well maintained and lubricated, too often it was stiff and required the driver to stand over it and use his upper body strength. A good, reliable steam reverser, that did not have its own opinion as to the cut-off, would have been an aid to drivers.

The cab was the cause of immediate complaint from the Running Department at Carr Loco and after a month another followed when the A1 was transferred to Kings Cross. In less than a month GREAT NORTHERN went into the Works to have the Gresley cab restored and large smoke deflectors fitted. The A1 was equipped with electric lighting similar to the A2/1s, but the axle-driven generator was replaced by a steam-driven version at a later stage. The engine was also fitted with discs as were the A2/1s, but electric headlamp lighting and discs met the same fate as on the A2/1s. A Flaman speed recorder was initially fitted but was removed in 1951: one would imagine that there was nothing to record in the first few post-war years by any express locomotive. A BR standard Smith-Stone speedometer was fitted in 1961, but the locomotive, which had been re-designated A1/1 in 1948, was withdrawn less than two years later. Originally without smoke deflectors, as mentioned above No.4470 acquired a pair of large deflectors that were not especially effective, to judge from drivers' comments. The Gresley standard high-sided A3 tender No.5582 remained with the locomotive from before the rebuilding throughout the rest of her life. The new A1 was exhibited at Edinburgh Waverley on June 19th and 20th as part of the NBR Centenary celebration in dark blue livery with her old LNER number. Despite the understandable wish to display the new locomotive, perhaps the choice of GREAT NORTHERN was somewhat tactless!

At Kings Cross GREAT NORTHERN was tested in comparison with A4 No.4466 SIR RALPH WEDGWOOD. The trains were the 10.30 to Leeds as far as Grantham, returning on the 15.25 from Leeds, both heavy trains averaging 480 tons tare

and no doubt 500-510 tons gross. The A4 worked from November 5th-9th, and the A1 on November 13/14/16th, and on the 19th and 20th the following week. The testing was simply a 'weighed on and off' series of trips, and the coal consumption figures were identical. This was as one might expect from two locomotives with the same boiler and grate, and with no call to exert much in the way of power. The A1/1 showed a complete mastery of heavy loads, but the lower factor of adhesion necessitated a greater degree of care at the regulator. There were some criticisms of a lack of smoke deflection, but if the engine had been harder pressed that may have been less of a problem. No doubt there were some caustic comments about the cab which didn't reach the test report.

The engine was tested again in April-May 1947 whilst still at Kings Cross, and then in August 1947 by which time she was at Gateshead. No report has been located of the first tests, but the NE and Scottish Area tests are documented. GREAT NORTHERN was now sent to Haymarket and was tested against that depot's A4 GOLDEN PLOVER. The test trains were the 10.00 Edinburgh to Dundee and 14.43 return, then the 10.15 Edinburgh to Newcastle and 15.22 return. The loads were 380 or 400 tons northbound to Dundee and 350 return: to Newcastle they were 475 tons for the A4 and 490 for the A1. Although both engines had the same boiler and grate, the draughting was different, and the A4 had been significantly weakened with the middle cylinder lined to 17in so that when pulling hard at low speeds, she was at a disadvantage. Also the extent of the testing was two runs to Dundee and one to Newcastle by each locomotive, and with so few results to consider, it must be recognised that it must have been difficult to eliminate variations due to the quality of the enginemanship in the trials. In addition, it must be remembered that the Edinburgh-Dundee route, although short, as mentioned earlier was full of TSRs for colliery workings and curvature. On the Dundee tests, the A4 averaged 47.2lbs/mile, while the A1 was down at 41.7lbs, and on her second run, went down further to an excellent 36.9lbs. On the Newcastle tests, the A4 burnt 39.2lbs/mile and the A1 40.9lbs. Perhaps the longer runs, better speed and less frequent slowing and accelerating suited the A4.

GREAT NORTHERN returned to Kings Cross where she worked turn and turn about with the newer Pacifics, until in 1950 she was sent to New England. Being sent there was hardly a vote of confidence, but with the reorganisation of locomotive diagrams in September 1951 she was despatched to Grantham where she went into the newly constituted top link, where each pair of drivers had their regular A1, similarly

to Kings Cross with A4s. At the time the shed had nine A1s, which was inadequate for a twelve man top link with regular manning, and GREAT NORTHERN was drafted in to improve cover. She ran for about two months on the up 'White Rose' and other expresses before being displaced by one of Grantham's eight or so A1s, the newer engines being much more reliable.

For a period in the middle 1950s she was a regular sight on the 12.40 slow from Grantham to Doncaster, returning on the 16.40 from Doncaster. A notice in the cab exhorted would-be borrowers to return the engine to Grantham. The reason for this was that the engine's coupled wheels were thought to be shifting, and she was kept under observation from Doncaster Works for some while. The Pacific was gainfully employed as a pool engine, working reliefs and occasionally standing in for one of her newer brethren. However, she was not a common sight on the principal services. All of the Thompson Pacifics were said to be poor riders, although that must be a subjective judgement. In their last hours three went to Scotland where the crews appreciated them. It depended whether one was used to an A4 or a Black Five. GREAT NORTHERN could fly, as indeed she ought, with 10in valves and a double Kylchap, and I remember a lightning descent of Stoke, admittedly with a smallish train of 9 coaches, reaching and sustaining 96mph easily before steam was shut off.

It was no surprise, therefore, that when withdrawal of the Pacifics started she should be one of the early ones. I have heard that it was mooted that she was considered for rebuilding to a standard A1, but if so, it came to nothing. It would have required a change of boiler and repositioning the cylinders, together with detail alterations, and the first generation diesel electrics were not far off. The rebuild ran a slightly higher annual mileage when rebuilt, about 52,200 as opposed to 50,000, but modern thinking would view the investment in the project as highly unremunerative unless it was regarded as a necessary preliminary to the introduction of the A1 class. I think that attitudes to the locomotive were perhaps prejudiced, maybe because it rode less well, maybe because of its history. Attitudes can be founded in emotion as well as reason: while the rebuild was an improvement and a pointer to the future, it is still a pity that Thompson was not persuaded to utilise a less prominent A1, or better still, settle for unequal connecting rod lengths. Had the rebuilt GREAT NORTHERN looked and performed like the unfortunately named No.60114 (see Chapter 7) attitudes and locomotive history would have been very different.

No.60114 W P ALLEN arriving at Kings Cross with what I assume is the 9.50 Leeds-London express. It is the first week of May 1949, with the comparative trials between the A1 and BRONZINO, and the dynamometer car is behind the A1. (Paul Chancellor Collection)

One of the first photographs of the new A1s to be published was one taken at New Barnet. No.60114 ran without a name for only two months, and despite being a Kings Cross engine, she was not an everyday sight for those of us at school. Here she is on the 17.50 Newcastle on June 24th 1949, in splendid condition, going well by the look of the exhaust.

Notes

_____

_____

_____

_____

_____

_____

_____

_____

_____

_____

_____

_____

Blind Veterans UK

Thank you for remembering blind veterans who have made sacrifices for our freedom.

22342_SL

CHAPTER SEVEN
THE PEPPERCORN A1 PACIFIC

Edward Thompson had a series of sketches prepared to outline his thoughts on the question of improving – as he saw it – the Gresley Pacific. Both the conventional layout with the bogie beneath the outside cylinders, and the design that was ultimately developed for GREAT NORTHERN were produced in sketch form. Both progressed further after the A1/1 was rebuilt, and early in 1946 a semi-streamlined version of the A1/1 was mooted. Ironically, its shape appeared to be derived from the first two Mikados. Amazingly, in April 1946 the conventional layout was developed into a fully streamlined version beneath an A4 cladding, with a corridor tender. From what we have been told of Edward Thompson's character, unless it was with his approval, it would not have been too late for the perpetrators to be ceremonially boiled in cylinder oil. It shows that he was prepared to consider the use of the successful A4 streamlined envelope.

Meanwhile the authorisation for the 1945 Locomotive Building Programme, which included 30 A2s, was followed by a policy decision on April 26th 1945 on a five-year building programme in accordance with Thompson's programme of standardisation. This envisaged no less than 75 A1s and A2s. The 1946 Programme contained 16 A1s and 13 A2s, and the 1947 contained another 23 A1s and 7 A2s. The 20 A2s were to be built by Beyer Peacock, but their tender price was too high and the order was replaced by another 10 A1s. So when he retired, Thompson had 49 A1s on order, and construction had started on the 30 A2s. The number of Pacifics existing and on order was now so big that it was impossible to use all of them economically. As we saw later on, a number weren't. This poses the question whether the traffic levels forecast were hopelessly optimistic. In my experience they were nearly always unrealistic. Alternatively, perhaps it was intended to start withdrawing the early Gresley Pacifics before too long. One wonders.

Earlier I had questioned where Arthur Peppercorn had been in 1938. Despite Gresley's careful investigation into the role of the double Kylchap exhaust on MALLARD's epic run, leading to his complete acceptance of the superiority of the design, then Thompson's as well, Peppercorn had continued to use single blast. In July 1946, no doubt spurred by the need to get the Drawing Office working on the A1, another sketch appeared. It was a combination of the A4 envelope and the cylindrical A3 smokebox, with the double chimney cast aside in favour of a single one. One hesitates to condemn, but it would have looked curious at least, and if the A2 was anything to go by, it would have been limited by its evaporative capacity. The SNCF Baltics of classes 232R, S and U combined a semi-streamlined profile with a cylindrical smokebox, but much more effectively. Immediately another followed in which the A4 shape was further corrupted in order to include the A3 smokebox. The next sketch showed a return to the A3 outline first mooted by Thompson, but with a single chimney, dome and a corridor tender. The penultimate sketch was almost like the A2, but with smoke deflectors, a single chimney, dome and a corridor tender. Of these, the final design only retained the Peppercorn smoke deflectors, and mercifully a double Kylchap was restored at a late stage.

As mentioned earlier, a CME was the leader of a large mechanical engineering organisation. His primary task was to have enough locomotives to work the timetabled duties economically, plus those disabled for repairs or servicing, for one reason or another. Design was a small but rewarding part of that responsibility. Arthur Peppercorn was greatly liked as a chief, and as a manager appears to have excelled, but as a designer he seemed to lack the instinctive touch and feel of his mentor Gresley, and even at least the academic understanding of design of Thompson. He had considerable personal tragedy in his life and one must allow that it would have affected his professional life. Because he was a popular and kindly chief, his staff did their best for him, a good team led by his Assistant CME, Freddie Harrison, and the experienced and able Chief Draughtsman, Teddy Windle. It is relevant to recall that in late 1947 it was seriously proposed – and rightly so in my view – to streamline the A1s, but with the shadow of state ownership falling over the Big Four, the CME designate, R A Riddles, vetoed the proposal. A pity: even the LMSR had streamlined engines, very good ones. It is sad that, when it was too late, having retired and then learnt the real benefits of streamlining in smoke deflection, he admitted that he was mistaken. Likewise he accepted that his opposition to the use of double Kylchaps was also a mistake.

DESIGN

The A1 was simply an enlarged version of the A2 BRONZINO. There were minor adjustments to accommodate the larger coupled wheels, including the smallest splashers of any design, three inches high. The Diagram 118 boiler of the A2s was also used in the A1 design. The wider A2 cab and running plate were included in the design. Divided drive was retained with connecting rods of different length, 10ft 9in outside and relatively short inside rods of 7ft 2in length. The valve travel was reduced by a sixteenth of an inch, and it was not considered necessary to alter the dimensions of the combination lever to correct the travel. Electric lighting was provided, with a Stone's turbo generator tucked behind one of the deflectors, although not all A1s got the generating set when new. Two large two gallon mechanical lubricators were provided on the driver's side, except for the roller-bearing engines which had lubricators for the cylinders only. The roller bearings were lubricated with grease and sealed. Flaman mechanical recorders were fitted to the first Doncaster batch and a number of the Darlington engines, but the equipment was removed in the early 1950s even though the supporting brackets remained in some cases. From 1960 the standard Smith-Stone electric speedometers were fitted to all of the class except No.60115.

The double Kylchap blastpipe had twin 5in orifices, and although the smokebox was large, it precluded the use of self-cleaning screens since the double Kylchap was close to the front. Thus the steaming of the A1s was not prejudiced by the equipment as were other classes. In retrospect, while one approved of the use of the exhaust to avoid a singularly unpleasant task – emptying smokeboxes – it always seemed one which lent itself better to a mechanical solution. In fact the apparatus seemed to be more effective in spark arresting and blinding the smokebox screens, thus throttling the steaming capacity of the locomotive and filling the smokebox. Steam brakes were fitted to the locomotives combined with vacuum for train working. No.60149 was the first to be fitted with experimental ATC, followed by 13 others, all likely to find themselves on the experimental New Barnet-Huntingdon section. Significantly, the A1s were not often used in the higher speed testing, the A4s – usually the Kylchap engines – being preferred. It was expected that the A1s would take over the 'Non-stop' in the 1950s, but the cost of converting the corridor tenders to steam brakes was not thought to be worthwhile since the A4s were coping well.

The first five A1s from the last batch of ten built at Doncaster were selected for the experimental use of Timken roller bearings. Three A4 tenders had been equipped with Timken, Skefco and Hoffman roller bearings in 1938, and had performed perfectly well, justifying the initial investment by reducing servicing and repairs, and reducing the incidence of hot boxes. It was particularly galling for a perfectly serviceable locomotive to be failed in traffic because of a hot box on the tender. With this in mind, the drawing office were keen to apply the use of roller bearings to the locomotives. However, roller bearings were a costly addition in new locomotives. Individuals had suggested or proposed their use in previous years, but during the war years they were simply unavailable. Post-war austerity prevented the experiment being carried forward into new construction. With nationalisation, the Railway Executive assumed responsibility, but they were concerned with their own standard classes and not anything else from the 'Big Four'.

If one considered the number of occasions a steam locomotive was failed on the road, then broke that down into main (carrying) bearing failures, and then calculated the overall cost to the railway as a whole of each disruption, the savings that would have accrued from the general fitting of roller bearings at least to the express locomotives would have made an attractive investment proposal. The addition of manganese steel liners to the axleboxes would have made the case even better. Such an investment case was made for re-draughting the A4 class, of course. The roller bearing experiment was requested by the Railway Executive as part of the preparation of the BR standard designs. The five engines were fitted with larger special axleboxes on all axles, which remained with them throughout their working lives. The roller bearings were not cheap and the building cost of the five A1s was increased by approximately £3,000. This outlay was retrieved quite quickly since the five engines ran considerably higher mileages between overhauls, and at a significantly higher rate than the rest of the A1s.

There were a number of variations in letters and numerals used, including the rogue Doncaster 6 or 9, and the two BR totems made their appearances in 1949 and 1956. The smokebox door had the conventional Doncaster appearance, with the BR numberplate just below the top lamp iron. The latter was set forward to allow the oil headlamps that were compulsory, to clear the electric headlamp. Apart from the difficulty in reaching up to place or remove a headboard or recalcitrant oil lamp, when a headboard was carried

the exhaust was again pulled down by the turbulence behind the board as in the case of the A2s, which could prejudice the driver's view ahead. The lamp iron was lowered, and the numberplate was secured below the handrail, on the top hinge. The A1s ran in this condition until their last years, when the lamp iron was lowered still further and the handrail was replaced by two short handrails. Of course as in most classes there were variations in detail, and a few engines such as HAL O' THE WYND, KENILWORTH and GUY MANNERING had the numberplate placed close to the upper hinge, with the handrail above. Most numberplates were renewed when they were moved, but for example PATRICK STIRLING's was reused.

CONSTRUCTION and NAMING

Doncaster started work on the 16 A1s authorised in 1946, and Darlington started on the 23 of the 1947 Programme. The later 10 were built at Doncaster after No.60129. Under Thompson's direction, Doncaster had adopted the considerably cheaper snap-head rivets where possible, and the new tenders were studded with rivet heads. Darlington, however, 76 miles away from Authority, persisted with countersunk rivets, and the new tenders had a smooth appearance which enabled everyone to distinguish the builds. The smaller and neater smoke deflectors initially introduced by Peppercorn on his A2 were continued on the A1. The chimney was a very short plain double stovepipe with a half inch round beading at the top.

The sixth engine of the second batch built at Doncaster, ABERDONIAN, was built with a lipped chimney, first seem on HUMORIST in the 1930s. The original drawing, interestingly, shows a lipped chimney at the outset. Lipped chimneys were introduced from late 1950 onwards. Despite the chimney being necessarily double and very short, a successful and pleasing design resulted. The A1 overall was a very handsome and impressive locomotive. Of the Doncaster build, Nos.60114-60126 were turned out in LNER apple green with BRITISH RAILWAYS on the tender, and Nos.60127-60129 wore the new BR blue livery with black and white lining, and the tender carried the BR totem. The A1s looked particularly good in the short-lived BR blue livery. No.60127 was unique in that the cylinders were lined out in red. The Darlington batch was built a little quicker, and the engines were all apple green. The blue livery was applied to the green A1s at overhaul, but the 49 A1s were all in BR blue for only three months before the ubiquitous Swindonian khaki beloved of the west began to be used. This remained the livery till withdrawal.

Apart from the prototype, the A1s were not named at first, but the

Railways Executive of the British Transport Commission having decided that such a prestigious task could not be delegated, formed (what else?) a Naming Committee. By 1950 of course we had retreated from the 1922 Grouping Act, and the old LNER was now three independent railways functioning under a fourth – BR – which was a railway organisation without its own railway. Each contributed a list of suggested names, and it was the task of the Naming Committee to decide. The Railway Executive (RE) had already decided to name the first A1 W P ALLEN after the RE member for personnel. This worthy was a prominent ASLEF trade unionist who was given a seat on the Railway Executive, and who started his career on the GNR in motive power, progressing to driver before leaving the footplate to concentrate on union matters. To say that the choice of name was unfortunate is a massive understatement: it was quite the most terrible choice at that time. I suppose we should be thankful that the Railway Executive stopped at one name: the thought of some of the other BTC names that might have got on to A1 smoke deflectors brings a shudder to the system! No.60114 was the only A1 to carry a name when apple green.

The names chosen seem to have been pulled out of the Doncaster drawing office waste-paper basket in some ways. The naming of the A1s was a typical example of committee deliberations. Any idea of a naming theme such as those beloved of the old GWR – sensibly so if not overdone in my humble opinion – was swiftly discarded. With the BTC and three different Regions having different ideas about names, inevitably 13 were racehorses, 18 were names from Scott novels or names carried by earlier locomotives, 6 each were either CMEs or birds (four of them removed, sadly, from A4s), four were pre-Grouping railway companies, and BALMORAL sounded like something from Scott but wasn't! At least with the Royal Scots hard at work nobody wanted to commemorate any more regiments of the Army. The racehorse names at least avoided some of the excesses of the dear old A3s, SANDWICH, SPEARMINT and PRETTY POLLY, but hadn't quite the poetry of a SOLARIO or the panache of a ROYAL LANCER. On the whole, the Scott names had a style and a swagger about them and were some of the best, although some were not quite the same once one learnt of the person and context! Four, plus GREAT NORTHERN, were selected to carry special nameplates bearing the coat of arms of the company concerned. These A1s were fitted with special nameplates with a raised portion over the middle that carried a plate with a hand painted coat of arms, and the A1/1 GREAT NORTHERN was refitted with her third set of plates in her lifetime. The engines concerned were the last to be named. The first names of the A1s other than No.60114 were applied from April 1950 when No.60133 was named POMMERN, shortly followed by No.60141 ABBOTSFORD. The naming process took just over two years, and the result was agreeable. We never learn, and the names of the 22 Deltics some 15 years later were the same strange mix of turf and famous regiments, although at least D9000 was not named Marples or Beeching!

COMPARATIVE TRIALS

The A1 could not of course participate in the 1948 Exchanges, and so in May 1949, W P ALLEN and BRONZINO were tested so as to provide comparative figures. I doubt whether the trials made the slightest impact on the minds at the Railway Executive. J F Harrison, Peppercorn's Assistant CME who had been closely involved in the design and building of the A1s, went to Derby as Mechanical Engineer (LM Region). Harrison always maintained that the A1s were the engines that Gresley would have built post-war, although I think it would have taken considerable pressure to make the latter abandon his cherished conjugated gear. No doubt at one time the use of poppet valves was seen as the way forward, replacing the conjugated gear.

The tests took place on the 13.00 to Leeds and 9.50 return, (498 and 490 tons respectively), and the 10.00 'Flying Scotsman' to Grantham and the up train leaving at 16.20. The loads were specially made up to 612 and 604 tons between London and Grantham. W P ALLEN and BRONZINO had run 47,000 and 40,000 miles respectively. Significantly, after the widely varying results of the tests of the Thompson Pacifics, the importance of good and experienced footplate discipline was addressed, and top link Driver Ted Moore drove both Pacifics in the trials. Ted Moore was also the driver on LORD FARINGDON in the 1948 Exchanges, running on the LM and Eastern Regions. The testing was as follows:-

April 26 -29th No.60539: 13.00 to Leeds twice returning on the 9.50 from Leeds the following day.
May 3-6th No.60114: 13.00 to Leeds twice returning on the 9.50 from Leeds the following day.
May 10-13th No.60114: 10.00 to Grantham and 16.20 return each day.
May 17-20th No.60539: 10.00 to Grantham and 16.20 return each day.
NB: The up run on May 18th was not taken into account as the steam brake was dragging.

The tests examined two almost identical locomotives in considerable detail, and as it represents most of what we know about one of our best express locomotives, it is worth studying in some detail. In addition to the care taken with footplate work, care was taken in preparation as well. The coal was weighed on and off the tender and particular care was taken at the time to ensure that the weight in the firebox was the same and the boiler water level was brought to a constant level. The coal used was analysed to establish its calorific value, so that the consumption figures could be corrected. But despite the obvious care with which the tests were carried out, there are some variations in consumption that can only be explained by unrecorded signal checks or speed restrictions, of which there were 8-14 per run. Comparing the Leeds tests, No.60114 was under power 18 minutes less on her second run down but the work done was almost the same. Coming back the disparity was still 12 minutes but again the work done was similar. Interestingly, there was a constant difference of about 10-15% in work done between the down and up journeys. The fuel consumption was similar for coal going down, but on the up run the coal consumption was 9-12lbs/mile lower. Indeed with 11 checks and a signal stop, on one run the A1 returned the amazingly low specific coal consumption of 2.694lbs/DBHP.hr. Clearly Driver Moore's fireman, who is not identified, was particularly skilled at maintaining pressure whilst running with a thin fire, and using his fuel economically. It was a skill that was not so widely encountered as one would have liked. The A2 was only a whisker behind, but having 'batted first' one needs to allow for the fact that the fireman was acclimatising to the larger grate.

When we come to the high power tests between Kings Cross and Grantham, the most striking feature is again the greater disparity in the amounts of work for the down and up runs, despite the hard start from Grantham and the long pull up to the Chilterns. The total effort was 15-25% less in the up direction, which goes a long way towards explaining why even the 500 tons 'Flying Scotsman' could manage to get below 100 minutes in the up direction, but hardly ever on the down. Grantham is of course higher than Kings Cross which would account both for the difference in work done, and the increase with trainload. The A1's coal consumption was higher, 45-50lbs/mile, but as the power output was higher, the specific coal consumption varied between 2.91 and 2.78. The A2 burnt less, and remarkably, achieved figures of 2.79-2.82. The water consumption was good on the Leeds runs, but on the high power tests to Grantham, it was high. The results were then compared with the 1948 A4 figures in Appendix H, and it will be seen that the new Pacifics, if handled properly, were fine engines.

Steam locomotive testing was a considerable skill and provided useful information. The unpalatable truth, however, is that a railway is not a laboratory, and it would have been only too easy to test two identical engines with two crews – or even one – and produce fuel consumption figures with a noticeable, if not significant, difference. It was simply not possible to test locomotives exhaustively, with a sufficient number of runs, to average out the perturbations of operating life and variations in firing skill. Two round trips, sadly, would only ask more questions than provide answers. Gresley was right in persisting with his plans for a testing station. It also needs to be pointed out that given the practical limitations of testing on an operating railway, differences of 5% or less fall 'within the limits of experimental error'. Despite having produced evidence to prove a design feature saved fuel, such were the ingrained habits of drivers and firemen that it was quite another thing to actually realise it. Locomotive Inspectors did not always appear to be so concerned with technical matters so much as operational and disciplinary matters, and did not command the same respect in technical matters as they did in France for example. However, the test results were excellent, and some of the best of the steam era.

The report then continued to comment on aspects of the testing and the future use of the locomotives. It is perhaps cynical, but a prerequisite of writing reports, at least on BR, was an understanding of what was expected or at least hoped for by the recipients. Of course if investigations revealed an outcome quite at odds with that expectation, then it required all one's political skill and wit to say so in a manner likely to be accepted without unnecessary pain! As the report stated, clearly the schedules and loads were not such as to tax either locomotive. The use of a locomotive with such a large grate on lighter loads was uneconomical, even when fired with care and skill, compared with a smaller type, and when not fired carefully could be wasteful. The report stressed that the locomotives should be used on the heavier duties where their increased grate area would have been an advantage.

That, with respect, was obvious without going to the trouble of testing, but there followed a tortured argument to reinforce the point, based on the rate of combustion of the A1 firebed compared with that of an A4. For anyone who has ridden on an express loco, the idea of timing the rate of combustion *per inch* of firebed depth must seem far-fetched. I would guess that this value was deduced from the rate of firing at the time, assuming the fireman was maintaining a firebed of roughly 6 inches. That would give a rough idea of the coal consumption at the time, as distinct from the overall figure usually given, which is the amount consumed

The second A1 has been joined by the third at Haymarket in May 1959. HAL O' THE WYND, No.60116, had one of the finest A1 names, even though perhaps it was more euphonious than the character deserved. Heaton worked rather more turns northwards, and after losing the 17.35 from Kings Cross in September 1951, their A1s were rare visitors down south. (D H Beecroft, Transport Treasury)

on the run, corrected for lighting-up and standing. Obviously it varies quite widely throughout the run. In my experience the Gresley Pacifics were fired largely to the back corners and below the trap door, leaving the engine to 'help herself' on the inclined grate, so that the firebed consisted of near-fresh fuel at the back and near-burnt out coal at the bottom or front of the grate. A thin fire would have been about 6 inches *average* in the centre of the grate, but the depth would be greater at the back and at the front there would be an accumulation of burnt-out coal. The report then went on to assume a higher rate of combustion for the A4, with a smaller grate, based on the coal consumption recorded in the 1948 Exchanges. In fact the rate of combustion multiplied by the grate area will give the total coal consumption, and if the A4 consumption was more economical or not, no amount of juggling with hypothetical rates of burning will alter that fact. In fact the higher rate of combustion might well have resulted in a higher firebox temperature with beneficial effects on the evaporation rate.

On firmer ground, the report then commented on the larger grate area and firebox heating surface, which gave rise to an increased evaporation rate round the firebox, but resulted in a

larger temperature drop from the firebox to the front tubeplate. With a shorter boiler and a strong draught, I would have expected a higher smokebox temperature as well, but there are no comparative figures. Without using more sophisticated forms of superheater element, the superheating surface was significantly reduced, and it was felt that it was inadequate to deal completely with the wet steam that was being evaporated in the firebox area. The smaller A2 smokebox was thought to have impeded an ideal distribution of heat across the tube bank, although BRONZINO recorded the marginally higher power outputs, 2,138 DBHP, which would equate roughly to 2,600 IHP. The A1 needed to be driven slightly harder than the A2 to achieve similar power outputs, but the report spoke diplomatically about the latter's lively riding. The Report concludes that since important information was not measured in the 1948 Exchanges, comparison was not possible, and further tests including an A4 would enable the team to make a more detailed study of the designs. A reading of the Report makes it quite clear that both the A1 and A2 acquitted themselves well, and were excellent designs. It is a great pity that the copy sent to Marylebone seemed to have been ignored or lost in the post!

In the very early 1950s it was rumoured that there was to be an exchange between the Haymarket A1s and the Polmadie Duchesses. Now there would have been some fascinating memories! Big Lizzies, or Big 'Uns as they were known at Crewe, shaking the neighbourhood as they thundered up to Cockburnspath! However, it was subsequently rumoured that the Stanier Pacifics were too tight a fit for the structure gauge in force between Newcastle and Edinburgh. Exactly whether such an exchange was mooted officially or not has been impossible to discover, but certainly three Haymarket A1s, Nos.60152, 60160 and 60161, went for a spell to the Glasgow depot in early 1951. None were recorded as having travelled so far south as Euston, despite Polmadie Pacifics working through with the 'Royal Scot' in the summer, but they worked as far south as Crewe, which set lineside imaginations a-buzz. Indeed I seem to remember that an A4, No.60012, was also loaned briefly at the time. I cannot imagine that Polmadie was short of power with, usually, some 9 Stanier Pacifics, and although the A1s were well-liked, I also cannot imagine that they were ever likely to displace the Big Lizzies in the affections of the Polmadie drivers. I believe that the firing technique there normally amounted to 'filling the firebox' in order that the powerful exhaust should not pull holes in the fire once the hard work started. No doubt the A1s ran happily with this treatment. Crews were surprised at the economy in coal and water of the strangers, but of course with heavy loads and long banks, the extra ton or so of tractive effort was important. Reports of footplate trips while they were at Polmadie noted the substantially lower coal and water consumption of the A1s, but also to a constant and at times heavy lateral swinging at the cab end.

OPERATIONAL ASPECTS

One wonders whether the Motive Power Department was consulted at all in the design stage. After all, they had to use the locomotives. Wiser counsels prevailed after the period of thinking aloud, due to the experience and judgement of the Drawing Office team as much as anything else, and a splendid locomotive resulted. The Doncaster Pacific had been progressively enlarged from the original in 1922, and despite the success of the A4, the escalation in loading in the war indicated that further enlargement was judged necessary. Taking soundings, looking into the future and coming to terms with the implications, was not a process that the railway was good at, no doubt because the conclusions were often unwelcome and required a fresh approach. Railwaymen always wanted people to use the railway. The A1 was a case in point, designed with express service loadings of 600 tons anticipated for the post-war years. With the bulk of inland freight on the railways, the number of expresses was smaller in the 1930s, but they were heavy multi-portioned trains. It was assumed that this service format would continue after the war.

With the rapid growth of road transport, there was in fact little reason for such an assumption, and trainloads at their heaviest were generally around 500 tons with only one or two services approaching 550-600 tons. Gradually the railway had to move towards a more frequent service, which of course involved smaller trains. By the late 1950s the A1s were working trains that were of streamliner weight, for which the large grate was less important than the large piston valves. The dawn of lighter, faster and more frequent services began on the East Coast Route within eight years with the 1956 winter book. We can see this in hindsight, and one must allow that it would have been less obvious at the time. The LM electrification, for example, was designed around the haulage of 16 coach, 600 ton trains initially. Never is an absolute that is ill-advised in railway life, but 600 ton loadings were rarely achieved in normal operation on BR.

It was a great pity that the operators did not allow the use of electric lighting.

No doubt there would have been problems in daylight, not being obvious just what class the locomotive was hauling, but white discs were the obvious answer. At night, however, the electric lights were far superior. I remember the sight of the Gateshead roller bearing A1 night after night on the heavy 22.15 'Night Scotsman' as it made its way north, sweeping almost silently down the GN main line, the two unblinking open lights clearly obvious before the sound of the A1 could be heard. In the same way the identity of the express was immediately obvious as the lights of the Grantham A1 could be seen south of Cemetery signalbox, racing into London with the up 'Heart of Midlothian'. In fact one could tell when an A3 was standing in for an A1 when the electric lights had been replaced by much dimmer oil lamps. For the signalman, much of the time the headcode carried was less important since the bell code described the train, but it provided confirmation of identity. If the signalbox was one which reported passing times to Control, it was much more important to get the train right! The lamps were not headlights by any stretch of the imagination, but they were the only means of announcing the presence of an approaching train, especially if other locomotives or machinery were drowning its sound. A number of us campaigned for effective headlights on locomotives and multiple units, and more than a few railwaymen would have lived to old age if they had been provided earlier.

PROBLEMS IN SERVICE

The A1s were almost completely trouble-free, but one aspect of their running which drew some criticism was their riding. Much of what we know of the A1s has been contributed by a few engineers who either led their design or were in charge of their operation and maintenance. In consulting the engineers who worked with the A1s, one hears two distinctly different points of view, namely that their riding was (a) quite normal or (b) definitely not all right. What makes it more difficult to present a considered verdict is that individual locomotives differed sharply in their riding. The weight of evidence from engineers involved favours (b) although, as Professor Joad might once have said 'What is defined as bad riding?'

On straight track the locomotives developed a steady lateral swing (hunting), increasing with speed but on reaching curved track the hunting stopped and the riding calmed down. In some cases a steadily increasing degree of hunting culminated in a heavy lurch, followed by steady running until the hunting started again. The practical response to the problem at depots such as Kings Cross, Copley Hill and Gateshead, was to tighten the drawbar

between the engine and tender, so that the tender restrained the rear of the engine through the drawbar and buffing gear, and the locomotive rode as a sort of 4-6-2+8. Riding was further improved by keeping the clearances of the Cortazzi and leading tender axleboxes to a minimum. Locomotives returned from general overhaul had been restored to design criteria, but rode poorly until modified by the depot. Provided an A1 had been treated in this way the riding was good. The A1 was very reliable, failures on the road were unusual, there was power in abundance to time services and provided the hunting had been restrained, crews would run with them.

The former Shedmaster at Kings Cross, Peter Townend, who in earlier days worked at Doncaster Plant, had considerable experience of them and has shared those experiences with many railwaymen and enthusiasts, including the author. It is of course relative, and if a driver was used to the slippered ease of an A4 footplate, he might well have regarded the A1 as lively, when, by comparison with the hard ride of a BR standard or a B1, or the wild riding of an Ivatt Atlantic or B17, they were fairly good. Some A1s were prone to sudden sharp lateral swings: George Carpenter was riding on EDWARD FLETCHER with Archie Waugh, one of Gateshead's senior men, north of York when, at 60mph or so the A1 started to swing laterally, progressively. As the speed rose, the movement became more aggressive until George and the driver exchanged glances, and the latter eased the regulator.

Peter Townend had received three A1s at Top Shed in September 1956 ostensibly for the new Newcastle lodging turn involving the Scots (or 'Scotch') Goods, 266 down, returning on the following day on the 'Northumbrian'. In fact the A1s worked turn and turn about with the A4s and later, A3s, but complaints of bad riding began to accrue. On a run to Peterborough with GREAT EASTERN, the riding was so poor that an experienced top link fireman found difficulty in hitting the firehole door. As the driver in one case was Bill Hoole, it was not a surprise. On questioning Drivers Duckmanton and McKinley, the regular drivers of GREAT CENTRAL, their A1 was held to be faultless. In order to see for himself, Peter went to Grantham to meet No.60156, and told the driver to push the A1 hard to test her riding at high speed. Horace Duckmanton was much more concerned that he was about to lose his treasured regular mount! The speed down Stoke bank almost certainly ran into three figures, but the precise speed was of no great concern, since GREAT CENTRAL was rock steady. I remember in their early years – and mine – watching them running through New Southgate on the down main, and realising that halfway

ALCAZAR – INDICATOR READINGS (IHP)

Speed mph	Cut-off %	Left Cylinder			Middle Cylinder			Right Cylinder		
		Forward Stroke	Backward Stroke	Difference	Forward Stroke	Backward Stroke	Difference	Forward Stroke	Backward Stroke	Difference
77.0	10	178	173	-5	162	290	128			
54.2	15	205	203	-2	218	253	35	183	186	3
57.0	15	172	221	49	199	274	75	195	197	2
68.0	15	168	199	31	240	318	78	178	200	22
74.5	15	226	223	-3	201	317	116			
50.5	25	276	262	-14	221	359	138	244	268	24
56.8	25	284	303	19	255	411	156	246	307	61
65.5	25	304	251	-53	245	415	170	209	284	75
72.0	25	281	340	59	211	302	91	238	238	0
40.0	35	324	306	-18			0			
52.5	35	318	313	-5			0			

through the station the engine and tender often seemed to shake, with the occasional bombardment of coal from the tender. It seems that this was quite a well-known trouble spot, and although the track ballast left something to be desired, the alignment, coming off a long curve, was in order. The climax came one night with ABERDONIAN hauling her namesake, as a huge block of coal smashed into pieces on the platform where I had been standing.

In his reminiscences Peter told of his trouble with GREAT EASTERN, which hunted violently at speeds over 60 mph on straight track and although a fine machine, was refused by drivers. Arguments with the Shopping Bureau followed, a general overhaul being refused since the locomotive was well short of her shopping mileage. Fortuitously, a Technical Assistant from the CMEE's office at Doncaster was travelling north, and was invited to ride with the driver of GREAT EASTERN on the 'Tees-Tyne Pullman'. The latter was told that, unless the visitor had been made vividly aware of the problem, further complaint to the Shedmaster would be pointless. By Hitchin it was accepted that the driver had made his point, and the speed reduced: she went into Doncaster Plant shortly afterwards. When the locomotive was dismantled, the springs went with all others as usual into the 'bosh' to be cleaned and serviced. When she returned from Doncaster, GREAT EASTERN was mechanically identical, but it is quite likely that the springs refitted were not those removed earlier. On returning the riding of the A1 was much improved, and she continued to run until at 197,000 miles she was called for general overhaul.

The problem remained, and it was decided to test an A1 in service and ALCAZAR, fresh from overhaul, was chosen. Preparatory to testing the A1 was sent to Doncaster for valve setting and weighing, where it was found that the middle steam chest front liner had shifted $\frac{1}{32}$in. This required the valve to be adjusted, then all three were set, and an expansion allowance also of $\frac{1}{32}$in was made. Then the engine went into service and was indicated. One of the principal arguments deployed by detractors of the 2:1 gear was that the distribution of power between the three cylinders was unequal and that inequality varied substantially with speed. Therefore with three independent sets of valve gear one might have supposed that the distribution was equal and unvarying.

The results showed that in reality a very different state of affairs existed.

The readings would have been determined from indicator cards taken on the A1 in the indicator shelter, far from laboratory conditions. Also the valve setting involved working to a 32nd of an inch, taxing in itself, and it was quite possible that the sum of the clearances in the axleboxes, motion and valve gear of even a newly overhauled locomotive could have an effect on the output of individual cylinders. The test results for ALCAZAR's middle cylinder showed that the distribution of power was anything but equal, with the backstroke developing 40-80% more power than the forward stroke. Clearly something was wrong, and it was suspected that the middle cylinder had moved relative to the outside cylinders. MEG MERRILIES was marked up and the distances between the marks recorded. The A1 was then run in service and when the marks were remeasured it was found that the frames had expanded a sixteenth of an inch as the A1 warmed up and worked the diagrammed turns. As a result the expansion allowance was not made to the middle cylinder of the A1s. Darlington Works did not apply any allowance, and it was not until the A1s built there passed through Doncaster Works that they conformed to the rest of the class.

Discussions followed and it was decided to fit ALCAZAR with a similar bogie to an A4, wherein the weight was carried on the bogie centre rather than on side bearers. Due to the frame construction of the A1 the bogie had to be customised to fit, but the resulting ride was much improved, almost like an A4. At the same time the inclination of the Cortazzi top inclined planes was changed from 1 in 7.1 to 1 in 10.66 to balance the lateral resistances front and rear. No.60136 kept her unique bogie until it failed, whereupon it was replaced by a standard bogie. No action was taken on the rest of the class; with diesel locomotives beginning to arrive, it was too late.

While this was interesting and important, it had not shed any light on the original problem of rough riding. Curiously, there were similarities with the case of the X type classes of Pacific of the East India Railway in the late 1930s, excellently recorded by E S Cox, a member of the investigating team. Uncontrolled hunting had caused track distortion and derailments, and yet just over ten years later, we had a similar problem ourselves. The first point of enquiry in such cases is the effectiveness of the horizontal control springs. J F Harrison, in retirement, was sure that the stiffness of the horizontal control springs on the bogie had been increased. The load was originally set at two tons, but this was thought to be inadequate, and although it was increased to four tons, there seems to be no record of that change. Harrison felt that a loading of 3.2 tons was ideal. He also felt that the stronger springs had been substituted in the case of GREAT EASTERN above. The modification was not felt to be worth recording, apparently, with diesel traction only a year or two away. However, he thought that the cause was at the rear of the locomotive rather than the front, and was quite sure that the Cortazzi axlebox sliding surfaces were not being properly maintained. Harrison was sceptical of the effectiveness of the Cortazzi arrangement in post-war conditions, and on DUKE OF GLOUCESTER, which he regarded as the logical development of the A1, he used a standard trailing truck. The East Indian Pacifics, very significantly, also had Cortazzi axleboxes.

On track, a locomotive tended to hunt due to irregularities in the track, curvature, surging in boiler and tender, and the thrusts of the pistons. In the last respect one can understand that a three cylinder locomotive with six pulses per cycle approximated to an ideally smooth pull better than two or four cylinders with four – with the notable exception of the 'Lord Nelson' 4-6-0s. The conicity of the wheel tyres stimulated the hunting at a low level, but tended to restrain stronger hunting. The energy dissipated in hunting came from the speed, and the higher the speed, the greater the movement and its frequency, at least until other factors came into play such as the limit of movement in the machine and the gauge. The locomotive tended to swing about the vertical axis through its centre of gravity, and the solution was normally a correction of the stiffness of the bogie control springs.

Gresley used the Cortazzi sliding axleboxes in the original GREAT NORTHERN, and in trailing axles on his Pacifics and Green Arrows. It was very successful. When used with the De Glehn type bogie, the riding was poorer at least and often worse. Why? In plan, the boxes should slide along a path that is tangential to an arc that has its centre on the middle coupled axle, which is assumed to be the centre of the symmetrical fixed wheelbase. That is not necessarily where the centre of gravity was. While the Gresley locomotives all rode well, one might assume from their general construction that the trailing axle was a similar distance from the centre of gravity in each case, and therefore the Cortazzi design functioned well. With the adoption of divided drive and a different bogie the Gresley concept had been substantially altered, and with all the benefit of hindsight, the design of the Cortazzi should have been revised, or even replaced with a Bissel truck. The restoring force at the rear due to the inclined planes on the Cortazzi was not great, and with inadequate control at the front, it was insufficient by itself to prevent hunting. With the damping provided by the palliative measures taken at depots, it did. The anecdotal evidence seems to me to indicate that the problem was caused firstly by inadequate lateral control in the leading bogie, but principally in the design and construction of the Cortazzi axleboxes. Recollections of the occasional lateral lurch or jolt might be due to the Cortazzi axleboxes binding and then being freed by the movement of the locomotive. That seems, at least, to point to the seat of the trouble if not the cause.

The A1s had the same smokebox saddle as the Thompson Pacifics, and were troubled with fracturing bolts, although they were fitted bolts, or the rivets holding the smokebox wrapper to the boiler. This continued to be a cause for concern with particular locomotives. The stretcher bracket carrying the middle cylinder valve gear also supported the boiler, and registered with a bracket which had no clearance, and this was thought to prevent expansion of the boiler barrel. The bracket was altered, but it was noticed that the rear boiler supports, which were intended to allow expansion, were in fact baulked by imperfections in some adjacent countersunk bolts.

Another problem arose from the fitting of a BR standard feature called a strumbox beneath the well of the tender. On the BR standards it was fitted on the right-hand side and was therefore obvious. The strumbox contained a filter plate or sieve, and a stop cock which allowed the removal of the filter for cleaning without emptying the tender first. On GREAT EASTERN,

hauling the down 'Flying Scotsman', the stop cock had gradually closed with the vibration of daily use, causing the injectors to stall at New Barnet. With a long run to Newcastle in mind, the fireman had built a big fire, which then had to be thrown out on the main line. The sieves tended to blind with grit or waste picked up from the troughs, and so the plates and stop cocks were removed. Even so, the strumbox imposed a constriction in the water feed to the engine, which had to be enlarged. The divided drive gave very little trouble, but attention was required to ensure that the middle eccentric was properly lubricated. Ironically the 2:1 gear gave little trouble when it was grease lubricated, but the middle eccentric was awkward to reach and it was oil lubricated. If the driver had not secured the reservoir cork, or had not checked the oil, the engine could run hot, and damage the eccentric.

There were differences in the water supply, which considering the work done by the LNER, was surprising. The ER water was treated to soften the feedwater, so that at washing-out the precipitate was soft and easily flushed out. It allowed priming, but with the use of polyamide as a deflocculator, the problem was controlled. One of the problems with BR was that the Regional structure, especially on the old LNER, imposed 'Chinese walls' which prevented a free exchange of information. It was quite commonplace to find another Region working in a better way, or one which had consigned a system to the waste bin, simply because of poor communication. So it was not surprising to hear that the NER had trouble with mixed waters, priming and more frequent washing-out as a result of trips south. The roller-bearing twins, BON ACCORD and BORDERER were prone to this problem, working as they did through the length of the main line. In Scotland the water was softer, and the boilers did not need so much maintenance, and there was little complaint of priming.

THE A1s in SERVICE
The operation of the services on the East Coast main line had changed considerably in ten years of war and austerity. The trade unions, particularly ASLEF, had much more influence than pre-war through their LDCs (Local Departmental Committees) in negotiating which depots worked which service, although any decision of political import was retained by the Union's Executive. Nationalisation had imposed a Regional Structure, and the three Regions comprising the old LNER worked as separate railways again. Nationalisation had also, by implication, required that trade union negotiation and consultation were now part and parcel of managing and operating the railway. Individual Depot LDCs lobbied hard for their members,

especially where 'mileage' turns were concerned, to boost their pay. As a result, diagrams appeared which seemed to have no justification, but road knowledge and the improvement in pay through the sharing of overtime and mileage turns were necessary considerations.

The intervention of trade unions could have been a force for good and there were many cases where they were, but in fact it was something that caused the railway management immense frustration, and the cost of the regular adversarial charades throughout the system and their consequences over the years must have run into tens if not hundreds of millions of pounds. Most managers strove to act fairly, recognising that without the co-operation of the staff the railway was a dead duck, but the trade unions, especially the politically motivated ASLEF officials, were often determined to impose a form of Marxism by frustrating management. I doubt whether, apart from salary increases negated by inflation, in retrospect the footplateman's lot was much the better for it all in the steam age.

So the A1s emerged from Darlington and Doncaster, 49 Pacifics built in 16 months. Before long they had swept many of Gresley's A3s aside and the Thompson Pacifics as well. The allocations are interesting. Obviously a number of depots were having difficulties with staff and/or locomotives, and the new A1s were allocated despite depots already having a number of A3s or, in the case of Kings Cross, Gateshead and Haymarket, A4s as well. The major change was the strengthening of the Copley Hill fleet from two Gresley A1s pre-war to six new Peppercorn A1s, as it replaced Doncaster in working the bulk of the West Riding services. The initial allocation was:-

Kings Cross: Nos.60114, 60120, 60122, 60139, 60156, 60157, 60158 (7)
Grantham: Nos.60117, 60133, 60148, 60149 (4)
Doncaster: Nos.60123, 60125, 60130, 60144, 60146 (5)
Copley Hill: Nos.60118, 60119, 60128, 60131, 60134, 60136 (6)
York: Nos.60121, 60129, 60138, 60140, 60141, 60153 (6)
Gateshead: Nos.60115, 60124, 60132, 60135, 60137, 60142, 60143, 60145, 60147, 60151, 60154, 60155 (12)
Heaton: Nos.60116, 60126, 60127, 60150 (4)
Haymarket: Nos.60152, 60159, 60160, 60161, 60162 (5)

At Leeds Copley Hill, by the early 1950s that total had increased to 11 despite three A1s being transferred away. At Gateshead, despite the presence of 11 A3s and 8 A4s, a sizeable fleet of new A1s had accumulated. By the end of 1951, the situation had changed, the

A4s having been concentrated on Kings Cross, Gateshead and Haymarket, while Kings Cross and Doncaster lost their allocations of A1s altogether. With the introduction of engine changing at Grantham, five more A1s arrived, including the two roller bearing examples from Kings Cross. At Copley Hill the large fleet was strengthened further still, and the large fleet at Gateshead was enlarged still further to 15 engines. By the end of 1951 the allocation was as given below.

Grantham: Nos.60128, 60130, 60131, 60136, 60148, 60149, 60156, 60157, 60158 (9)
Copley Hill:* Nos.60114, 60117, 60118, 60119, 60120, 60123, 60125, 60133, 60134, 60139, 60141, 60144 (12)
York: Nos.60121, 60138, 60140, 60146, 60153 (5)
Gateshead: Nos.60115, 60124, 60129, 60132, 60135, 60137, 60142, 60143, 60145, 60147, 60150, 60151, 60154, 60155 (15)
Heaton: Nos.60116, 60126, 60127 (3)
Haymarket: Nos.60152, 60159, 60160, 60161, 60162 (5)
*includes Nos.60123 and 60144 allocated to Ardsley but used indiscriminately by Copley Hill.

One of the fascinating features of the changes in A1 allocation was the movement of apparently identical locomotives. Three left Copley Hill and nine arrived. At Grantham three of the four left, but eight others, different only in their numbers, arrived. It had been decided to alter the ER distribution, but instead of merely increasing or decreasing the depot fleet size, there was a baffling interchange. BONGRACE left Copley Hill only to be replaced by POMMERN, admittedly just from overhaul, and ABBOTSFORD replaced KINGS COURIER in the same way which one can understand, except that the latter returned to Copley Hill, run-down, a year later. While this was enormously entertaining to the lineside youth, like the solitary A2 variants mentioned earlier, it challenged the logical mind. If it were a case of an experienced Shedmaster passing a troublesome locomotive on to an unsuspecting colleague, one can understand why, but as the A1s were as trouble-free as any class, especially in steaming, one was much the same as another.

When it was decided to split the 7P BR classification into 7P for locomotives with less than 35,000lbs tractive effort and 8P for those above, the move affected the allocation of Pacifics to diagrams. If the diagram specified an 8P then a 7P A3 was inadequate, unless the driver was prepared to take her. Curiously, once re-draughted with a double Kylchap, the A3s were regarded as the equal of the A1s and A4s by many crews. The increased power of the A1 was noticeable particularly at starting, and always provided that the locomotive was started carefully, there was nothing that they would not pull. An excessively optimistic use of the regulator, wet or greasy rails could precipitate an explosive start just like any other steam engine of course. The use of the sanders in wet weather appeared to be more frequent with the A1s when the locomotives were pulling hard. The very heavy 'Aberdonian' and 'Night Scotsman' were lifted off the mark and the A1 made her way up the gradients out of London with skill but without any great effort. The double Kylchap tended to make them quieter runners than the lusty roar of the single blast Gresley Pacifics, and on up services it was unusual to hear a sharp edge to the Kylchap exhaust south of Stevenage.

The A1s were equipped with ATC in its various forms as it was developed, culminating in the fitting of AWS. They were also fitted with steam brakes which were useful when working freight, and some of the diagrams worked farther north included some fast freight work. South of Doncaster it was unusual. One of the minor modifications to the A1s was necessitated by the hollow roar of the vacuum ejector exhaust in the large smokebox drowning the sound of the public address system. The public address system of the steam age was severely limited by comparison with contemporary equipment, and its maintenance was bedevilled by inadequate staff numbers and investment, and it was a constant source of complaint if not downright ridicule, but traction as well was far noisier in steam days. A small silencer was devised, which was successful in reducing the noise.

Willie Yeadon's Register dealing with the A1s makes reference to frequent visits to Doncaster Works by some of the class for weighing. I think that this may well have been a check on the weight distribution which could have been the result of complaints about poor riding. Their appearance changed very little in their short life: I have described the livery with which they were built, and both apple green and dark blue were superseded by dark green starting in August 1951. This is probably the livery in which they are best remembered, and it suited them.

PERFORMANCE IN SERVICE
At Haymarket, generally the A1s did not displace the A4s from the top link and were used by the second link, although in practice they were often on the top turns instead of A4s. The A1s were generally kept in sparkling condition, but SAINT JOHNSTOUN, the last A1, was the regular engine of Driver Willie Bain, and he saw to it that his A1 was absolutely immaculate. It was difficult to overstate the magnificence of his locomotive as can be seen from the illustrations. Having pursued the cleaners, Willie and his fireman then supplemented the efforts themselves in their spare moments. Despite the superb finish of the A4s, especially those working the 'Non-stop', No.60162 exceeded even that standard, and for much of the time would have made a Royal engine look drab by comparison. I doubt if there was a cleaner engine in the post-war steam years. North of Newcastle on the 'Non-stop', if a train passed hauled by an engine that seemed to glow whatever the weather, one knew which engine it was instinctively. The A1s worked the 'Heart of Midlothian', 'Aberdonian', the down 'Flying Scotsman', up 'Queen of Scots', both London-Glasgow services, together with balancing services. Most of the engine diagrams are set out in Appendix F.

At Kings Cross of course, the A4s ruled the roost together with the W1 and a solitary A3 or two until 1956. Three A1s returned in September 1956 ostensibly for the new Newcastle lodging turn with the down 'Scots/Scotch Goods' and up 'Northumbrian'. Of the three, GREAT CENTRAL impressed Shedmaster Peter Townend as being almost the ultimate locomotive, reliable, smooth riding and a popular machine, the best A1 at Top Shed at the time. Her riding was in complete contrast to her sister roller bearing A1, GREAT EASTERN, in which the riding was bad as described above. The A1s worked alongside the A4s and the re-draughted A3s with great success, although the A4s tended to take the attention with faster running when necessary. It was amusing to see the Scots Goods making its way north behind a gleaming A1, when a more prestigious express such as the 15.20 Newcastle had a much more travel-stained sister engine in charge. The A1s certainly did clean up very rewardingly.

At Gateshead the DMPS ruled that as the newest, strongest and freest steaming express locomotives, the A1s should be the principal express power, and the A4s were the substitutes very often. Only three turns were for an A4, and even then an A1 was often used instead. The preference was easy to understand. Nevertheless, there were problems with the larger grate, especially when the driver was heavy handed. There were a considerable number of services worked by Gateshead engines, and the system used involved the engines being allocated to a particular diagram, for example No.60142 EDWARD FLETCHER worked the 22.35 from Kings Cross on from Newcastle to Edinburgh, returning with the up 'Flying Scotsman' for a number of years.

Although the Gateshead top link were unwilling to lodge at the turn of the 1950s, a volunteer London link was formed and three of the crews were willing to continue. Their duties comprised the up 'Night Scotsman', or its first portion, to London returning the following night with the down service. The 268 miles would be regularly run on 5 tons of coal, giving a remarkably good consumption of 42lbs/mile with a heavy train. Then while the crew rested, the A1 would work forward to Edinburgh and return to Newcastle with the 'North Briton' service.

Kings Cross, realising that a perfectly good A1 was on shed all day, in steam, often used the A1 for a trip to Grantham on the 10.40 semi-fast or the 12.18 'Northumbrian', returning on the 'Flying Scotsman' or 'White Rose'. In this way the A1s accumulated 800 miles for the two-day diagram, but often that was inflated to almost exactly 1000 miles. For this they had the two roller bearing A1s, BON ACCORD and BORDERER, and these two remarkable locomotives dominated this diagram for years. Of course they needed to be washed out, inspected and maintained, in which case one of the other A1s substituted. BORDERER, in its short life, exceeded a million miles while BON ACCORD was not far short. We have no way of knowing how the mileages accrued since mileage records ceased for steam traction early in the 1960s, but we can estimate roughly. The locomotives were fully used for seven years before loads were reduced, then another three until the advent of diesel traction when the London turns were more widely shared, after which their rate of accumulation slowed down over six years to a trickle. Making allowance for down time, an

annual mileage of 90-100,000 seems reasonable up to winter 1956. As loads were cut and the number of Grantham trips reduced in winter 1956 it would have fallen to say 70-80,000, falling three years later to 50,000, and then to 15-20,000. Certainly in the 1950-56 period the locomotives were often running just over 3,000 miles a week, nearly 500 miles per day for long periods, and the annual mileages must have passed 100,000 at times. There can be little doubt that this was one of the finest demonstrations of consistency and economy in the steam era.

One of the many inconsistencies of the post-war steam era was that while matters at Gateshead proceeded as I have described, a few miles north, in the same city and under the same management, matters at Heaton were rather different. There one had the impression that Gresley's engines were better liked, and they were certainly better cared for. Heaton received three A1s including the last apple green and the first BR blue ones to be built at Doncaster. They were usually reasonably clean at least and often well turned out. But things are rarely as they appear and of course there were other factors to consider – there was more room at Heaton than in the older depot to clean engines, and the demand for firemen in the Newcastle area from the outlying depots meant that at Gateshead, the senior depot, promotion from cleaner to fireman could be swift.

The result was that, as was painfully obvious at times, little or no cleaning was done at Gateshead.

Heaton worked the down 'Queen of Scots' from Leeds to Newcastle as well as, for the first year, the 'Tees-Tyne Pullman' changing crews at Grantham. Until No.60116 arrived, No.60115 was borrowed from Gateshead for this duty. They also worked the 7.53 from Sunderland to Kings Cross, returning on the 17.35 to Newcastle, until September 1951. Youthful enthusiasts in the south were regaled with the sight of hitherto infrequent visitors, and the new blue No.60127 joined SUNSTAR, THE WHITE KNIGHT, SIR HUGO *et al* in those heady days. After September 1951, the Heaton Pacific came off at Grantham and returned north with the 'Northumbrian', and another worked the 7.50 from Newcastle to Peterborough, returning with the down 'Heart of Midlothian' to Newcastle. It was very, very unusual for Gateshead or Heaton to appropriate a Haymarket Pacific even in times of urgent need, and with the sizes of their fleets, one can understand why. Nevertheless, late in the steam era, Heaton borrowed one, and used it on, amongst other duties, the 7.50 to Peterborough and return 'Heart of Midlothian'. It just happened to be HOLYROOD, arguably the rarest A1 to visit the south!

As a result of this metamorphosis, Copley Hill's A1s displaced Doncaster from the principal Yorkshire services. One each worked up to Kings Cross with

An excellent study of 60117 BOIS ROUSSEL at New England. The period is 1961 or thereafter. (B Richardson, Transport Treasury)

the 'West Riding' and 'Yorkshire Pullman', returning on the same day with the down 'West Riding' and 18.18 to Leeds, and two others worked up the 'Queen of Scots' Pullman and the 18.17 from Bradford and Newcastle (the up 'Bradford Flyer'). The crews lodged and then took the 7.50 to Bradford and Newcastle (the down 'Bradford Flyer') and the 12 noon 'Queen of Scots' Pullman. It was perfectly possible to service the A1s and, if no repairs had been booked, use them on the diagram all week. The schedules of the services from the West Riding were not demanding until the introduction of the 8.00 'Bradford Flyer' in 1952, which never actually carried its nickname, and only late in the steam age became 'The West Riding'. Unusually, only the down service was named, and the 7.50 from Leeds retained its name. It took a long while for the train to become established, as businessmen were less eager to make an early start. The train was quite fast, calling at Hitchin, and running from there to Doncaster. The 127 minute timing was reduced to 113, an average of 65.9mph. Initially the train was worked by Kings Cross, but was taken over by Copley Hill in September 1953 when the service started at 7.50 and was extended to Newcastle. The train was then later scheduled to be divided at Doncaster, serving Newcastle and Huddersfield, and called at Retford to provide a connection to Sheffield. The timing to Retford was 96 minutes, an average of 66.7mph, while a Doncaster A3 worked the 6 coach Newcastle portion forward to Darlington at 63.7mph. The treatment meted out to the train varied, but anything up 15 minutes delay could be inflicted on what should have been a prestige service. Curiously, I have not come across any record of running on the up service, but I know from experience that it was not a good timekeeper, having to run the gauntlet with the early overnight freights and the Hull and New Clee fish trains. Nevertheless, with a keen crew that were on their way home, a number of fine performances were recorded over the years. The Doncaster men must have enjoyed a 224 mile gallop with their A3s on a light load.

The 7.50 was weekdays only, and on Saturday the A1 returned on the down 'White Rose'. On Sundays there were the usual balancing turns so as to start off correctly on Monday. Another A1 came up to Grantham with the 7.25 from Leeds and returned with the 10.18 from Kings Cross taking over from the top link A4. Relief services at weekends and in the summer were also worked by A1s. The crew working the up 'Yorkshire Pullman' returned after a rest with the down 'West Riding', the longest turn of duty on the East Coast main line. It was not worked by the same crew through the week, for apart from fatigue, the earnings in the one week would have

been excessive due to mileage payments and were better equalised over the ten weeks there. For every 15 miles in excess of 200 the crews earned an hour of overtime, paid at an enhanced rate, and I calculate that a week on this hard turn would bring at least 66 hours overtime at time and a half!

It has to be said that the schedules of the Pullman services were quite slow considering the moderate loadings, and a determined crew ought to have been able to cope with a faster schedule. The up 'Queen of Scots' Pullman, non-stop from Leeds to Kings Cross, 10 Pullmans, about 400 tons gross, was timed at 159 minutes from passing Doncaster to arriving in London. It was hardly surprising that 581 up, the Hull fish with 1A link men and a Top Shed B1 in splendid condition, was often right on the tail of the Pullman. Having given 'Train out of Section' for the Pullman, it was not unusual to receive 1-3-1 for the B1, and immediately 'Train on Line', on having accepted it! The 'West Riding' prior to 1959 was a heavy 14 coach train, and the 15.45 down was booked to run non-stop from Kings Cross to Wakefield in a fairly easy timing. At holiday times the down train was preceded by a relief that called at all the principal stations and took a minute longer to reach Wakefield than the non-stop!

No.60128 went new to Copley Hill, and dominated the 'West Riding' duty in the summer of 1949. The following year, No.60133 POMMERN was transferred there, and again dominated the duty for the summer of 1950. Despite its large fleet of A1s, Copley Hill occasionally used its three or four A3s on the top duties, and the gentle morning commuting routine with an N2 0-6-2 tank and its quad-art set was enlivened with either the hissing roar of an A1 getting into her stride, or occasionally the rousing sound of BLINK BONNY or her sisters speeding north with the 'Flyer'. Copley Hill also possessed three V2s, as did Ardsley as well, for the freight turns that each depot worked to London. The V2s were kept in splendid condition, but when they were unavailable it was not an A1 that was used – with its steam brake as a useful extra control – but a B1 4-6-0. Sometimes something even smaller was used such as a J39 0-6-0 or, on one memorable occasion, a J6 0-6-0!

The A1s, meanwhile, ran the 'Flyer' with great success, and although the top speeds were usually below that of their streamlined sisters, the uphill work was good, reflecting the greater tractive power of the A1. In terms of individual locomotive performance, the work on this service is the high-water mark for the A1s. As the load had risen to 350-370 tons, work of pre-war streamliner quality was being achieved daily, sometimes even exceeded uphill, despite the shortcomings of the operators and the attentions of the

CCE. Although the latter maintained, in my judgement, the best main line track in the country, the operators never seemed to plan his work so that the impact of TSRs gave the drivers a chance to recover time. As a result the train suffered a level of delay and lost time that would never have been tolerated pre-war with the streamliners. The A1s never sounded unduly pressed although they must have been, and their work was not appreciated generally. As will be seen in Appendix G & H, it was on Stoke bank that the drivers, no doubt with a thick fire on the grate, pushed the A1s hard. Performances where 2,000 IHP had been developed were fairly common, while those selected were in the 2,300-2,500 IHP category. The pick must be the work of Driver Nichols and Fireman Higson on KESTREL, storming up the last three miles at 1 in 178 to Stoke at a steady 70.5mph, an amazing effort. It is a salutary thought that the A1 nearly out-performed COCK O'THE NORTH. As far as I recall, the Copley Hill top link was 12 strong, and included Brown, Cartwright, Clarke, Crossley, Jeffs, Mattock, Mayhew, Merritt, Nichols, Smith, Wadsworth and Wood. There was also a Driver Higton and a Fireman Higson just to add to the confusion. The Leeds depot neither used regular manning nor regular diagramming of engines to trains, and it was very much a lucky dip as to which locomotive was turned out. As they were identical in their capability it was immaterial of course.

The allocation of five A1s to York, which already had seven A2s of different sorts plus an enormous fleet of V2s, always struck me as a curiosity. York had two passenger turns to Kings Cross, one with a sleeper which seemed to comprise more parcels than slumbering passengers, returning with the 8.00 to York, and the other with the 9.00 from York and Hull, returning with the 16.50 second portion of the down 'West Riding'. When the latter duty was taken over by Doncaster for several years the situation became still more odd. York provided a north and south facing pilot, as did a number of stations, but it was a task which could and indeed was, pre-war, devolved to V2s, which often stood in valiantly. York had two further London turns on fast freight, but these were dominated by V2s. Quite often a B16 4-6-0 was pressed into service in place of a V2, and they seemed to cope very well on what was an extremely long and heavy haul. Whether that view was shared by the firemen is no longer possible to ascertain! If a Pacific was used, it was an A2, but such occasions were extremely rare.

Quite why the first of the roller-bearing A1s, FLAMBOYANT, was sent there defies understanding. The fitting of roller bearings was an experiment at the request of the Railway Executive, and it is possible that the A1 was kept close at hand to observe and report. In which case when the experiment was concluded in 1951 the locomotive should have gone to a shed which could make better use of it. I have a theory that those who determined the destinations of locomotives were under the impression that the roller-bearing quintet was Nos.60154-60158, rather than 60153-60157; when one looks at the allocations of the former, they were shared between Gateshead and Kings Cross, where the ability of roller-bearing engines could be utilised. As a potentially very useful locomotive it was wasted. Although York had three A1 diagrams, they were well within the capacity of an A3 or even a Green Arrow (V2) in good condition. One would have thought that the five A1s should have gone to depots which could make better use of them, and their places taken by single chimney A3s. There were a number of inconsistencies about locomotive allocation, some already referred to, which leads me to suspect that it had more to do with personalities and motive power politics than logic. As it was though, the mileage of FLAMBOYANT was only (very roughly) 75% of her sisters.

There is no doubt in my mind that, in the work of the remarkable roller-bearing locomotives, their fine record of performance on the Bradford Flyer, and their work in the Grantham top link represented the high water mark for the A1 class. Their reliability, for steam traction, was excellent, although less than we came to expect from diesel traction once initial teething troubles had been overcome. The Grantham top link consisted of twelve crews in September 1951, each sharing an A1 as follows:-

Drivers Jarvis and Walton
60122 CURLEW
Drivers Healey and Brownsell
60128 BONGRACE
Drivers Atterton and Barnes
60131 OSPREY
Drivers Measures and Marshall
60149 AMADIS
Drivers Thompson and Taylor
60156 GREAT CENTRAL
Drivers Ross and Hudson
60113 GREAT NORTHERN

The A1/1 did not last in the top link for very long and was displaced by a newer A1. By 1955 the top link had changed almost completely, some engines had been transferred away and others came in, and three remained in the top link:

Drivers Royce and Widdowson
60128 BONGRACE
Drivers Johnson and Watson
60144 KINGS COURIER
Drivers Bednall and Harrison
60149 AMADIS
Drivers Agg and Newbury
60156 GREAT CENTRAL
Drivers Brownsell and Kirk

60157 GREAT EASTERN
Drivers Clayton and Simpson
60158 ABERDONIAN

The duties worked in the early to mid-1950s were as described in Appendix E. Of course there were minor changes from timetable to timetable, as regardless of Region the operators seemed incapable of leaving schedules alone. Very few trains retained the same timing with each new timetable, which generated a vast amount of work which could, and should have been avoided. My recollection of the locomotive diagrams is incomplete but the main services are listed, supplemented with information from such as Eric Neve and Ken Hoole. It should be understood that adherence to the diagrams was not absolute, indeed I would be surprised if a week went by without some variation somewhere on the main line. Locomotives failed, or were stopped on shed for repairs, which meant that another deputised, sometimes of another class. Then they had to be worked back home. Boilers were usually washed out once a week, and complete examinations of various aspects of the engine's functioning would keep it out of action for a day or so at least. Each duty was worked for two weeks, one with each driver, so that in 12 weeks, 4,600 miles were run at an average of 383 miles/week, and in a year of 46 weeks and 6 days' operation, an engine could in theory achieve 100,000 miles in the year. In fact BONGRACE was said to have reached 90,000 miles, and as noted earlier, GREAT CENTRAL reached nearly six figures. When one of the six engines was stopped for examination, repair or overhaul, another simply took its place. The duties had regular days for boiler washouts when another A1, or an A3 would take its place, but it is a measure of the domination of the A1s that the A3s, until re-draughted, were uncommon on the main duties and were usually on the reliefs.

The period from September 1951 to April 1957, when the increase in services with through working by Kings Cross and Gateshead brought a reduction in Grantham's role on the East Coast route, was remarkable for the consistency of the Grantham top link running. The schedules were unchallenging, the loads heavier than post-1957, and so the work was not especially spectacular, but the A1s nevertheless established a high water mark for operation, much as did the A4s on the pre-war streamliners when new, but I suspect without the same attention. The A1 standing at the buffers at Kings Cross in the early morning as one hurried past to the office was usually the same one that appeared on the up 'Heart of Midlothian' in the late evening. While it was good to see the A4s and then the A3s after re-draughting coping with

faster, lighter and more numerous services, there was a tinge of sadness that a depot with a long history that had served the railway conspicuously well was now relegated to a supporting role.

As mentioned earlier, at Kings Cross the A1 arrivals worked turn and turn about with the A4s, and later the double Kylchap A3s. Hot boxes were almost unknown on the A1s, and with the lighter loads a thin fire was quite feasible and they were economical despite the larger grate. With so many Pacifics, it became difficult for Kings Cross to keep up with inspections, and it was arranged that Doncaster Works would do the work, over the weekends if necessary, together with the maintenance arising. The drivers who set great store by punctuality, of whom Bill Hoole was the best known but not the only one, seemed not to mind the rough riding, although no doubt they preferred the 'Blue 'Uns' as the Cockneys knew the A4s.

I cannot remember any occasion down south when an A1 was turned out for a Royal train, but it did happen once at Kings Cross. The engine was GREAT EASTERN, and as it was told me by Peter Townend, Shedmaster at the time, it illustrates perfectly the necessity of attention to detail. Otherwise, as I have said before, if it can go wrong, it probably will, if it hasn't already. No doubt with this in mind, Peter asked Frank Knight, one of the Locomotive Inspectors and a particularly valuable colleague, to oversee the preparation of the A1. No doubt she was prepared and immaculate, but Peter asked Frank to check her over himself, especially using a ladder in the inspection pit to check that the corks to the oil reservoirs for the middle engine had been securely screwed home. Sure enough the one on the middle big end was sitting nearby, the driver having forgotten to replace it!

There were the occasional incidents when the injectors failed on a visiting A1 and I recall a fireman, I think from Copley Hill, being hoist with his own petard, so to speak. He had filled the firebox with a big fire as usual, no doubt with the intention of letting the engine chew through it as the driver made his way up to Potters Bar. When the injectors both failed within a few miles of the terminus, there was no alternative but to dump something like a ton of fire. Comments from the local ganger afterwards would have made interesting reading. Over the years it happened several times, and at least the unfortunate fireman had a rocking grate to expedite the process. The old Kylchap hands would start from Kings Cross with a fire that looked thin and dead, enough to alarm one not in the know. They knew that the ferocity of the draught, with a round of firing as the engine started away, was enough to have

60117 BOIS ROUSSEL under repair at Doncaster Works. One can understand diesel engineers not wanting to work in apparent chaos, but if one was brought up in it, it was understood and accepted. Some very fine work was done in such conditions. It does not feel as though the A1 is still new, indeed it feels much more like the last few years when repairs were limited, and if the requirements were excessive, the loco was withdrawn. The boiler has not been lifted and shows no sign of inspection or repair. On the rare occasions one saw an A1 without the deflectors the kinship with the Thompson Pacifics could be seen, particularly emphasised by the long smokebox. (Paul Chancellor Collection)

the fire white and hot and the pressure gauge rising as the driver opened out.

The major achievement of the A1s was their reliability, as has been well illustrated above. Having established their ability and economy, and disposed of the BTC costing system to the annoyance of the maroon adherents there, the A1s continued as the mainstay of the East Coast main line with the A4s. J F Harrison, in his Presidential address to the Institution of Locomotive Engineers, felt that it was high time the success of the A1s was proclaimed, and did so. For his address, some statistics were prepared, and in such cases a less eminent assistant does the devilling for his Chief: senior engineers did not dig around the record cards and mileage records themselves.

Some startling figures emerged. While the Works Accountants' figures were susceptible to all sorts of errors and assumptions, as well as unchecked mistakes by disinterested typists, we have to take them at face value. Without individual figures to guide us, we have to make an intelligent guess. At the time, in twelve years service the five roller-bearing A1s had accumulated 4.8 million miles. FLAMBOYANT, at York, was substantially below the others at 600,000 or so, leaving the other four at 4.2 million, of which BORDERER was

the first to exceed a million. The unique record of the Gateshead pair has been examined earlier. If we take an average cycle between general overhauls, allowing for all the usual stoppages, an A1 locomotive worked about 188 days per annum. Having calculated the age of the four, I estimate their daily mileage as 445 per working day and 229 per calendar day. That is remarkable.

Far be it for an armchair engineer to suggest that a senior engineer made a mistake, but Harrison went on to claim that the whole class (49 not 50) had by then accumulated 48 million miles. It gave daily mileages not too far short of the roller-bearing engines, which seemed too high. I do not believe it, for although they ran well, the 44 plain bearing A1s would have had more down time, and with the under-utilisation of engines at Copley Hill and York, for example, individual mileages were more varied depending on their use. Also it was simply impossible with the multi-Regional diagramming to achieve the long runs of the West Coast main line. Working Harrison's daily calendar mileage back, a gross figure would be nearer 42 million, which equates to 363 miles per working day and an annual mileage of about 68,300, which sounds about right. Nevertheless, despite the inaccuracy, Harrison's point

was well made. The A1s were unsurpassed as a strong, economical and reliable locomotive, and an operator's dream. Yes, of course Stanier's Pacifics, with their long runs, could accumulate high mileages as could the Britannias, intensively used on the GE. However good the CME's locomotives, unless the operators use them fully, their potential cannot be realised. Just like the Mikados in fact.

INDIVIDUAL PERFORMANCES
The performance of the A1s was adequate and reliable if unspectacular for much of the time. The railway operators set much store by reliability and punctuality, and it has to be said that spectacle is all very well if it has no impact on other services. Running in 15 minutes BT may thrill enthusiasts, but if it has caused operational mayhem in the process then it was not a good idea! Crews understood that a double Kylchap with that big grate could burn coal unless the reverser was well pulled up. Many of the drivers had learnt their skills on single blast engines, and were deprived of one of the principal means of judging the working of the A1 by its quiet exhaust. Their process of familiarisation did not endear them to their firemen, shovelling hard to keep the large grate

covered while their fire was being pulled by the strong draught caused by longer cut-offs than necessary.

Net times comparable with the streamliners were occasionally achieved, suggesting that for all their deficiencies in riding at speed, they would have timed the streamliners comfortably. Considering the close relationship between the A1 and A4, for all the arguing over the merits or otherwise of the 2:1 gear, that is hardly remarkable. The list of published runs by A1s and all varieties of A2 is in Appendix G and as can be seen the spread of fast running went across the A1 class. A considerable number of fast runs were recorded between Hitchin and Retford or Doncaster with the Bradford Flyer. The uphill work was good, especially on Stoke bank, again bearing out the Gresley philosophy of increasing uphill speeds rather than down.

Whilst on the subject of Stoke bank, one run bears mention. On this occasion the train was the down 'Heart of Midlothian', a heavy 13 coach train, worked by Top Shed to Peterborough and a Heaton engine north thereof. Cecil J Allen, who wrote monthly articles on locomotive performance, happened to be on the train, fortunately. The engines were changed and Heaton's SIR VINCENT RAVEN took over the 13 coaches of 470 tons gross. Although the train left on time, as the speed rose quicker than usual north of Peterborough it was apparent that the driver was in a hurry. By Helpston the speed had risen to 69, and by Tallington it had risen to 76½ – with 470 tons! By then it was only too clear that something very unusual was going on. The speed was still 74 at Little Bytham, and SIR VINCENT completed an amazing climb with a minimum of 67 at Stoke. The train was right time at Peterborough, and by Grantham it was no less than 6 minutes early, so the considerable effort was not justified by the schedule. The A1 had been working at 2,000 IHP and more from north of Werrington to Stoke. There was obviously a huge effort involved in accelerating this big train by Tallington, of the order of 2,100-2,300 IHP depending on the actual rate of acceleration. The speed levelled off and then fell, but there was a mighty effort over the last three miles or so in the region of 2,500IHP by Corby Glen. Most drivers in my experience were responsible and skilled men, to whom driving was a simple daily task which they enjoyed to one degree or another. Despite the calm exterior however, given a challenge, sometimes they could surprise. The driver seemed a sporting character, and knowing railwaymen, I suspect that there was a challenge or a wager as an incentive for this heroic effort. I hope the fireman was suitably rewarded! Of course it was just asking for trouble, and operators and engineers between them managed to delay the train so badly that it was late at York!

One of the finest fast runs made with an A1 occurred when a Type 4 diesel on the up 'Talisman' failed at York, and the south pilot, A1 No.60140 BALMORAL was commandeered. The load was 308 tons tare, say 320-325 gross, the same as the summer loading of the 'Coronation'. The driver was Dick Turner of Kings Cross, one of the Sparshatt school of GN driving, who was known never to be late if he could possibly help it. It was a name that one encountered frequently in cases where fast running was required to make up lost time. The up 'Coronation' was allowed 162 minutes from passing York, and the 'Talisman' 193 minutes, without the protection of double block working. The train had three heavy signal checks, one signal stop and three TSRs in 55 miles, two of which were only 16 miles apart. So much for planned engineering speed restrictions! Dick Turner made a superb run with BALMORAL, restarting from York 26 late and reaching Kings Cross 2½ minutes late. But for the signal stop at 'Star Brush Halt' (Holloway South up) he would have been on time. The running time was 169 minutes 12 seconds, but the net time was 158 minutes. I feel that the latter was a shade parsimonious, and was in fact lower still. The uphill work was of high quality, and the downhill speeds were fully in the main line tradition with 92½ at Crow Park, a sustained flight down Stoke bank with a maximum of 100½, and a rousing 90 through Welwyn Garden City!

Dick Turner was widely known as 'Colonel Bass' due to a love affair with the beverage that was life-long, an affable man who later retired and became a passenger guard. His florid countenance, betraying his affiliation, together with his comments generally on the alertness of the platform staff and his N2 driver enlivened many an evening commuter journey. Footplate crews worked hard in steam days, and a little strong drink was perfectly normal and allowable refreshment.

A number of runs were published in various magazines showing the A1s could attain 100mph and just from a standing start at Grantham, usually with a light load but not invariably. 102mph seemed to be the maximum and it was always on the dash 'down the hill' through Essendine. Their greater tractive effort made a faster climb to Stoke possible but from there the A4s, if pressed, were faster.

When discussing performance and fast running the name of Bill Hoole automatically springs to mind. His colleague and rival, Ted Hailstone, rarely had an A1, but Bill, two years younger, drove A1s. An approximate record of his running with AMADIS is in Appendix H. Although he ran fast, his fastest running was with A4s, but the few runs on record with A1s were hardly slow. When Grantham's three stalwarts, Nos.60149, 60156 and 60157 moved to Kings Cross in September 1956, it was for a new diagram. The engine and men went down with 266dn, the heavy Scots Goods, and returned with the 'Northumbrian' the following day. No.266 left Kings Cross Goods at different times with each timetable, but generally around 15.15, which required it to step aside for the 15.20 Newcastle, then the 15.45 'West Riding', the 15.50 and then the 16.00 'Talisman' as it made its way north. The 'Talisman' was hauled by an A4 with 8 coaches, and like the Pullman, had a fast schedule.

Freight operation was quite an imprecise art in those days by comparison with today, and once a crew had left Kings Cross Goods and gained the main line, it was every man for himself. Once the Newcastle was clear and 266 was turned out, a keen driver would get as far north as he could before being turned back in, because that often meant delay, perhaps trailing behind a WD 2-8-0 hauling coal empties at 20mph. North of Peterborough, the freight was booked to be turned in for the three expresses to pass, but the main tussle was with the 16.45 'Tees-Tyne Pullman' which caught up on the two-track section north of Grantham.

On the occasion in question, it is not certain which of the three A1s that Bill had but, with the injectors needing attention, he was booked away at 15.38 with 47 on, 23 late, two minutes ahead of the 15.45. No.266 down was a class C freight, the fastest category, fully braked, but on the day in question it was very fast. By Hitchin he had left the 15.45 for dead, and the famous Hitchin-Huntingdon racing stretch was covered in 20 minutes – an average of some 80mph – before he was stopped by Huntingdon with a hot axlebox. Having detached the offending vehicle at Peterborough, he was ready to resume, but the signalman held 266 until the three following expresses had passed before letting him out on to the down main. That day the Control log recorded '266 checked by Grove Road, waiting for the Talisman to clear the section.'

Probably the most remarkable performance by an A1 was described to me by Peter Howe. I had heard of a tremendous performance in which an A1 had achieved 3,600 IHP, and was trying to verify the story. In fact the figure was exaggerated. The approval by HM Railway Inspectorate of the automatic warning system, that would prevent an accident in which a driver had misread or mistaken his signals, had taken a long while. The GWR contact system that had worked well over the years was set aside, and a non-contact system was required, the Hudd system being developed as the ATC. Later it was re-christened AWS to distinguish it from the various development phases of the ATC. Development had entailed the running of many special trains on Sundays, screeching to a stop from high speed with the regulator open, testing all of the permutations that the Civil Service and the railway operators could imagine. The Power Brakes Sub-Committee of the BTC were asked to test the system with the vacuum in the train pipe reduced at the rear by air leakage, certainly a real risk.

So events led to a Saturday evening in the saloon bar when the Dynamometer Car staff, staying at Grantham, were joined by Inspector Sam Jenkins of 126 mph fame, and Driver 'Curly' Royce, the test train driver, whose regular A1 was BONGRACE. 'Curly'? No hair. Amid many reminiscences, the next day's plans were discussed, and it was required that the test train should be travelling at 90 mph at milepost 95½. Many would have thought that, from a standing start, with no less than 462 tons hooked behind the tender, that was next to impossible, but Curly Royce promised that he would make his A1 run as never before.

On Sunday September 25th 1955, he took BONGRACE away from Grantham and roared up to Stoke, passing the summit at 58 mph. She must have sounded like the wrath of God, accelerating hard downhill, but the speed at the location was only 89 mph – only! While a practical railwayman might dismiss 1 mph as being neither here nor there, they were dealing with the Civil Service and our friends in the Inspectorate. Then there was the honour of the driving fraternity at stake, and this was failure for Royce. I have passed milepost 95½ at 90 mph, but this was on a non-stop run, not starting from Grantham, and with 425 tons, not 462! However, there was a second chance in the afternoon, with a full firebox and no need to be concerned about pulling the fire, and despite some uncertainty as the A1 started away, with the reverser at 45% indicated and probably nearer 50% actually, BONGRACE stormed up the hill to Stoke, passing the summit at 57 mph. Stoke Tunnel was full of fire as Royce roared through at full regulator and 45-50% cut-off, and the time to passing Stoke with such a load was amazing at 8 minutes 55½ seconds. With such a load 10 minutes and 50 mph was pretty good. At full regulator and the reverser left unchanged BONGRACE charged

downhill, and this time the speed was 90 mph and honour was satisfied. Presumably Driver Royce and his fireman were the recipients rather than the donors of refreshments that evening! As the cut-off indicator was out of adjustment, it is likely that the value was nearly some 5% higher.

Comparison of the readings from the dynamometer car shows that the performance of BONGRACE was completely in line with the results of the 1949 testing of W P ALLEN at the lower speeds achieved. The maximum EDBHP was in the region of 2,300 at 60-65mph just south of Stoke, while the climb to Stoke from Great Ponton involved 2,200-2,300 EDBPH. Normally an estimate of the power developed would be pointless in cases where the dynamometer car is involved, but in this instance there was a difference between what was measured and an estimate based on the normal resistance formula. The reason was that the test specified a loss of vacuum in the train pipe at the rear, which increased its resistance. The maximum recorded drawbar pull would suggest a brief maximum IHP of 2,600-2,700, the highest for the class. The A1 was a powerful locomotive, especially at lower

speeds, as the two ascents to Stoke proved.

REFLECTIONS

As soon as one touches on the development of high power outputs, there is inevitably a comparison to be made between the Pacifics of Gresley and Stanier, and now Peppercorn. Since the three designs have the same boiler pressure, similar coupled wheel diameter, and a free steaming boiler the limit of which has not been reached, any dimensional difference comes down approximately to cylinder volume, and it is clear that the 'Duchess' is some 15% bigger than an A4 and an A1. So it is not surprising that the DUCHESSES OF HAMILTON and SUTHERLAND can develop 3,600IHP and possibly more, roughly some 500-600 IHP more than an A4. For a locomotive marginally more powerful on paper than an A4, it is curious that no A1 has bettered MALLARD's performances. BONGRACE, SIR VINCENT, KESTREL, W P ALLEN and no doubt others have run her close but not surpassed her.

There was a difference in the philosophy of the old LMSR and the old LNER as regards their express

locomotives. The LNER designers used small clearance volumes, but not excessively so, so as to produce designs that were competent and economical. They were not built to break records for developing high power. The result of that philosophy was seen in the 1948 Locomotive Exchanges in which, despite the shortcomings of the trials, the A4 was the most economical of the express types tested. It was a remarkably economical locomotive, as was the A1, developed from it.

However, the West Coast main line enjoys substantially heavier gradients than its counterpart, and for its heavier services, William Stanier designed a magnificently powerful Pacific. The critical difference was that the Stanier Pacific could handle higher steam flows through a well-laid out, capacious front end, and develop significantly higher maximum power outputs. The downside of this philosophy was that larger ports and passages inevitably led to higher clearance volumes and less economy. The downside of the LNER philosophy was that despite high tractive efforts and the free-steaming combination of the Doncaster boiler and double Kylchap exhaust, there was an upper limit on the power outputs achieved. When a locomotive was working at full power, the ability to handle high steam flows became far more important, and four steam chests, eight live steam ports and four cylinders had the edge on three. On the other hand, a fireman on the former LNER might have reflected on how much more coal his counterpart had to move in order to get up Shap and Beattock! As a Doncaster man remarked to me, the LNER built Pacifics with enough power to do their work economically, not to break records.

Suppositions about which were the best locomotives and the worst has always been part of the lore of railway enthusiasm, much of it subjective and partial. Drivers would take against an engine known to be shy of steam, or a bad rider. All of the A1s were free-steaming engines, and there was nothing to choose between them. The riding varied and that might have made some drivers partial to some and prejudiced against another. The roller-bearing quintet was in a class apart in terms of reliability, but as I have instanced earlier, their riding varied from one extreme to the other.

With Nationalisation, Riddles and his LMSR team took over, with J F Harrison, his assistant, as the only ex-LNER senior member. One of the first moves was to install the LMSR locomotive costing scheme, confident that the economy of the LMSR designs would serve as an example to others and also would justify their perpetuation in standard form. Alas for such hopes. The scheme demonstrated the economy of the LNER Pacifics and before long, for some reason it was

discontinued! Roland Bond, in a lecture to the Institution of Locomotive Engineers in 1953, gave details of the mileages between overhaul of the principal classes. But for the Stanier Class 5s equipped with manganese steel axlebox liners, the A1s achieved the highest mileages of all, 93,363. The figure included the five with roller bearings, but it should be remembered that there were 44 without. It is an interesting demonstration of the effectiveness of the manganese liners that those Black 5s so equipped achieved 97,291 miles; those without, only reached 56,969. Even the A4 with all the shortcomings of single blast, 2:1 conjugated gear and the notoriously susceptible middle big end achieved 86,614 miles. Horses for courses.

One of the curiosities of railway history post-war on the East Coast was the resurgence of the Gresley Pacifics, once fitted with double Kylchaps in the later 1950s. Whereas the newer Pacifics were preferred for their free steaming and reliability, once the A4s – and more remarkably, the older A3s – were improved, the situation was reversed and the A1s worked turn and turn about with their predecessors. A notable exception was Copley Hill, which continued to handle the West Riding services using a fleet of A1s, together with Kings Cross. They worked the harder turns, and credit for much of the best work of the class over the years should go to the staff and drivers there.

Fortunately we have BLUE PETER preserved to remind us of the A2s, and when TORNADO is completed and running, we shall once again enjoy the sight of a Peppercorn A1 hauling express trains. Fitting heirs to the Gresley tradition – the Pacific that Gresley might have built after the war, had he lived

I have included a number of Appendices covering the dimensions, the individual histories, their work and performance. I have given some estimates of power developed during the best known performances. Considerable efforts have gone into making this a reasonably accurate record. If there are mistakes, I apologise. Otherwise, enjoy reading about some remarkable locomotives in days long ago.

A magnificent study of 60121 SILURIAN at Doncaster, fresh from general overhaul, on April 4th 1957. A rebuilt ex-NER B16 4-6-0 stands on the adjacent road and an M&GN 'Black Pig', No.43156, lurks in the shed. (P Groom)

GREAT NORTHERN at New England on a date given as May 27th 1951. I would query that date since she would have been just out of Doncaster after a heavy overhaul according to Yeadon, with the Flaman recorder removed, although the drive is still there. New crested nameplates would have replaced the earlier plain nameplate. It would have been at least two months earlier, and she would still be in BR blue livery. She has been consigned to that depot, hardly a vote of confidence, but later in 1951 she would be moved to Grantham. In an excellent study, one can see quite clearly the Gresley engine, up to the leading coupled axle, with the new front end designed by Thompson. The long exhaust ducts are clearly visible, and the De Glehn bogie with its side bearers. In the rebuilding, the bracket carrying the radius link has been redesigned, a fabricated version replacing the previous casting. The engine still has a plain stovepipe double chimney. The pipe attached to the boiler bands was the electrical conduit with the supply to the electric headlights. She was always coupled to A3 non-corridor tender No.5582. (B K B Green, Initial Photographics)

A close-up of the driver's side deflector showing the excellence of the coat of arms carried on the special nameplate. It is sad to reflect that today an immaculate plastic transfer would be applied in moments. A minute detail, but the shape of the plaque carrying the company's coat of arms varied across the five engines with the special nameplates. Clearly the engine has been in service some years by now bearing the heat and burden of the day, and it looks as though the connections for the deflector securing brackets have required repair and reinforcement. The date is not given, but I would guess at February 1961 after her last general overhaul.

THOMPSON and PEPPERCORN PACIFIC PORTFOLIO

GREAT NORTHERN pulls out of Kings Cross on June 28th 1946. (G O P Pearce)

GREAT NORTHERN waits for the road from Kings Cross (old platform 4) in summer 1961, alongside the new D5000 Type 2 diesel that brought in the 13.05 ECS. (P J Coster)

Above. The official picture of GREAT NORTHERN rebuilt, bearing the old number 4470 but with the Gresley cab reinstated. Although the locomotive was painted with a lined-out dark blue approximating to the blue of the old GER, the tender had only the letters 'NE', a wartime measure that seemed incongruous as part of a splendid livery.

Below. GREAT NORTHERN, bearing her new 1946 LNER number, in the glory of the lined apple green livery. Surely even Edward Thompson's Pacifics looked splendid in this livery.

60114 W P ALLEN at Doncaster on September 25th 1955 with the 15.05 Leeds-Kings Cross express. The prototype was allocated to Grantham at the time. The train was 849up, originally a FO semi-fast worked by Doncaster, but it was later extended to Leeds and Bradford. A bureaucratic point, but the WTT number was not changed from the GN 800 series to the West Riding 900 series. It was worked by Grantham and Kings Cross, changing engines at Grantham. (B K B Green, Initial Photographics).

No.60114 W P ALLEN pulls away from Preston with a railtour on September 28th 1963. (A W Battson, Transport Treasury)

The works plate of the first new A1, No.60114. Compared with the pre-war version, the new plate is more terse, in the spirit of austerity. However, amid the hand painted numbers, Doncaster's rogue 6 is alive and well! (R E Vincent, Transport Treasury)

60114 W P ALLEN is headed for home on June 16th 1951 with the 14.18 from Kings Cross to Leeds at Marshgate Junction, north of Doncaster. The East Coast main line is to the left, and the A1 is on the down Leeds. It must have been a novelty at Copley Hill, for so long an Ivatt Atlantic shed, to receive new Pacifics, the prototype among them. The A1 is carrying the old code for the Leeds shed. (R E Vincent, Transport Treasury)

MEG MERRILIES was a curious name for an express locomotive, we lads thought at the time, unused to some of the more extravagant Scott names of the 'Director' and NBR 4-4-0s. Here, at Marshgate Junction, Gateshead's A1 makes her way back north with the 15.30 from Kings Cross on June 16th 1951. (R E Vincent, Transport Treasury)

The Gateshead A1, uncharacteristically clean for a locomotive awaiting her second general overhaul, at Doncaster Works on April 29th 1951. She is in BR blue livery, and retained that livery after repair. (B K B Green, Initial Photographics).

On May 21st 1955 the up 'Flying Scotsman' was hauled from Edinburgh to Newcastle by 60115 MEG MERRILIES. One of the Waverley J83 pilots is on the right. (www.vintag-images.co.uk).

60116 HAL O' THE WYND on Gateshead shed in 1957 with Haymarket's PEARL DIVER in the background. The A1 has the smokebox handrail and numberplate transposed, as a few did. She looks out of steam, and either has paid a visit to Gateshead Works or is about to. (C J B Sanderson, J W Armstrong Trust)

The train is said to be the 23.45 Edinburgh-Kings Cross parcels, but it looks very much more like one of the Sunday morning fast freights, which were often fish. It is March 5th 1950, between Welwyn Garden City and Hatfield and the train is headed by new No.60117 in LNER apple green livery. Curiously, Grantham received the fourth new A1s from both Doncaster and Darlington, Nos.60117 and 60133, and both seemed to work north more often than south. It was not until both went to Copley Hill three months later that they became more familiar in the Metropolis. (E D Bruton, Gresley Society Trust)

60117 BOIS ROUSSEL brings an up express into York across the north junction. The name, lipped chimney and the 35B shedplate pin the time down to summer 1952. (J Robertson, Transport Treasury)

Above. ARCHIBALD STURROCK enters Peterborough North with the 18.18 Leeds express on June 23rd 1954. (R E Vincent, Transport Treasury)

Left. No.60118 ARCHIBALD STURROCK at Leeds Central with 'The Harrogate Sunday Pullman'. The train survived well enough some fifty years ago, but would not even be remotely contemplated on today's railway. Everything in the picture has gone, the A1, the train, even Leeds Central, all have gone.

60119 PATRICK STIRLING at Doncaster shed. The date is not given but it must fall after August 1958 and before 1961. (J Davenport, Initial Photographics)

60119 PATRICK STIRLING pulling away from Leeds past Wortley Junction with a fast freight. At the time she was a Doncaster engine, so the date must be after August 1958. (P Wilson)

60120 KITTIWAKE at Copley Hill in March 1963. She looks somewhat travel-stained and in nine months was withdrawn. The Flaman bracket is still in place – why was it not removed during the umpteen works visits over the last ten or more years, I wonder? Among the footplate furniture in the photo, the pile of firebricks might suggest that the brick arch needed rebuilding. Fire irons and a flame shield lay discarded and unwanted. (J Davenport, Initial Photographics)

Warm bearing? 60120 KITTIWAKE was another long-term Copley Hill engine being carefully examined by the relief crew. She is standing in old platform 4 at Kings Cross on June 1st 1963 within days of steam being banned south of Peterborough. The only up service worked by Copley Hill (during daylight) with ordinary stock during the week was the up 'West Riding'. On Saturdays, as this was of course, there were extra services bringing Leeds Pacifics into London. Do you remember those trains of platform barrows clattering around the station, and those piles of vestibule end boards? (A R Scarsbrook, Initial Photographics)

60120 KITTIWAKE emerges from a tunnel portal probably with an up express. As the A1 is on the left-hand road, we must be on a four track section with two twin bores, and the only ones that spring to mind are Hadley North and South, and Potters Bar, but the new down tunnels are just out of sight for confirmation. I would plump for the last-named, since the overburden is higher for the other two. Date probably 1959 just after opening the four-track section in May of that year. The Signal Engineer would not be at all happy if those cables were operational: the section was resignalled and the cables are probably the earthly remains of the 1932 scheme that replaced Hadley Wood, Ganwick and Mimms Hall signalboxes. (J G Walmsley, Transport Treasury)

60120 KITTIWAKE heads a down express north of Hadley North Tunnel in 1961-62. From the look of the trees it is spring 1962. The A1 seems to be making light work of its load, probably the 13.18 from Kings Cross, nominally an Ardsley turn. (J G Walmsley, Transport Treasury)

No.60121 SILURIAN at Gateshead MPD. It looks very much like October 23rd 1964, when the last A4 service trip was made, UNION OF SOUTH AFRICA, left Kings Cross with the 'Jubilee Requiem' railtour. SILURIAN was standing nearby at Gateshead when the A4 arrived for servicing.

60121 SILURIAN at Doncaster shed in October 1964. The A1 now has the modified smokebox door with the top lamp bracket in its lowest position, and with two short handrails either side. The 9F alongside was a one-time Somerset & Dorset resident, and I believe has been preserved. (J Davenport, Initial Photographics)

60121 SILURIAN stands in York roundhouse on November 15th 1964. Three of York's A1s stayed at the one shed throughout their existence, 60121, 60138 and 60153. York kept them in good external condition, even in their last years.

60122, as yet without name, in apple green livery at Doncaster shed in February 1950. (J Davenport, Initial Photographics)

60122 CURLEW cruises down the gradient from Potters Bar with an up express. By now the A1 has moved to Doncaster, fixing the date at after 1959. (P Ransome-Wallis)

60122 CURLEW with the Sunday 'Flying Scotsman' has been diverted over the down slow at New Southgate, and is about to regain the down main, in the summer of 1957. It was unusual to pull No.6 lever, the starter from down slow to main, as the crossover was seldom used. (P J Coster)

Allocation to Ardsley ultimately proved the end of 60123 H A IVATT. She was badly damaged at Sandy on the collision-prone Ardsley goods, 1357up, and subsequently withdrawn as the first A1 casualty in the great throwaway of the 1960s. Condemned on October 1st 1962, she stands at Doncaster Works on October 7th. She was the A1, most appropriately, that hauled the returning Ivatt Atlantic special from Doncaster to Kings Cross on November 26th 1950, pausing at Biggleswade to detach an incinerated GCR restaurant car. The last C1 62822 had of course worked the down train, and was withdrawn on reaching Doncaster – alas! (Paul Chancellor Collection)

The 'Harrogate Sunday Pullman' was probably diverted over more odd bits of railway than any other named train, due to engineering works of all sorts taking place on the day it ran. No.60123 H A IVATT runs light, tender first, through Woodlesford, east of Leeds, on Sunday November 6th 1960. This was normally the only through working to and from London and that is probably, but not certainly, the diverted train that the A1 is travelling to or from. (Transport Treasury)

60124 KENILWORTH pauses at Darlington on July 28th 1958 with the 19.05 Newcastle-Bristol cross-country express. (M Mensing)

The 'Night Scotsman' waits in old platform 8 at Kings Cross, with Gateshead's KENILWORTH at the head. The A1's fire was prepared with care, and the engine was let down to the station early, since there were up to six locomotives following to power the various night services out of London, as well as those arriving, to be released. Together with the ECS movements, it was a busy two hours. Inattention to the big fire on the grate could result in an explosive roar from the safety valves and disciplinary action as a result. (George Heiron, courtesy Mrs Shirley Heiron, The Transport Treasury)

SCOTTISH UNION running into Peterborough North with an up Pullman service. It is August 28th 1962, and I would assume that, as the A1 is a Doncaster engine, it is more likely to be the 'Yorkshire Pullman' than the 'Tees-Tyne Pullman', but one never be certain that the Doncaster pilot has not been commandeered to take over the latter from a failed Pacific. (A E Bennett, Transport Treasury)

60125 SCOTTISH UNION was another ER A1, now working from Doncaster, probably on an up Hull express in old No.5 platform at Kings Cross. We are now into the 1960s and Brush diesels; Gorton's B1, No.61179, with a freshly repainted smokebox door, had migrated to pastures new with an outer suburban service at Kings Cross. (B W L Brooksbank, Initial Photographics)

60125 SCOTTISH UNION stands at Carr Loco on May 7th 1960, with one of Immingham's Britannias standing behind. (F Hornby)

60125 SCOTTISH UNION heads an up express in the vicinity of Peterborough in 1962 or later. The A1 is working hard to gather speed, for the section south of Peterborough over the Fens was notorious for strong winds. The train is south of Fletton Junction, gathering speed past the extensive brickworks that used to be on the down side. The up side was linked by an overhead bridge carrying a ropeway that existed for years. A colleague of mine inspected it and was deeply impressed that it was still standing: it was condemned. (B Richardson, Transport Treasury)

Doncaster's last apple green A1 was 60126. Later named SIR VINCENT RAVEN after the famous NER CME, she was a long-term Heaton A1, only moving to York in her last few years. She was a very infrequent visitor to London in the 1950s, as were all of Heaton's trinity of A1s. The location is New England shed, and the A1 has probably worked in on the 7.50 from Newcastle, to return on the down 'Heart of Midlothian'. The period is after June 1960. (B Richardson, Transport Treasury)

SIR VINCENT RAVEN gathers speed south of Fletton Junction with an up express. For a Heaton engine, she is looking unusually dirty, with a blow on the inside cylinder somewhere. The date is after June 1960, and it is clear that standards are beginning to fall. (B Richardson, Transport Treasury)

Heaton's brand new gleaming blue A1 No.60127 waits at York with what looks like a troop train of the period, with special number 458. No.60127 was unique in that the cylinders were also lined red, as this was omitted from subsequent liveries. (Paul Chancellor Collection)

The third member of the Heaton A1 triumvirate was 60127 WILSON WORSDELL. She was the first blue A1, and the BR Caley blue suited the A1s very well, I thought. She stands at Haymarket, in excellent condition, alongside the home shed's V2 No.60927. Heaton worked northbound services rather than south, and the Heaton Pacifics were less common in the south than their Gateshead cousins. The date is difficult to pin down with the A1s, but I would estimate mid-1952 to early 1954. (R K Blencowe)

No.60127 WILSON WORSDELL approaches Grantham from the north on September 1st 1952. Almost certainly the train is the 7.53 from Sunderland, which Heaton engines worked through to London, but she will have come off at Grantham and returned with the down 'Northumbrian' (R E Vincent, Transport Treasury)

60128 BONGRACE arrives at old platform 8 at Kings Cross on August 28th, 1951 with an up express, the 7.20 from Leeds Central. She is in blue livery, unlipped double chimney, and the Flaman drive fitted to the early A1s is visible. She would have worked the light but fast 5.15 parcels and newspapers as far as Grantham before returning with this heavy train. The Copley Hill engine off the 7.20 would later return to Leeds with the 10.18 from Kings Cross. (B K B Green, Initial Photographics)

Grantham's No.60128 BONGRACE waits in the loco spur by the Yard signalbox at Grantham, ready to take over an up express in 1952.

60129 GUY MANNERING slows for the Permanent Speed Restriction (PSR) at Selby swing bridge, passing the BOCM factory between Barlby Junction and Selby, on August 1st 1953. A V2 stands on the up goods waiting for the road. (J Robertson, Transport Treasury)

A filthy 60129 GUY MANNERING approaches Retford with an up Newcastle relief on August 7th 1956. The A1 seems to be running well despite the neglected appearance, and perhaps the clean cylinder is an indication of recent repairs. (B K B Green, Initial Photographics)

No.60129 GUY MANNERING standing at the head of a fast freight. As the A1 is displaying a light engine headcode, I assume that she had either just uncoupled or coupled. The location looks rather like the eastern end of Newcastle Central with the train having crossed the High Level Bridge. Those who know the location better...

60129 GUY MANNERING, looking reassuringly more like a Gateshead A1, pauses at York with a down express in the late 1950s. It was a time when the fair sex had yet to discover the joys and fulfilment of soot, char, oil, grease and perspiration! (Transport Treasury)

60130 KESTREL was the first express Pacific to be built by Darlington since Raven's design, and one can readily distinguish Darlington's A1s by their smooth tenders, countersunk rivets having been used rather than snap head ones as at Doncaster. Although Ardsley had a few A1s for their London passenger lodging turn, in fact the actual engines varied from day to day. Copley Hill deployed its A1 fleet, including Ardsley's, and whether Ardsley had their own engines to use or those of its neighbour seemed not to matter. Here the Copley Hill Shedmaster has been caught red-handed, with Ardsley's KESTREL at the head of the 15.45 down 'West Riding' before returning to West Yorkshire on March 10th 1956. (A G Forsyth, Initial Photographics)

60130 KESTREL drifts into Hadley North Tunnel with an up express in the early 1960s. (J G Walmsley, Transport Treasury)

No.60130 KESTREL, approaching Sandy at speed and magnificently caught as a 'pan' shot on August 7th 1961. It was easy to blur the background with a lower shutter speed, but all too easy to blur the locomotive as well! Unlike the picture here. (M Mensing)

KESTREL emerges from Hadley South Tunnel, running light on May 15th 1952. This was a curiously uneconomic turn. The A1 on the up 'Northumbrian' returned from Kings Cross on the 17.35 Newcastle, and in the winter book, the next three-four up expresses were all worked by Kings Cross, returning from Grantham or Peterborough. There was no balancing up train duty for the Grantham A1 working the down 'Aberdonian', and so it was sent up light, except on Fridays when a Lincoln-Grantham train was extended to Kings Cross, unadvertised, and worked by the A1. The down 'Aberdonian' was a heavy train, and the Grantham A1 worked through to York, the top link crews changing at the Grantham stop. (R E Vincent, Transport Treasury)

'The Harrogate Sunday Pullman', diverted over the New Line. 60131 OSPREY mounts the sharp 1 in 50 climb up to Wood Green flyover with little effort. The period must be between 1951 and 1954. (S Creer, Transport Treasury)

60132 MARMION coasts into Berwick with the 6.50 slow from Edinburgh on May 22nd 1962. The A1 was now a Heaton engine, which accounts for its clean appearance no doubt. For those of us not conversant with Scott literature it was slightly disappointing to find that MARMION did not come from that quarter, but from an elderly NBR Clyde paddle steamer! I believe that the name itself meant a lament. (M Mensing)

No.60132 MARMION comes on to Haymarket shed having turned and coaled. The period must be 1951-54.

On a Sunday afternoon at Haymarket the engines not needed for service until Monday were stabled alongside the main line, presenting passing enthusiasts with a splendid display of main line power. 60132 MARMION, a visitor from Gateshead, stands at the head of the queue on October 12th 1952, six months from general overhaul when it was painted in BR dark green livery. She is probably rostered for one of the overnight services to London later in the evening. The right-hand smoke deflector appears to have been re-secured recently. (J Robertson, Transport Treasury)

No.60133 POMMERN, the first to be named other than the prototype, in her first week as a Leeds engine with the 18.20 Kings Cross-Leeds express on June 9th 1950. Shortly after this the A1 took over the 'West Riding' duty for most of summer 1950. (R E Vincent, Transport Treasury)

No.60133 POMMERN at Top Shed on May 8th 1954, turning after bringing up the 'Yorkshire Pullman'. Notice how tight a fit the A1 is on the turntable. (M N Bland, Transport Treasury)

A five month old 60134 on the south curve at Hatfield near Red Hall signalbox on April 16th 1949. Still in apple green livery, with BRITISH RAILWAYS rather than the ferret and dartboard on the tender, she has yet to be named. The distinctive Darlington tender lining is apparent: perhaps a short painter or a short ladder?

No.60134 FOXHUNTER was always a Leeds area engine, Copley Hill, Ardsley or Neville Hill at the end. Here she is at Doncaster shed on September 9th 1951, when she was in BR blue livery. The A1 was named after a winner of the Doncaster Cup, and not, as most would assume, Col. Harry Llewelyn's famous show jumper. (B K B Green, Initial Photographics)

60134 FOXHUNTER pulls out of Kings Cross with a down express. It feels like evening, and I would plump for the 18.18 to Leeds, the stock having arrived in platform 8 earlier as an up express. I would put the date quite specifically at late September 1951, which means that the A1 is in BR blue livery. FOXHUNTER would have arrived on the up 'Yorkshire Pullman' with Copley Hill men, but Doncaster men are taking her home. Sister engine BONGRACE waits in the station loco yard for the 'Aberdonian', with another A1 – PEREGRINE, I think – behind for the first part of the 'Aberdonian'. Both A1s would not have been turned and ready much before 17.30. Meanwhile one of the station pilots, N2 No.69521, slumbers by the York Road platform. (R A Ellis, Transport Treasury)

No.60135 MADGE WILDFIRE on Haymarket turntable in April 1955. (W Hermiston, Transport Treasury)

A filthy 60135 MADGE WILDFIRE near Retford on August 7th 1956 with 860 down, a curious service from Harwich to Doncaster. Not only had the intrepid souls been travelling nearly six hours by then, but it was a curious turn on which to find a Gateshead A1. Even by the latter's standards the engine is a disgrace, but let us be charitable and assume that it has just been repaired after failing and laying idle somewhere! (B K B Green, Initial Photographics)

The spot on or by Haymarket turntable was a gift to a photographers, provided one could avoid any unwanted protrusions from the boiler top. No.60135 MADGE WILDFIRE is nicely posed in the 1951-55 period.

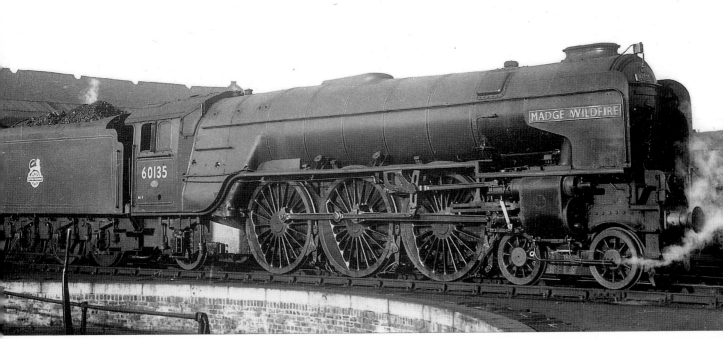

No.60136 ALCAZAR runs into Retford station in the late 1950s/early 1960s. (J Davenport, Initial Photographics)

A wonderful panorama of lunchtime Kings Cross in the late 1950s. ALCAZAR looks to have lost her feet, probably with the 13.05 Leeds departure. A loco inspector (trilby) glances while a guard looks on. Small boys in 1950s short trousers and uniform enjoy this demonstration of unbridled power, and a permanent way man waits the departure of this noisy engine before he can return to cleaning the tracks of rubbish. (G F Heiron, courtesy Mrs Shirley Heiron, The Transport Treasury)

No.60137 REDGAUNTLET, probably at Haymarket, about to leave for Waverley. The engine is in BR blue livery and has yet to receive a lipped chimney. The date lies between June 1950 and January 1953. (J Robertson, Transport Treasury)

60138 BOSWELL was always a York A1, and here she is at her home shed between two visitors, a Jubilee and a 9F, on May 19th 1964.

60138 BOSWELL at York on August 11th 1965, within weeks of her withdrawal, dumped on the buffer stops. The nameplate has already been removed, legally one hopes. (Peter Groom)

60139 SEA EAGLE at Doncaster shed on June 4th 1950, just fresh from general overhaul at the Plant, newly named and in BR blue livery. (B K B Green, Initial Photographics)

No.60139, only three months from the Works, gets a down Leeds express away from Kings Cross in March 1949. Again, the sanders are on, and the column of exhaust is impressive. (R E Vincent, Transport Treasury)

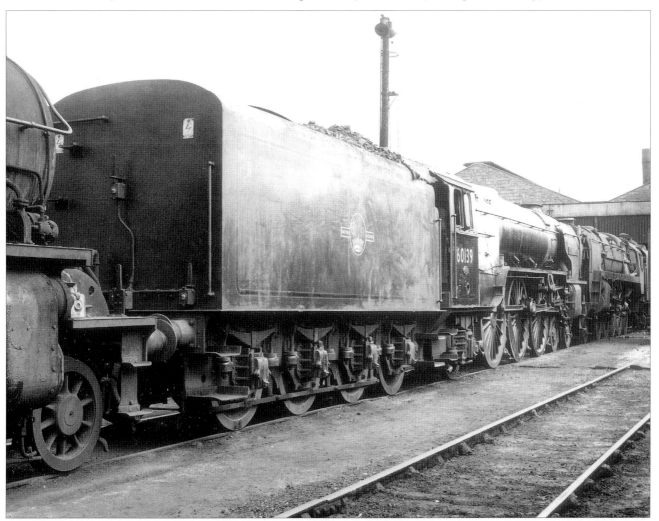

60139 SEA EAGLE at Doncaster shed on June 9th 1963. (Transport Treasury)

Here I must admit defeat. The photograph is bereft of all detail save the identity of the A1, SEA EAGLE; the class D freight on the slow is hauled by an A4, possibly 60022, 60023 or 60032. The signalling is standard LNER upper quadrant, although the high signal gantry is unusual and might be a clue. With CWR on the main lines it is almost certainly the East Coast with four running lines and additional tracks beyond. Quite possibly the four tracks funnel down to two through a station, which is why the A4 is held on the slow line. There also appears to be a structure behind resembling a walkway or overline conveyor. (Transport Treasury)

60140 BALMORAL at speed with a special train on the Plain of York. It is impossible to tell whether it is a down or up train, but I would plump for the down. It may be a special company train to the ICI works at Billingham. The date is likely to be in the mid-1950s to judge from the track; not only is it jointed rail but it is bullhead. (Paul Chancellor Collection)

No.60140 BALMORAL passing Cross Gates with the 9.00 Liverpool-Newcastle express on August 31st 1958. This is a challenging location with factory and its excrescences behind. Presumably today it would be a 3 car DMU!
(B K B Green, Initial Photographics)

A long-term resident at York, apart from seven months at Top Shed, No.60140 BALMORAL is at York in July 1963.

60140 BALMORAL passes King Edward Bridge Junction at Gateshead with a up express. From the latter's stock I would say that it is the up 'Heart of Midlothian', in which case BALMORAL has been borrowed by Gateshead for a trip to Grantham and back. She was a long-term York A1, apart from eight months at Kings Cross in her second year. Her name might be thought to be connected to Scott literature, or to be that of the Royal Deeside palace, but both would be wrong as BALMORAL was another NBR Clyde steamer. The date would lie between late 1951 and 1954. (www.vintage-images.co.uk)

BALMORAL stands in old platform 6 at Kings Cross. That platform was used by the 9.15 from York and Hull for years, which was a York turn, and I would imagine that is the duty BALMORAL is on. (G F Heiron, courtesy Mrs Shirley Heiron, Transport Treasury)

No.60141 ABBOTSFORD at the buffer stops at Kings Cross old platform 5. The date is probably in the early 1960s, and the service must be from Leeds as the A1 was a long-term Leeds engine.

The southbound 'Yorkshire Pullman' headed by 60141 ABBOTSFORD in BR blue livery approaches the site of the old Ganwick signalbox on September 2nd 1952. The famous bottleneck was a perennial nuisance, especially on summer Saturdays, but it had a rural charm which has been lost thanks to the roar of the M25 just over the horizon above the tunnel. The Pullman was never given a timing that exercised engine or crew, and it was not until the arrival of the Deltics that its stately pace was rudely accelerated. Yet in a less frantic age, it was the way to enjoy travelling.

No.60141 ABBOTSFORD in blue livery, going hard up the bank from Holme to Abbotts Ripton with the 7.20 Leeds-Kings Cross, June 10th 1950. (R E Vincent, Transport Treasury)

60142 EDWARD FLETCHER at Doncaster in March 1953. She was given a general overhaul a month or so before, as evidenced by the chalked number still on the bogie stretcher, but returned for some attention. Gateshead engines did not normally work into Doncaster rather than through, to Grantham, Peterborough or Kings Cross. (J Davenport, Initial Photographics)

The Peppercorn A1 in its apple green glory. 60142 stands at Haymarket in 1949-50. (J Robertson, Transport Treasury)

The up 'Flying Scotsman' departs from Edinburgh Waverley on March 24th 1951. 60142 EDWARD FLETCHER is named and in blue livery, and has been superbly cleaned, even the smokebox hinges having been burnished. Normally Gateshead paid little attention to cleanliness, perhaps through an inability to recruit cleaners, or perhaps 60142 has been on Royal duties. 1951 was Festival of Britain year, and the newly created British Railways made much of their named expresses and added some new ones such as the 'Heart of Midlothian', all with fine headboards. Initially as a new engine, No.60142 was seen in London but after the timetable and diagramming revision in September 1951, she went into purdah. Gateshead allocated their A1s to the main 8P diagrams and kept specific engines on each duty as far as practicable. No.60142 was kept to the Newcastle-Edinburgh down sleeping car service leaving Kings Cross, I believe, at 22.35 and returning on the up (or down if you are Scots!) 'Flying Scotsman'. She looks a grand sight. (Transport Treasury)

60143 SIR WALTER SCOTT pulls away from York with the 10.5 Kings Cross-Edinburgh and Glasgow, July 1st 1951. The A1 is in blue livery, and her driver has got the heavy train underway past the engine shed. Pacifics looked awfully large when passing alongside, and a swift check to ensure that one was well clear of the sleeper ends was always wise. A glance at the tender to anticipate falling coal was not a bad idea as well! Better still to stand well clear in the proverbial place of safety advised in the Rule Book. (B K B Green, Initial Photographics)

Four A1s and a K1 2-6-0 stand at York, dead and unwanted. From left to right they are SIR WALTER SCOTT, SIR VINCENT RAVEN, NORTH EASTERN and WILLBROOK, the K1 being No.62058. The date is October 3rd 1964. (Ray Farrell)

No.60144 KING'S COURIER stands at Copley Hill shed on May 25th 1952. After nine months in BR blue she was repainted dark green whilst a Leeds engine. Copley Hill usually kept their A1s clean. (B K B Green, Initial Photographics)

60144 KING'S COURIER, released from an up train, moves to the station loco yard for turning and servicing. The date must be about 1953-54. Immingham's B1 No.61328 is being coaled before turning: the B1s on this turn usually went to Top Shed. (G F Heiron, courtesy Mrs Shirley Heiron, Transport Treasury)

60145, now named SAINT MUNGO, stands at Haymarket alongside Waverley pilot J83 No.68457. The date is March 30th 1951. (J Robertson, Transport Treasury)

No.60145 SAINT MUNGO pulls away from Peterborough North late in the steam era, March 16th 1963, with the 13.15 Kings Cross to Leeds. The A1 has passed the junction with the up excursion road and is at the point where the down goods line joins in. (Alec Swain, Transport Treasury)

60146 PEREGRINE was another York engine for many years. She is at Doncaster shed on March 15th 1953, and during a recent heavy intermediate repair at the Plant has been repainted. (R J Buckley, Initial Photographics)

60146 PEREGRINE at York shed in July 1951 when in BR blue livery. (J Davenport, Initial Photographics)

No.60146 PEREGRINE, coming on to shed at Copley Hill on March 28th 1959.

60147 heads an up express through Escrick station, between York and Selby. It is unnamed and in Darlington's apple green livery, and has yet to receive the familiar 52A shed plate. The train looks like the 'Flying Scotsman' with its Newton/Thompson coaches, and the A1 looks fairly new. I would put the year at 1949, possibly 1950, but no later. (Cecil Ord)

60147 NORTH EASTERN pauses at York with the summer 13.05 Newcastle-Kings Cross on July 3rd 1955. This was a Sunday service, and the Gateshead A1 would have taken the train to Peterborough where a London engine would have taken over. Notice the intriguing LMS coach in the bay platform. (B K B Green, Initial Photographics)

Four close up studies of 60147 NORTH EASTERN at New England shed. Notice that the A1 has lost the footstep welded to the smokebox door. The coat of arms, in this case the NER, is painted separately on a metal plate whose shape differed between the five A1s, and was fastened in the space on the special nameplate. The right-hand cab side has been repaired and no doubt awaits a touch of paint. The A1 is now a York engine, which puts the date as post-September 1963. (B Richardson, Transport Treasury)

No.60148 ABOYEUR is opened out for the sharp climb from Peterborough North with a Leeds-Kings Cross express. More curious is the 'Ugly Duckling' No.43094 bearing down on the photographer with express 'open lights'. Having moved beyond the connection for Peterborough East and East Anglia, it can only be heading for London, which was unusual to say the least, even in 1961-63. The 2-6-0 is leaking so much steam it is a wonder that there is enough to spare for forward motion! (B Richardson, Transport Treasury)

A dishevelled 60148 ABOYEUR at Grantham shed in June 1960. (D H Beecroft, Transport Treasury)

60148 ABOYEUR stands in old platform four at Kings Cross on May 22nd 1963. (J A C Kirke, Transport Treasury)

A scene so familiar in the 1950s as heavy expresses pounded up the bank to Holloway North with towering exhausts and a haze over the railway. This is a superb shot of No.60149 AMADIS passing Holloway South Down with the heavy 10.18 Kings Cross-Leeds on September 20th 1953. Holloway South Up signalbox is on the left-hand side, on the platform. (R E Vincent, Transport Treasury)

60149 AMADIS was a Grantham top link for many years, then moving to Top Shed where she ran many useful miles. In March 1962 she was a Doncaster engine, and is seen at speed passing Welwyn Garden City. (A G Forsyth, Initial Photographics)

60149 AMADIS was one of the regularly manned Grantham A1s for many years before it was one of three A1s that moved to Kings Cross for the extra Newcastle lodging duties. It is at York on August 20th 1960. (Peter Groom)

No.60149 AMADIS stands on the up platform one at Doncaster. The period would be 1958-61. (Transport Treasury)

60150 WILLBROOK eases back on to her train at Edinburgh Waverley July 25th 1953. The A1 is reassuringly scruffy, as befitted a Gateshead engine. (J Robertson, Transport Treasury)

One can almost hear the shunter calling 'blow up!' as the driver of 60150 WILLBROOK creates 21 inches of vacuum, ready for the brake test. The date must be about 1960-61 and it is of course, old platform 10 at Kings Cross. (C Martin, Transport Treasury)

A scruffy and uncared-for 60151 MIDLOTHIAN pulls out of Berwick-on-Tweed with the 6.55 Newcastle-Edinburgh slow on May 22nd 1962. A sad decline for one of Gateshead's splendid Pacifics. (M Mensing)

No.60151 MIDLOTHIAN stands at the north end of Grantham station to take over a down express. A new DMU on a Grantham-Boston service waits alongside. The time is probably the middle 1950s. (Transport Treasury)

60151 MIDLOTHIAN stands at Darlington shed on July 3rd 1949. The A1 is only a few days from its building date, and is in apple green livery. It is a joy to see a locomotive in such magnificent condition. Clearly the tender lining at Darlington has been the subject of official investigation, and either a taller painter has taken over the task of the lining, or a longer ladder has been provided! (Transport Treasury)

There was great disappointment in schoolboy circles when Darlington's last A1 went to Haymarket, and 60152 HOLYROOD remained the most elusive of the 49 down in the south. Here she is standing at Doncaster, about to go for her first general overhaul, the last apple green A1 and unnamed. Some in the North East might be excused for thinking that the A1 had just been overhauled and repainted rather than needing repair! No.60152 was the last A1 to lose its LNER livery, and the last to be painted BR blue. (B K B Green, Initial Photographics)

No.60152 HOLYROOD, the last A1 in BR blue livery, at Haymarket in 1951-52.

No.60152 HOLYROOD, in charge of the down 'Heart of Midlothian'. The location may be Berwick-on-Tweed or Dunbar, and the date is probably in the late 1950s. The A1 is in magnificent external condition.

No.60153 FLAMBOYANT at York in June 1950. The A1 was still in BR blue livery, and the deflectors have been drilled to take the nameplates which were fitted two months later. (J Davenport, Initial Photographics)

60153 FLAMBOYANT was the first of Doncaster's second batch of A1s and the first of five roller-bearing A1s. For some strange reason she was sent to York, which had far less main line work than most of the other main line depots such as Gateshead and Kings Cross, where the other four were allocated. For a long while she was kept on shorter turns before coming south. On Sunday September 25th 1955, she cruises through Doncaster with the 13.05 Newcastle-Kings Cross. (B K B Green, Initial Photographics)

At first sight hardly an example of economical utilisation. York's roller bearing A1 60153 FLAMBOYANT pauses at Selby with a stopping passenger service. Given the splendid condition of the A1, it is quite probable that it is August 1953 and she is running-in. (J Robertson, Transport Treasury)

60153 FLAMBOYANT at the rear of Grantham shed in June 1960. The A1 seems to be parked on the siding used for reblocking brakes, to judge from the foreground. (D H Beecroft, Transport Treasury)

No.60154 BON ACCORD was one of the two Gateshead roller-bearing A1s that dominated the solitary lodging turn from Gateshead to Kings Cross in the first half of the 1950s. Here she is just leaving the works after repair in the 1952-55 period, at Doncaster station. (B K B Green, Initial Photographics).

60154 BON ACCORD at Doncaster shed, just ex-Works. The date is given as October 1957, but the engine was overhauled in May and was not at the Works again until September 1958. Either the month or the year is wrong. (J Davenport, Initial Photographics)

60155 BORDERER was the other prolific roller-bearing A1 at Gateshead, and was the first A1 to aggregate one million miles. So many times had I and others watched her and her sister sail north effortlessly through the suburbs with their huge trains. Displaced by diesel traction, she was photographed in October 1964 at her new home shed, York. (J Davenport, Initial Photographics)

60155 BORDERER, without doubt the Gateshead lodging turn engine, standing at Kings Cross on May 9th 1954. The shed's V2 No.60903 and LORD FARINGDON are alongside, and I recognise beyond one of New England's old faithfuls, WD 2-8-0 No.90256. (A R Carpenter, Transport Treasury)

60155 BORDERER stands at New England depot in the early 1960s. (B Richardson, Transport Treasury)

The big Doncaster tender, an old friend leaning out of the cab – a nostalgic sight for former residents of old platform 10 at Kings Cross. The engine for the departing services would appear in the mouth of the up independent line in the middle bore and, as more came into sight, its identity became clearer until, as in the photograph, the number was revealed. 60155 BORDERER was one of the less common visitors, but in the early 1960s with impending dieselisation, things were changing. (Derek A Potton, Transport Treasury)

No.60156 GREAT CENTRAL. This was taken at a time when the Grantham A1s were bringing greater reliability to steam operation, the two roller bearing A1s being the stars. Here she is at Doncaster in October 1952. (J Davenport, Initial Photographics)

No.60156 GREAT CENTRAL pauses at Peterborough with an up express on August 8th 1961. (Ken Fairey)

60157 GREAT EASTERN, by then one of the six top link A1s that were regularly manned, at Grantham shed on October 4th 1953. (B K B Green, Initial Photographics).

60157 GREAT EASTERN on a down Leeds express at Saltersford Cutting between Great Ponton and Grantham in June 1960. (D H Beecroft, Transport Treasury)

60158 ABERDONIAN stands at Doncaster on May 30th 1953 with an up express, probably a West Riding/Hull train. (B K B Green, Initial Photographics)

60158 ABERDONIAN under repair at Doncaster Works with an A4 behind and Top Shed's B1 4-6-0 No.61394. (R K Blencowe)

60158 ABERDONIAN is at Cambridge in May 1958. The A1s were unusual visitors to Cambridge other than on Sunday diversions. Cambridge trips were usually used for running-in after repair, and as the A1s rarely broke down, they needed running-in less often. (J Davenport, Initial Photographics)

60159 climbs the 1 in 70 past North Queensferry with an up parcels train. The A1 is in BR blue livery, and as it is unnamed the date must be between 1950 and the middle of 1951. (J Robertson, Transport Treasury)

No.60159, with the southbound 'Queen of Scots' approaches Damdykes Crossing, near Seaton Sluice, north of Newcastle. The period must be 1953/54, with the old totem and numberplate position. Although it was early afternoon at the latest, the shadows are long, signifying wintry sun. Of interest are the early colour light signals, an LNER design whereby the semaphore signal arms were removed leaving only the spectacle plate, behind which was a powerful electric Adlake lamp. This enabled colour light signalling to be achieved without the concomitant costs of a full resignalling. (Jim Smith)

No.60159 BONNIE DUNDEE at Haymarket shed in September 1951.

No.60159 BONNIE DUNDEE at Haymarket on March 28th 1959. The open smokebox allows a view of the double Kylchap together with the ejector exhaust. One can understand the horror of those engineers west of Doncaster at the amount of smokebox equipment involved, since they presumably frequently had to gain access to blocked tubes. With a double Kylchap, frequent access was unnecessary.

No.60160 AULD REEKIE in BR blue livery at Haymarket in the early 1950s. The name, strongly reminiscent of Rabbie Burns, is the affectionate name for Edinburgh from the time of coal fires and steam locomotives.

No.60160 AULD REEKIE being serviced at Haymarket. I would put the date at about 1952-55 (R K Blencowe)

An unusual view of a gleaming 60160 AULD REEKIE, hauling a southbound fast freight, crossing the Forth Bridge. Few Shedmasters could claim that even the boiler tops of their locomotives were properly cleaned. (Bishop Eric Treacy)

60161 NORTH BRITISH stands at Haymarket in April 1957. A sister A1 stands alongside. (D H Beecroft, Transport Treasury) *Inset.* The nameplate of No.60161.

No.60161 NORTH BRITISH, superbly cleaned, stands at Haymarket in the 1952-55 period.

Above. For the time being, the last A1. Doncaster's final Pacific No.60162 SAINT JOHNSTOUN stands at Doncaster station, running-in after general overhaul on September 5th 1954.

(A G Forsyth, Initial Photographics)

Left. An immaculate SAINT JOHNSTOUN at some time between 1954 and 1957. I think it is at Dundee Tay Bridge and clearly the headcode is wrong for a light engine. Either she is off a Class C train and about to set back to the shed or, less likely, is about to take a train on to Aberdeen. Despite the gloom the attention to the A1's appearence is remarkable, even to the greasing of the burnished front buffers.

The prototype A2/3, 60500 EDWARD THOMPSON comes off the loco yard at Kings Cross to take a northbound departure, probably the 16.15 'Parley' to Peterborough, on July 11th 1953. Signalling Regulations, if I remember them correctly, required that the crew should set a light engine headcode, which is what it was, rather than an express. Maybe within Kings Cross station limits such requirements were considered unnecessary. (J Davenport, Initial Photographics)

The official photograph of No.500 EDWARD THOMPSON. In the south we rarely saw her looking superbly clean like this. The lining on the tender, at first sight, looks as though the short Darlington painter had originally moved from Doncaster. Although it may be a trick of the light, it certainly appears on the other side of the tender in other views.

60500 EDWARD THOMPSON is reduced to hauling unbraked mineral empties at Peterborough. The A2/3 is drawing forward off the down goods across Spital Junction. This move was necessary to enable down freight from the south and east to gain access to New England yard, which was located east of the main line. One can see from the second shot from Spital Bridge how this move completely blocked the East Coast main line, and reflect on the havoc that could be caused by a signalman injudiciously allowing a WD 2-8-0 on 60 wagons of coal across at the wrong time! The period would be 1961-63. (B Richardson, Transport Treasury)

E500 EDWARD THOMPSON in LNER apple green livery heads an up Newcastle express past Ganwick in 1948-49.

501 COCK O' THE NORTH, now a York engine, is at Doncaster on June 17th 1951. The engine is very clean considering she has been four months out of the Works, unusually so since it normally looked less presentable. The lack of large deflectors enables a clear illustration of the elongated front end with its exhaust steam ducts linking the valves with the saddle and blastpipe base. She has retained her special A3 non-corridor tender No.5565 with the welded superstructure. (B K B Green, Initial Photographics)

No.60501 COCK O' THE NORTH rolls into sidings with a Class E partially braked freight. The train seems to be a down service and the location looks as though it is on the old NE Region, perhaps Northallerton. The period would look to be the early 1950s.

The end. After sixteen years, the early hopes and plans reach their sad conclusion in Doncaster Works scrap yard, in the unlikely company of ex-S&D 2-8-0 No.53802 and Fowler 2-6-2 tank No.40057. (Frank Hornby)

No.60502 EARL MARISCHAL at Doncaster in May 1960, in the late evening of her existence. She seemed the best of an indifferent class, and if an A2/2 was on a principal service, it was usually No.60502. (J Davenport, Initial Photographics)

No.60502 EARL MARISCHAL pulls away from York on April 22nd 1959 with the Colchester-Newcastle service.

No.60502 EARL MARISCHAL pulls away with an express. The location is unknown and the date is later than 1954. (N Skinner)

60502 EARL MARISCHAL in York yard in April 1957. (D H Beecroft, Transport Treasury)

60503 LORD PRESIDENT stands in Doncaster Works, fresh from the Paint Shop, on July 28th 1957. Hitchin's J6 0-6-0 No.64251 stands behind. (A R Gault)

A down slow service departs from Kings Cross in the mid-1950s behind No.60504 MONS MEG. (D W Law)

60504 MONS MEG pauses at York with an up express. The date is unknown, but the middle 1950s seems a reasonable estimate.

60505 THANE OF FIFE in Doncaster Erecting Shop in August 1959. Among the collection of dismantled parts, bits of the brake rigging are on the right whilst on the left some of the components of the double Kylchap can be seen. (D H Beecroft, Transport Treasury)

THANE OF FIFE waiting at Doncaster showing the detail alterations that applied to the rebuilds. She retains the plain chimney, but now has a Diagram 117 boiler with the banjo dome cover in the forward position. Note that tender No.5576 has had the hole for tablet exchange apparatus filled in.

It is not normally my practice to include pictures of withdrawn and scrapped locomotives, but the view of 60505 THANE OF FIFE being dismantled is included for a specific reason. Sadly, but fortuitously, the A2/2 is standing alongside the remains of an A3, so that the substantial Gresley smokebox saddle can be compared with the smaller Thompson version. (B Richardson, Transport Treasury)

No.60506 WOLF OF BADENOCH at her home shed on May 11th 1958. The three New England A2/2s were much of a muchness, but when they were pulling hard climbing out of London, on the 10.5 Glasgow or, for a short period, the 10.00 'Flying Scotsman', they often had their own private fog around the front end, leaking exhaust heroically! (B K B Green, Initial Photographics)

No.60506 WOLF OF BADENOCH under repair in New England shops alongside a K3 2-6-0. (B Richardson, Transport Treasury)

A morning 'parley' calls at Hitchin on April 30th 1956 behind No.60506 WOLF OF BADENOCH. The 9F on Hitchin shed is certainly a change from the 'Hitchin Pacifics' of earlier times. (Frank Hornby)

60507 HIGHLAND CHIEFTAIN waits at Doncaster for a light repair in February 1959. Haymarket managed the A2/1s well and got good work out of them. The front end footplating looks very slightly out of line, and the firebox housing for the original steam reverser equipment has been retained to carry various pipes not hidden beneath the cladding with the reversing rod. She has the A4 non-corridor tender No.5675 off the bombed A4 No.4469, renumbered 703. (J Davenport, Initial Photographics)

60507 HIGHLAND CHIEFTAIN at Haymarket, probably between 1951 and 1954. The locomotive is in magnificent condition, even though, I assume, it has worked a night turn to Newcastle and back. The express headcode is strange since the locomotive must have come from Waverley as a light engine, unless of course the picture was posed.

At Damdykes Crossing near Cramlington, a gleaming HIGHLAND CHIEFTAIN is hard at work with a huge fast freight from Heaton Yard. This was an afternoon departure, and the driver needed to run hard to avoid being recessed before Berwick, if the 'Flying Scotsman' was not to catch him too soon. It is February 1955. (Jim Smith)

DUKE OF ROTHESAY heads a down express north of Sandy on June 26th 1954. From the look of the coaching stock, it is an Anglo-Scottish service, probably the 'Heart of Midlothian', on which the engines will be changed at Peterborough. (R E Vincent, Transport Treasury)

No.60508 DUKE OF ROTHESAY at an unspecified location, time and train. I think it is at Ganwick, coming out of Hadley North Tunnel: the lineside cabling looks familiar. It is in the early 1950s, and the fact that the engine is almost in mid-gear would indicate that the load – if any – is light. It has the feel of one of the 'parleys' that New England's Pacifics used as a balancing turn. (G F Heiron, courtesy Mrs Shirley Heiron, Transport Treasury)

No.60509 WAVERLEY stands at the west end of Edinburgh Waverley station in platform 11 with a northbound express in July 25th 1955. (A G Forsyth, Initial Photographics)

60509 WAVERLEY in LNER apple green livery at Haymarket between mid-1948 and mid-1950.

60510 ROBERT THE BRUCE, fresh from general overhaul. The location is not stated, nor the date, but early 1950s seems likely.

The 10.5 from Waverley to St.Pancras, 'The Waverley', gets under way behind 60510 ROBERT THE BRUCE in the early 1950s. A handsome rake of LMSR 57ft steel stock forms the train, but we became used to a rather better standard of cleanliness with Haymarket's locomotives than seen here. (J Robertson, Transport Treasury)

60510 ROBERT THE BRUCE is an unusual visitor to New England on May 31st 1953. Clearly the A2/1 has just left Doncaster Works and is running-in. One of the home shed's fleet of V2s, No.60842, stands behind; to the right just out of the picture is a B16 4-6-0, no doubt from York. (Frank Hornby)

60511 AIRBORNE spent most of her life at Heaton, and Tyneside A2s of all varieties were rare visitors to the capital. Much of their work involved cross-country passenger and main line freight, and this is the 8.05 Birmingham New Street-Newcastle. AIRBORNE is just pulling away from York with the sanders on, on July 6th 1957, having relieved a Stanier Class 5 from Saltley. (M Mensing)

No.60511 AIRBORNE waits at Doncaster Works for unclassified attention on June 4th 1950. Edward Thompson would not have been pleased at the presence of a Type 118 boiler on his A2/3, with its banjo dome. It was a boiler change that eluded the Yeadon Registers, unusually. Speedometers were originally fitted on the driver's side, unlike the Flaman design. Although they were later removed the bracket is still in position. AIRBORNE was rarely seen in the south, being a Heaton engine for many years. (B K B Green, Initial Photographics)

No.60511 AIRBORNE at Newcastle Central. Although she may be uncoupling, it is more likely that she is coupling on and the headcode has not yet been set. The newer totem and the power signalling suggest that the date is 1960 or later.

No.60511 AIRBORNE in splendid condition, in apple green livery, at Haymarket on April 17ᵗʰ 1949.

No.60512 STEADY AIM at speed through Pilmoor during 1953-56, with an up express. She was fairly common sight on the main line over the years, one of York's harder-working Pacifics. (Transport Treasury)

60512 STEADY AIM at Doncaster Works in August 1959, with A3s SCEPTRE and GRAND PARADE alongside.
(D H Beecroft, Transport Treasury)

60513 DANTE at Top Shed, Kings Cross, local B1 No.61200 alongside. (E D Bruton)

60513 DANTE in New England shops in the early 1960s, undergoing attention to the left-hand motion and cylinders. (B Richardson, Transport Treasury)

Cleaning DANTE.

60514 CHAMOSSAIRE with a tank wagon train on the freight lines avoiding Newcastle Central station on May 21st 1962. CHAMOSSAIRE was one of the two A2/3s that retained the plain double chimney. With steam traction it was a rule that barrier wagons should be marshalled between the locomotive and the tank wagons, to avoid the risk of fire. (M Mensing)

60514 CHAMOSSAIRE in Doncaster Works, probably for a non-classified repair in early 1962. (B Richardson, Transport Treasury)

No.60515 SUN STREAM waits at Grantham on September 7th 1959. The engine still has the BTH speedometer fitted. (Peter Groom)

No.60515 SUN STREAM at York on May 3rd 1962. (Jack Hodgkinson)

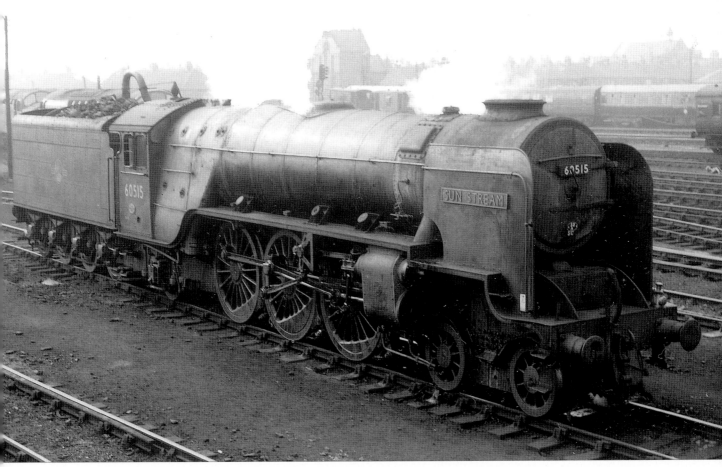

No.60516 HYCILLA at Doncaster on November 16th 1952. Roped to the smokebox door hinge is evidence of a calamity, probably on the road somewhere, requiring main works attention. (B K B Green, Initial Photographics)

No.60516 HYCILLA at Gateshead. (N E Preedy)

With the decline of steam traction, York became something of a concentration depot for displaced steam. 60516 HYCILLA moved there in mid-1960 and a year later, on August 7th 1961, she was on the 12.20 from Hull. The A2/3s could run fast, and here, at Sandy, HYCILLA is going well. (M Mensing)

60516 HYCILLA, standing in York shed, out of steam, in 1961-62.
(B Richardson, Transport Treasury)

60517 OCEAN SWELL at Berwick-on-Tweed, arriving from Edinburgh and then shunting the ECS off the 15.30 from Edinburgh into the down sidings. The date is May 24th 1962. (M Mensing)

No.60517 OCEAN SWELL coasts through Selby with an up express, having slowed for the PSR for the swing bridge and sharp reverse curve. It appears to be during the school holidays, to judge from the size of the audience. The engine is well turned out, and the train has the look of a cross-country service. The year is probably in the early 1950s. (J Robertson, Transport Treasury)

No.60517 OCEAN SWELL on shed, possibly Heaton, later than 1957.

No.60518 TEHRAN at Haymarket in the early 1950s.

60518 TEHRAN at Kings Cross after release from old platform 8. The date is April 26th 1959. (D Clayton)

No.60519 HONEYWAY was Haymarket's only A2/3, and again they managed to get good work out of the engine, the best aggregate mileage of the class. On May 17th 1959 she was at Perth bearing evidence of a previously overheated smokebox. HONEYWAY and CHAMOSSAIRE were the two A2/3s that never had their plain chimney replaced with a cast pattern. (R J Buckley, Initial Photographics)

In a scene strongly reminiscent of a Christmas card, 60519 HONEYWAY pulls out of platform 11 at Edinburgh Waverley. The period must be approximately the mid-1950s. (Transport Treasury)

In apple green livery, No.519 HONEYWAY at Haymarket in 1947-48.

HONEYWAY, splendidly turned out, heads south from Edinburgh with the 'Queen of Scots' Pullman in 1954-57.

No.60519 HONEYWAY at Carlisle Canal. The time must be later than 1957.

60520 OWEN TUDOR with the infamous – to crews of the up 'Elizabethan' at any rate – 827up, the 13.05 'Parley' from Peterborough. This was another slow service which ran as an express from Hitchin. By the early 1960s B1s had given way to Pacifics. The location is the Ganwick curve, sweeping into Hadley North Tunnel. (Transport Treasury)

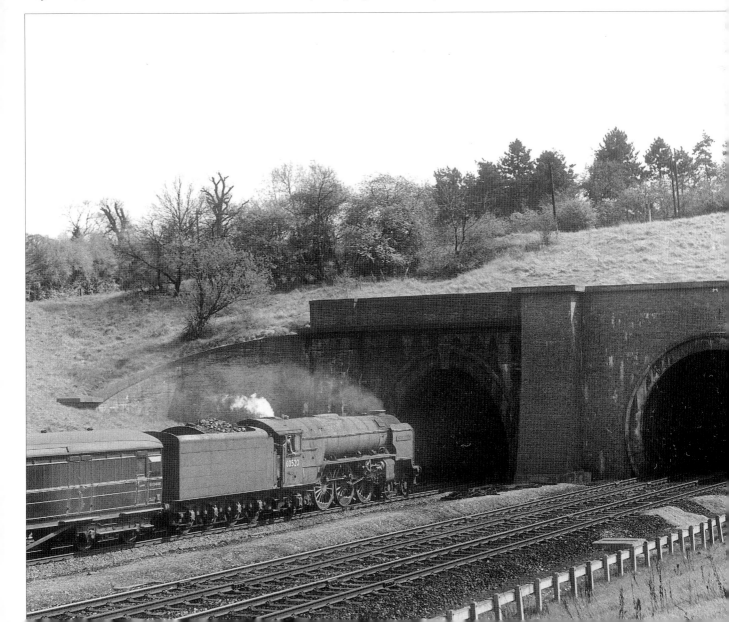

No.60520 OWEN TUDOR leaving Hatfield with the 16.10 down 'Parley' on May 14th 1959. One of Hatfield's N7 0-6-2Ts stands in the right background, on the Dunstable single line. (Peter Groom)

No.520 OWEN TUDOR in apple green livery in 1947-48. The location is likely to have been Doncaster as the A2/3 was allocated there.

60520 OWEN TUDOR hauls a slow freight on the down goods north of Westwood Junction, and has the signal into New England yard. It is probably near the end for the A2/3s, and what work merited the power of the A2s has been dieselised by now. (B Richardson, Transport Treasury)

No.60521 WATLING STREET at Haymarket on August 8th 1951, alongside a very dishevelled K3, and now with a lipped chimney. (A G Forsyth, Initial Photographics)

No.60521 WATLING STREET on the Haymarket turntable; the date must lie between 1950 and 1955.

WATLING STREET backs down on to her train at Edinburgh Waverley on August 29th 1953. (J Robertson, Transport Treasury)

STRAIGHT DEAL was a long-term resident at York, but her last two years were spent in new pastures on the West Coast main line at Polmadie with sister A2/3s STEADY AIM and HERRINGBONE, also from York. Having lost the Stanier Pacifics, the strangers were quite well used, their considerable strength being an advantage. Here she is at Carstairs on April 18th 1965 a few months before withdrawal. She looks to being standing pilot, but the air of desolation is obvious, even for the shed clock! (D Cousins)

STRAIGHT DEAL, brand new, outside Doncaster Weigh House on June 19th 1947. (R E Vincent, Transport Treasury)

No.60522 STRAIGHT DEAL having backed out of Kings Cross, pauses by Copenhagen Junction before going to Top Shed in 1961. Above the retaining wall behind the A2/3 is the formation of the connection between Goods & Mineral Junction and the GN coal depot at Caledonian Road on the North London line. (A E Durrant, Transport Treasury)

No.60523 SUN CASTLE was a regular sight down south for many years, residing at all the principal depots, chiefly New England. Here she is turning on the Kings Cross station turntable. The date is not given and the shed code is illegible, but the Class B headcode is virtually certain confirmation that the A2/3 is at New England, having worked up on one of the slow 'parley' services. The date must lie between 1949 and 1953, probably later rather than earlier.

The 18.17 'parley' from Kings Cross pounds past Copenhagen Junction behind No.60523 SUN CASTLE in 1963. An A4 waits by Belle Isle signalbox. (A E Durrant, Transport Treasury)

While at Doncaster SUN CASTLE appeared on different diagrams and here, on August 18th 1962, she is gathering speed past Wood Green Tunnel with a down express for Leeds and Bradford. A month later she moved back to New England. One of the Craven DMUs is on the flyover bound for Hertford North. (Peter Groom)

The familiar front of Top Shed on February 21st 1960, with SUN CASTLE prominent, LADAS to the left, BALMORAL to the right and GREEN ARROW beyond. The displacement of the V2s by the 9Fs had started and 92200 lurks in the shed beyond LADAS. (D Idle, Transport Treasury)

No.60524 HERRINGBONE, under construction at Doncaster Works in 1947. This view, taken while the lagging was being fixed in place, shows the longer front end, and the reason for the exhaust steam duct. The layout from the cylinder casting to the hole in the frames under the saddle left a great deal to be desired. Although it is August, the workshop gives every impression of being extremely cold in winter! (R E Vincent, Transport Treasury)

No.60524 HERRINGBONE with the 15.30 Postal at Perth on June 24th 1963. The Pacific took the postal vans forward to Motherwell, while the passenger portion continued to Glasgow behind BR class 5 No.73153. (D Cousins)

The up Glasgow-Kings Cross relief stands at Grantham in June 1960. No.60524 HERRINGBONE is taking water, which suggests that the troughs at Scrooby and/or Muskham were out of action. (D H Beecroft, Transport Treasury)

Two views of No.524 HERRINGBONE, brand new, probably at York in late 1947 and resplendent in apple green livery.

Ferryhill's No.60525 A H PEPPERCORN, the first A2, waits at Doncaster Works on November 29th 1953. This is a good illustration of the Scottish Region practice of using the Regional colour – sky blue – as the background to nameplates. (B K B Green, Initial Photographics)

No.60526 SUGAR PALM at Gateshead shed in 1953. (C J B Sanderson)

York's SUGAR PALM eases past the shed into the station in April 1950. (J Davenport, Initial Photographics)

No.60527 SUN CHARIOT under repair at Ferryhill. The A2 is unusually dirty, as Tay Bridge and Ferryhill kept their few Pacifics clean. The year would be about 1960. (B Richardson, Transport Treasury)

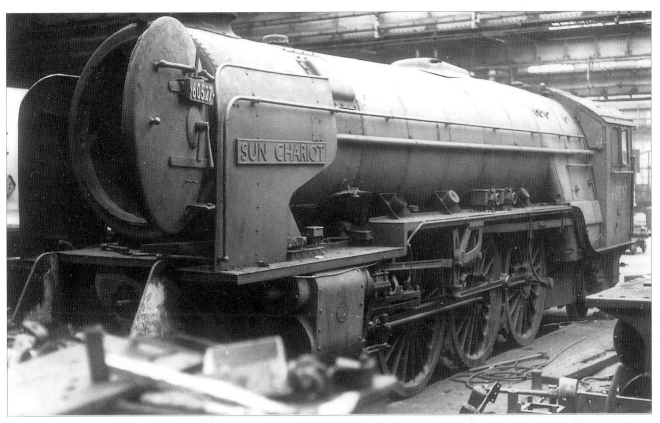

No.60527 SUN CHARIOT under repair at Darlington Works on March 9th 1964. (N Skinner)

No.60527 SUN CHARIOT at Tay Bridge in the late 1950s, in splendid external condition. (J Robertson, Transport Treasury).

No.60528 TUDOR MINSTREL at Doncaster, fresh from general overhaul at the turn of the 1950s. (C Spencer)

A Kings Cross-Newcastle express heads north between Beninbrough and Tollerton behind No.60528 TUDOR MINSTREL during her brief spell at Gateshead. (Cecil Ord)

Haymarket's PEARL DIVER at Eastfield on May 6th 1950. Once the solitary Scottish A2, by that time she had been joined by ten sisters. The superheater regulator was said to be an improvement on the Gresley regulator, but it was a pity about the external rodding, aesthetically. (J Davenport, Initial Photographics)

PEARL DIVER at Doncaster, fresh from overhaul, in October 1957. The lipped double chimney, apart from engineering considerations, gave the locomotive a more balanced look. (J Davenport, Initial Photographics)

PEARL DIVER at Haymarket on May 16ᵗʰ 1953. (A R Goult)

The down 'Flying Scotsman' at Damdykes near Cramlington, on a wintry day in February 1956. It is a splendid portrait of an A2, the one with the unpronounceable name, No.60530 SAYAJIRAO. Once again, the cleanliness of Haymarket's Pacifics at the time was a joy to see. (Jim Smith)

One of the last A2s in service, No.60530 SAYAJIRAO, at Tay Bridge on May 16th 1965. (A Scarsbrook, Initial Photographics)

No.60530 with an express near Grantshouse on June 29th 1957. No indication has been given, but I think it is an up train rather than down. (J Robertson, Transport Treasury).

No.60530 SAYAJIRAO at Tay Bridge on August 23rd 1966. (Transport Treasury).

No.E531 BAHRAM, a Gateshead engine when new, waits for her train at the east end of Waverley station in 1948. (J Patterson, Transport Treasury).

No.60532 BLUE PETER has come from Aberdeen to Doncaster Works for general overhaul, March 1961. (J Davenport, Initial Photographics)

No.60532 BLUE PETER on shed but not at Ferryhill. St Rollox seems a more likely location with the flats going up in the background. The date would be 1961-64, with the split smokebox handle, but the A2 has no electrification flashes.

The cab side of the soon-to-preserved Peppercorn Pacific, No.60532 BLUE PETER on August 14th 1966. (Transport Treasury).

No.60533 HAPPY KNIGHT was, after 1949, the sole representative of the class in the south. Much of her time was spent at New England where she was under utilised, and normally looking far from pristine, unlike this view at Doncaster shed. At the time she was a Grantham engine, although she was never in the top link, no doubt her lively riding being the reason. The date is May 6th 1956. (B K B Green, Initial Photographics)

No.60533 HAPPY KNIGHT in her early days as a single blast A2, hauling the up 'Yorkshire Pullman' at Ganwick. The year must be 1948 or early 1949. (D C Ovenden)

No.60533 HAPPY KNIGHT at New England, I think, in 1961, but now a Doncaster locomotive. (B Richardson, Transport Treasury)

A very unusual appearance of an A2 on the 'Tees-Tyne Pullman'. HAPPY KNIGHT spent several periods at Grantham, and was a Grantham engine at the time, which indicates 1959 as the year. Coincidentally another Grantham engine, ABERDONIAN, passes on the up slow. The timing from York to Darlington was tight, and Top Shed drivers had to run hard to keep time. No.60533 would have been accelerating hard through Tollerton. One possible explanation for the A2's appearance is that she is a replacement for an earlier failure. (Cecil Ord)

No.60534 IRISH ELEGANCE at Haymarket in the early 1950s.

Two gleaming Haymarket Pacifics. No.60534 IRISH ELEGANCE passing Haymarket with a down stopping service on March 2nd 1952; SAINT JOHNSTOUN stands on the shed siding. (J Robertson, Transport Treasury).

No.60534 IRISH ELEGANCE at Carlisle in 1957-58. (Transport Treasury).

One of those quizzical names that was drawn out of the Doncaster bowler hat for No.60535 – HORNET'S BEAUTY. Beauty would not be the first thought to cross the mind on seeing one – unless it was the sting! The A2 has arrived at Waverley from Dundee, and her fireman watches the unloading of the mail van. The shunter looks as though he is using his mobile, some decades before it became the universal body language, but he actually has his gloved hand to his ear. It is a fine atmospheric shot. (G F Heiron, courtesy Mrs Shirley Heiron, Transport Treasury).

An immaculate No.60535 HORNET'S BEAUTY at Haymarket in May 1959; not only did Haymarket clean Top Link engines, but most of the others as well. Some of the A2 names taxed the imagination; just who was the bewitching Miss Hornet? (D H Beecroft, Transport Treasury).

No.60536 TRIMBUSH waits at Waverley for the 'Queen of Scots' to arrive from Glasgow in the early 1950s.

The driver of No.60536 TRIMBUSH with an up Leeds express has evidently seen that Barnet North's distant is off, and opened the regulator. To judge from the exhaust, the cut-off is none too short either. The period must be 1948-49. (D C Ovenden)

No.60536 TRIMBUSH awaits general overhaul at Doncaster Works. The self-cleaning screens have been removed for examination, no doubt to discover whether Haymarket have been using illicit blastpipe tops again! A GE B17 4-6-0 waits behind the A2, but not for a general overhaul this time. The date is July 1959. (D H Beecroft, Transport Treasury).

Another curious name was BACHELOR'S BUTTON, strange for a racehorse and even stranger for an A2. This shot was taken in her early days at Copley Hill when discs were in use, about to leave Kings Cross with a heavy Leeds train.

No.60537 BACHELOR'S BUTTON at Haymarket in July 1959. (D H Beecroft, Transport Treasury).

Gateshead's VELOCITY photographed some time between October 1949 and 1955. The location is York Carriage Sidings, with the crew just warming up the steam sanders before the tricky start on the sharp curve at York. (Paul Chancellor Collection)

No.60539 BRONZINO at Grantham on April 5th 1961. No doubt she will be heading the 'Northumbrian' back north in a few hours. (Peter Groom)

No.60539 BRONZINO backs through York station in order to take over a down service. The date is June 9th 1951.

Heaton's No.60539 BRONZINO at Haymarket in 1950-53.

No.60539 BRONZINO, running light from Edinburgh back to Tweedmouth on May 30th 1962. (M Mensing)

APPENDICES

APPENDIX A. Individual locomotive histories in brief.

Date applied or Ex-overhaul	COCK O' THE NORTH
	Doncaster Works No.1789.
22-May-34	Completed as Cl.P2 three cylinder 2-8-2, with RC poppet valve gear, in LNER apple green livery Numbered LNER 2001, spl. welded tender No.5565, boiler no.8771and allocated to Doncaster.
27-Aug-34	Tablet exchange apparatus fitted
24-Nov-34	Infinitely variable scroll cams replaced by stepped cams at Doncaster.
5-Dec-34	Despatched to Vitry-sur-Seine Test Plant
21-Feb-35	Returned from Vitry-sur-Seine
30-Mar-35	RC poppet valve gear cooling system fitted at Doncaster
30-Sep-37	Withdrawn from traffic for rebuilding at Doncaster. Mileage 125,670 as a poppet valve engine.
14-Apr-38	Rebuilt with piston valves and streamlined front end. ACFI equipment removed.
24-Jun-44	Withdrawn from traffic for rebuilding as a Pacific at Doncaster. Mileage as 2-8-2, 362,136
14-Sep-44	Returned to traffic rebuilt as a Pacific, black wartime livery.
11-Aug-46	Painted as No.2001 in LNER apple green at Cowlairs.
12-Nov-46	Allocated LNER No.990, but renumbered 501.
22-May-48	Renumbered BR No.60501
21-Feb-50	BR dark green livery
Date Unknown	Fitted with a lipped chimney
22-Jan-60	Withdrawn from service
Life Mileage	125,670 (poppet valve), 362,136 as a Mikado, 616,461 as a Pacific, Life total 978,597

Date applied or Ex-overhaul	EARL MARISCHAL
	Doncaster Works No.1796.
6-Oct-34	Completed as Cl.P2 three cylinder 2-8-2, with piston valves, in LNER apple green livery Numbered LNER 2002, tender No.5575, boiler no.8785 and allocated to Doncaster.
17-Apr-35	Additional smoke deflectors fitted.
9-Jun-35	First transferred to Scotland (Haymarket)
14-Oct-36	Rebuilt with streamlined front end.
1-Apr-44	Withdrawn from traffic for rebuilding as a Pacific at Doncaster. Life mileage as 2-8-2, 360,907
23-Jun-44	Returned to traffic rebuilt as a Pacific, black wartime livery.
12-May-46	Allocated LNER No.991, but renumbered 502 by Cowlairs.
29-Mar-47	Painted in LNER apple green livery at Cowlairs
30-Jun-48	Renumbered BR No.60502 by Cowlairs.
7-Mar-51	BR dark green livery
Date Unknown	Fitted with a lipped chimney
26-Jun-61	Withdrawn from service
Life Mileage	360,907 as a Mikado, 673,947 as a Pacific, total 1,034,854

Date applied or Ex-overhaul	LORD PRESIDENT
	Doncaster Works No.1836.
13-Jun-36	Completed as three cylinder 2-8-2, with piston valves and streamlined front end, in LNER apple green livery. Numbered LNER 2003, tender No.5576, boiler no.8796 and allocated to Haymarket.
2-Sep-44	Withdrawn from traffic for rebuilding as a Pacific at Doncaster. Life mileage as 2-8-2, 246,283
17-Dec-44	Returned to traffic rebuilt as a Pacific, black wartime livery.
30-Jun-46	Renumbered LNER No.503
21-Dec-46	Painted in apple green livery at Cowlairs
18-Sep-48	Renumbered BR No.60503
31-Aug-50	BR dark green livery
Date Unknown	Fitted with a lipped chimney
27-Nov-59	Withdrawn from service
Life Mileage	246,283 as Mikado, 508,498 as a Pacific, total 754,781

Date applied or Ex-overhaul	MONS MEG
	Doncaster Works No.1839.
11-Jul-36	Completed as Cl.P2 three cylinder 2-8-2, with piston valves and streamlined front end, in LNER apple green livery. LNER No.2004, tender No.5577, boiler no.8798 and allocated to Haymarket. Built with an exhaust bypass to control smokebox vacuum
1-Jul-37	Bypass valve enlarged
1-Jun-39	Bypass valve modified
22-Aug-44	Withdrawn from traffic for rebuilding as a Pacific at Doncaster. Life mileage as 2-8-2, 294,243
3-Nov-44	Returned to traffic rebuilt as a Pacific, black wartime livery.
30-Jun-46	Renumbered LNER No.504
12-Mar-48	Renumbered BR No.E504
23-Mar-48	Renumbered BR No.60504 and painted in apple green livery at Doncaster
26-May-50	BR dark green livery
Date Unknown	Fitted with a lipped chimney
23-Jan-61	Withdrawn from service
Life Mileage	294,243 as a Mikado, 694,797 as a Pacific, total 989,040

Date applied or Ex-overhaul	THANE OF FIFE
	Doncaster Works No.1840.
11-Jul-36	Completed as three cylinder 2-8-2, single blast with piston valves and streamlined front end, in LNER apple green livery. Numbered LNER 2005, tender No.5576, boiler no.8799 and allocated to Dundee Tay Bridge
26-Oct-42	Withdrawn from traffic for rebuilding as a Pacific at Doncaster. Life mileage as 2-8-2, 246,283
18-Jan-43	Returned to traffic rebuilt as a Pacific, unnamed, black wartime livery.
6-Jun-44	Nameplates restored
25-Apr-46	Renumbered LNER No.994
12-May-46	Renumbered LNER No.505
5-Jun-48	Renumbered BR No.60505 and painted in apple green livery at Cowlairs.
4-Jan-52	BR dark green livery
After 1957	Fitted with a lipped chimney
10-Nov-59	Withdrawn from service
Life Mileage	246,283 as a Mikado, 673,464 as a Pacific, total 919,747

Date applied or Ex-overhaul	WOLF OF BADENOCH
	Doncaster Works No.1842.
5-Sep-36	Completed as 3 cylinder 2-8-2, with piston valves and streamlined front end, in LNER apple green livery Numbered LNER 2006, tender No.5579, boiler no.8934 and allocated to Haymarket.
28-Jan-44	Withdrawn from traffic for rebuilding as a Pacific at Doncaster. Life mileage as 2-8-2, 287,187
15-Apr-44	Returned to traffic rebuilt as a Pacific, unnamed, black wartime livery.
4-Jun-44	Nameplates restored
30-Jun-46	Renumbered LNER No.506
18-Oct-47	Painted in apple green livery at Cowlairs.
18-Dec-48	Renumbered BR No.60506
28-Jul-50	BR dark green livery
4-Apr-61	Withdrawn from service. Never fitted with a cast lipped chimney.
Life Mileage	287,187 as a Mikado, 629,013 as a Pacific, total 916,200

Date applied or Ex-overhaul	HIGHLAND CHIEFTAIN
	Darlington Works No.1930.
13-May-44	Originally Cl.V2, completed at Darlington Works and entered traffic with small deflectors and Group Std. 6 wh. Tender, in wartime black livery.LNER No.3696
28-Jun-45	Electric lighting equipment fitted
24-Dec-45	Coupled to 8 wheel A4 non-corridor tender No.5675, renumbered 703.
12-May-46	Renumbered LNER No. 507
21-Nov-46	Large smoke deflectors fitted.
29-Oct-48	Renumbered BR No. 60507
12-Oct-49	Changed from black to BR mixed traffic dark green livery
Date Unknown	Fitted with a lipped chimney
24-Nov-60	Withdrawn from service
Life Mileage	786,505

Date applied or Ex-overhaul	DUKE OF ROTHESAY
	Darlington Works No.1933.
30-Jun-44	Originally Cl.V2, completed at Darlington Works and entered traffic with small eflectors and Group Std. 6 wh. tender, in wartime black livery. LNER No.3697
20-Jul-46	Renumbered LNER No. 508
17-Jan-47	Large smoke deflectors fitted.
6-Feb-48	Renumbered BR No. E508
29-Oct-48	Renumbered BR No. 60508 and painted apple green
15-Jun-49	Coupled to 8 wheel non-corridor tender No.748, & painted BR dark green livery
Date Unknown	Fitted with a lipped chimney
20-Feb-61	Withdrawn from service
Life Mileage	754,952

Date applied or Ex-overhaul	WAVERLEY
	Darlington Works No.1944.
15-Nov-44	Originally Cl.V2, completed at Darlington Works and entered traffic with small deflectors and Group Std. 6 wh. tender, in wartime black livery LNER No.3698
2-May-46	Renumbered LNER No. 509.
26-Oct-46	Large smoke deflectors fitted and coupled to 8 wheel non-corridor tender No.706.
6-Aug-48	Renumbered BR No. 60509 and painted apple green
2-Jun-50	Painted in BR dark green livery
Date Unknown	Fitted with a lipped chimney
12-Jul-60	Withdrawn from service
Life Mileage	818,943

Date applied or Ex-overhaul	ROBERT THE BRUCE
	Darlington Works No.1950.
15-Nov-44	Originally Cl.V2, completed at Darlington Works and entered traffic with small eflectors and Group Std.6 wh. tender, in wartime black livery. LNER No.3699
7-Jun-46	Renumbered LNER No. 510.
28-Apr-48	Large smoke deflectors fitted and renumbered BR No. 60510.
2-Sep-49	Coupled to 8 wheel non-corridor tender No.759 and changed from black to BR dark green livery
Date Unknown	Fitted with a lipped chimney
17-Oct-60	Withdrawn from service
Life Mileage	815,528

	EDWARD THOMPSON
Date applied or Ex-overhaul	Doncaster Works No.2000
24-May-46	Completed at Doncaster Works and entered traffic with large deflectors and 8 wh non-corridor tender No.704, in LNER apple green livery LNER No.500
26-Feb-48	Renumbered BR No. E500.
7-Oct-49	Renumbered BR No. 60500 and repainted BR dark green livery
Date Unknown	Fitted with a lipped chimney
16-Jun-63	Withdrawn from service
Life Mileage	Approx 858,000

	AIRBORNE
Date applied or Ex-overhaul	Doncaster Works No.2002
20-Jul-46	Completed at Doncaster Works and entered traffic with large deflectors and 8 wh non-corridor tender No.705, in LNER apple green livery. LNER No.511
16-Apr-48	Renumbered BR No. 60511
23-Dec-49	BR dark green livery
Date Unknown	Fitted with a lipped chimney
4-Sep-58	AWS fitted
12-Nov-62	Withdrawn from service
Life Mileage	817,748

	STEADY AIM
Date applied or Ex-overhaul	Doncaster Works No.2003
24-Aug-46	Completed at Doncaster Works and entered traffic with large deflectors and 8 wh non-corridor tender No.707, in LNER apple green livery. LNER No.512
20-Mar-48	Renumbered BR No. 60513
6-Apr-50	BR dark green livery
Date Unknown	Fitted with a lipped chimney
19-Jun-65	Withdrawn from service
Life Mileage	Not known

	DANTE
Date applied or Ex-overhaul	Doncaster Works No.2004
31-Aug-46	Completed at Doncaster Works and entered traffic with large deflectors and 8 wh non-corridor tender No.710, in LNER apple green livery. LNER No.513
3-Nov-48	Renumbered BR No. 60512
15-Aug-50	BR dark green livery
Date Unknown	Fitted with a lipped chimney
27-Apr-63	Withdrawn from service
Life Mileage	Not known

	CHAMOSSAIRE
Date applied or Ex-overhaul	Doncaster Works No.2005
28-Sep-46	Completed at Doncaster Works and entered traffic with large deflectors and 8 wh non-corridor tender No.708, in LNER apple green livery. LNER No.514
23-Mar-48	Renumbered BR No. 60514
3-Nov-50	BR dark green livery
29-Dec-62	Withdrawn from service
Life Mileage	Not known

	SUN STREAM
Date applied or Ex-overhaul	Doncaster Works No.2006
19-Oct-46	Completed at Doncaster Works and entered traffic with large deflectors and 8 wh non-corridor tender No.713, in LNER apple green livery. LNER No.515
25-Jun-48	Renumbered BR No. 60515
20-Oct-49	BR dark green livery
Date Unknown	Fitted with a lipped chimney
12-Nov-62	Withdrawn from service
Life Mileage	690,352

	HYCILLA
Date applied or Ex-overhaul	Doncaster Works No.2007
2-Nov-46	Completed at Doncaster Works and entered traffic with large deflectors and 8 wh non-corridor tender No.711, in LNER apple green livery. LNER No.516
8-Oct-48	Renumbered BR No. 60516
7-Jun-50	BR dark green livery
Date Unknown	Fitted with a lipped chimney
19-Jun-65	Withdrawn from service
Life Mileage	833,050

	OCEAN SWELL
Date applied or Ex-overhaul	Doncaster Works No.2008
28-Nov-46	Completed at Doncaster Works and entered traffic with large deflectors and 8 wh non-corridor tender No.712, in LNER apple green livery. LNER No.517
27-Aug-48	Renumbered BR No. 60517
23-Feb-50	BR dark green livery
Date Unknown	Fitted with a lipped chimney
12-Nov-62	Withdrawn from service
Life Mileage	749,180

Date applied or Ex-overhaul	TEHRAN
	Doncaster Works No.2009
28-Dec-46	Completed at Doncaster Works and entered traffic with large deflectors and 8 wh non-corridor tender No.709, in LNER apple green livery.
15-Jul-48	Renumbered BR No. 60518 LNER No.518
1-Feb-50	BR dark green livery
9-Feb-54	Fitted with a lipped chimney
12-Nov-62	Withdrawn from service
Life Mileage	825,230

Date applied or Ex-overhaul	HONEYWAY
	Doncaster Works No.2010
1-Feb-47	Completed at Doncaster Works and entered traffic with large deflectors and 8 wh non-corridor tender No.714, in LNER apple green livery. LNER No.519
22-Oct-48	Renumbered BR No. 60519
21-Jul-50	BR dark green livery
18-Dec-62	Withdrawn from service
Life Mileage	Approx 920,000

Date applied or Ex-overhaul	OWEN TUDOR
	Doncaster Works No.2011
29-Mar-47	Completed at Doncaster Works and entered traffic with large deflectors and 8 wh non-corridor tender No.715, in LNER apple green livery. LNER No.520
13-Aug-48	Renumbered BR No. 60520
23-Jun-50	BR dark green livery
Date Unknown	Fitted with a lipped chimney
16-Jun-63	Withdrawn from service
Life Mileage	Not known

Date applied or Ex-overhaul	WATLING STREET
	Doncaster Works No.2012
8-May-47	Completed at Doncaster Works and entered traffic with large deflectors and 8 wh non-corridor tender No.716, in LNER apple green livery. LNER No.521
21-May-48	Renumbered BR No. 60521
15-Dec-49	BR dark green livery
19-Jul-51	Fitted with a lipped chimney
12-Nov-62	Withdrawn from service
Life Mileage	836,461

Date applied or Ex-overhaul	STRAIGHT DEAL
	Doncaster Works No.2013
19-Jun-47	Completed at Doncaster Works and entered traffic with large deflectors and 8 wh non-corridor tender No.717, in LNER apple green livery. LNER No.522
12-Feb-48	Renumbered BR No.E522
29-Sep-49	Renumbered BR No. 60522 and repainted in BR dark green livery.
Date Unknown	Fitted with a lipped chimney
19-Jun-65	Withdrawn from service
Life Mileage	Not known

Date applied or Ex-overhaul	SUN CASTLE
	Doncaster Works No.2014
2-Aug-47	Completed at Doncaster Works and entered traffic with large deflectors and 8 wh non-corridor tender No.718, in LNER apple green livery.
14-Jul-49	Renumbered BR No. 60523 and repainted in BR dark green livery. LNER No.523
13-May-54	Fitted with a lipped chimney
16-Jun-63	Withdrawn from service
Life Mileage	Not known

Date applied or Ex-overhaul	HERRINGBONE
	Doncaster Works No.2015
26-Sep-47	Completed at Doncaster Works and entered traffic with large deflectors and 8 wh non-corridor tender No.700, in LNER apple green livery. LNER No.524
26-Jan-49	Renumbered BR No. 60524
11-Apr-51	BR dark green livery
Date Unknown	Fitted with a lipped chimney
12-Nov-62	Withdrawn from service
Life Mileage	Not known

Date applied or Ex-overhaul	A H PEPPERCORN
	Doncaster Works No.2016
24-Dec-47	Completed at Doncaster Works and entered traffic with deflectors and 8 wh non-corridor tender No.701 in LNER apple green livery. LNER No.525
25-Aug-49	Renumbered BR No. 60525 and repainted in BR dark green livery.
19-Apr-52	Fitted with B1 blastpipe at Cowlairs
5-Dec-53	Fitted with BR exhaust at Doncaster
27-Mar-63	Withdrawn from service
Life Mileage	812,000 approx

Date applied or Ex-overhaul	SUGAR PALM
	Doncaster Works No.2017
9-Jan-48	Completed at Doncaster Works and entered traffic with deflectors and 8 wh non-corridor tender No.702 in LNER apple green livery. LNER No.526
26-Aug-48	Renumbered BR No. 60526
27-Oct-49	Fitted with a Multiple valve regulator, steam drier & Kylchap double blast, & BR dark green livery.
Date unknown	Fitted with a lipped chimney
12-Nov-62	Withdrawn from service
Life Mileage	718,432

Date applied or Ex-overhaul	SUN CHARIOT
	Doncaster Works No.2018
30-Jan-48	Completed at Doncaster Works and entered traffic with deflectors and 8 wh non-corridor tender No.719 in LNER apple green livery. Numbered BR No. E527
2-Jun-48	Renumbered BR No. 60527
13-May-49	BR dark green livery.
21-Nov-53	Fitted with BR exhaust
24-Apr-65	Withdrawn from service
Life Mileage	Approx 850,000

Date applied or Ex-overhaul	TUDOR MINSTREL
	Doncaster Works No.2019
21-Feb-48	Completed at Doncaster Works and entered traffic with deflectors and 8 wh non-corridor tender No.720 in LNER apple green livery. Numbered BR No. E528
25-Jun-48	Renumbered BR No. 60528
10-Jun-49	BR dark green livery.
21-Dec-54	Fitted with BR exhaust at Doncaster
24-Apr-66	Withdrawn from service
Life Mileage	Over 850,000

Date applied or Ex-overhaul	PEARL DIVER
	Doncaster Works No.2020
9-Jan-48	Completed at Doncaster Works and entered traffic with deflectors and 8 wh non-corridor tender No.721 in LNER apple green livery. Numbered BR No.E529
26-Aug-48	Renumbered BR No. 60529
16-Sep-49	Fitted with a Multiple valve regulator, steam drier & Kylchap double blast, BR dark green livery.
Date unknown	Fitted with a lipped chimney
12-Nov-62	Withdrawn from service
Life Mileage	Over 850000

Date applied or Ex-overhaul	SAYAJIRAO
	Doncaster Works No.2021
4-Mar-48	Completed at Doncaster Works and entered traffic with deflectors and 8 wh non-corridor tender No.723 in LNER apple green livery. Numbered BR No. E530
17-Nov-48	Renumbered BR No. 60530
9-Dec-49	BR dark green livery.
18-Jun-52	Fitted with B1 blastpipe at Cowlairs
26-Feb-54	Fitted with BR exhaust
19-Nov-66	Withdrawn from service
Life Mileage	Not known

Date applied or Ex-overhaul	BAHRAM
	Doncaster Works No.2022
12-Mar-48	Completed at Doncaster Works and entered traffic with deflectors and 8 wh non-corridor tender No.722 in LNER apple green livery. Numbered BR No. E531
25-Nov-48	Renumbered BR No. 60531
23-Jun-49	BR dark green livery.
9-Mar-54	Fitted with B1 exhaust at Doncaster
10-Dec-62	Withdrawn from service
Life Mileage	Over 850,000

Date applied or Ex-overhaul	BLUE PETER
	Doncaster Works No.2023
25-Mar-48	Completed at Doncaster Works and entered traffic with deflectors and 8 wh non-corridor tender No.724 in LNER apple green livery. Numbered BR No.60532
28-Sep-49	Fitted with a Multiple valve regulator, steam drier & Kylchap double blast, BR dark green livery.
Date unknown	Fitted with a lipped chimney
31-Dec-66	Withdrawn from service for preservation
Life Mileage	Over 850,000

Date applied or Ex-overhaul	**HAPPY KNIGHT** Doncaster Works No.2024
9-Apr-48	Completed at Doncaster Works and entered traffic with deflectors and 8 wh non-corridor tender No.725 in LNER apple green livery.
7-Dec-49	Fitted with a Multiple valve regulator, steam drier & Kylchap double blast, BR dark green livery.
Date unknown	Fitted with a lipped chimney
15-Jun-63	Withdrawn from service for preservation
Life Mileage	Approx 800,000

Date applied or Ex-overhaul	**IRISH ELEGANCE** Doncaster Works No.2025
23-Apr-48	Completed at Doncaster Works and entered traffic with deflectors and 8 wh non-corridor tender No.726 in LNER apple green livery. Numbered BR No.60534
24-Mar-50	BR dark green livery.
9-Jun-54	Fitted with BR exhaust
29-Dec-62	Withdrawn from service
Life Mileage	Over 850000

Date applied or Ex-overhaul	**HORNETS BEAUTY** Doncaster Works No.2026
5-May-48	Completed at Doncaster Works and entered traffic with deflectors and 8 wh non-corridor tender No.727 in LNER apple green livery. Numbered BR No.60535
19-May-50	BR dark green livery.
24-May-52	Fitted with B1 exhaust at Cowlairs
19-Jun-65	Withdrawn from service
Life Mileage	Over 850,000

Date applied or Ex-overhaul	**TRIMBUSH** Doncaster Works No.2027
14-May-48	Completed at Doncaster Works and entered traffic with deflectors and 8 wh non-corridor tender No.728 in LNER apple green livery. Numbered BR No.60536
21-Jul-50	BR dark green livery.
16-Jul-54	Fitted with BR exhaust at Doncaster
31-Dec-66	Withdrawn from service
Life Mileage	Over 850000

Date applied or Ex-overhaul	**BACHELOR'S BUTTON** Doncaster Works No.2028
11-Jun-48	Completed at Doncaster Works and entered traffic with deflectors and 8 wh non-corridor tender No.729 in LNER apple green livery. Numbered BR No.60537
30-Aug-50	BR dark green livery.
31-Jul-52	Fitted with B1 blastpipe at Doncaster
29-Dec-62	Withdrawn from service
Life Mileage	Over 850,000

Date applied or Ex-overhaul	**VELOCITY** Doncaster Works No.2029
18-Jun-48	Completed at Doncaster Works and entered traffic with deflectors and 8 wh non-corridor tender No.730 in LNER apple green livery. Numbered BR No. 60538
28-Oct-49	Fitted with a Multiple valve regulator, steam drier and Kylchap double blast, BR dark green livery.
12-Dec-62	Withdrawn from service
Life Mileage	890,627

Date applied or Ex-overhaul	**BRONZINO** Doncaster Works No.2030
27-Aug-48	Completed at Doncaster Works with a double Kylchap exhaust and entered traffic with deflectors and 8 wh non-corridor tender No.732 in LNER apple green livery. Numbered BR No.60539
14-Apr-50	BR dark green livery.
Date unknown	Fitted with a lipped chimney
12-Dec-66	Withdrawn from service
Life Mileage	769,552

Date applied or Ex-overhaul	**GREAT NORTHERN** Doncaster Works No.1536
25-Sep-45	Rebuilt at Doncaster Works from 180lb Gresley A1 and entered traffic with small chimney side deflectors and 8 wh A3 non-corridor tender No.5582 in dark blue GER livery. Numbered LNER No.4470.
13-Dec-45	Modified with full depth cab and large smoke deflectors, carrying the nameplates.
8-Oct-46	Renumbered LNER 113
16-May-47	Repainted LNER apple green
1-Oct-48	Renumbered BR 60113
6-Jan-50	Repainted BR blue
18-May-51	Nameplates replaced with crested pattern and Flaman recorder removed.
21-Aug-52	Repainted BR dark green
2-Feb-61	BR speedometer fitted
19-Nov-62	Withdrawn Estd. life mileage: 1,220,000 as Gresley A1, 950,000 as rebuilt, total 2,170,000

Date applied or Ex-overhaul	W P ALLEN
	Doncaster Works No.2031
6-Aug-48	Completed at Doncaster Works and entered traffic with 8 wh non-corridor tender No.731 in LNER apple green livery. Numbered BR No. 60114
26-Oct-48	Named
16-Nov-49	Repainted BR blue
15-Aug-52	Repainted BR green
26-Dec-64	Withdrawn

Date applied or Ex-overhaul	MEG MERRILIES
	Doncaster Works No.2032, but actually carried 2026.
3-Sep-48	Completed at Doncaster Works and entered traffic with deflectors and 8 wh non-corridor tender No.733 in LNER apple green livery. Numbered BR No.60115
2-Jun-50	Named and repainted BR blue
19-Sep-52	Repainted BR green
12-Nov-62	Withdrawn

Date applied or Ex-overhaul	HAL O' THE WYND
	Doncaster Works No.2033
8-Oct-48	Completed at Doncaster Works and entered traffic with 8 wh non-corridor tender No.734 in LNER apple green livery. Numbered BR No. 60116
22-Mar-50	Repainted BR blue
1-May-51	Named
22-Aug-52	Repainted BR green
14-Jun-65	Withdrawn

Date applied or Ex-overhaul	BOIS ROUSSEL
	Doncaster Works No.2034
22-Oct-48	Completed at Doncaster Works and entered traffic with 8 wh non-corridor tender No.735 in LNER apple green livery. Numbered BR No.60117
6-Jul-50	Named and repainted BR blue
20-Nov-51	Repainted BR green
21-Jun-65	Withdrawn

Date applied or Ex-overhaul	ARCHIBALD STURROCK
	Doncaster Works No.2035
12-Nov-48	Completed at Doncaster Works and entered traffic with 8 wh non-corridor tender No.736 in LNER apple green livery. Numbered BR No. 60118
12-May-50	Repainted BR blue
13-Jul-50	Named
22-Jan-52	Repainted BR green
4-Oct-65	Withdrawn

Date applied or Ex-overhaul	PATRICK STIRLING
	Doncaster Works No.2036
26-Nov-48	Completed at Doncaster Works and entered traffic with 8 wh non-corridor tender No.737 in LNER apple green livery. Numbered BR No.60119
7-Jun-50	Repainted BR blue
13-Jul-50	Named
19-Feb-52	Repainted BR green
31-May-64	Withdrawn

Date applied or Ex-overhaul	KITTIWAKE
	Doncaster Works No.2037
10-Dec-48	Completed at Doncaster Works and entered traffic with 8 wh non-corridor tender No.738 in LNER apple green livery. Numbered BR No.60120
31-Mar-50	Repainted BR blue
1-May-50	Named
4-Oct-51	Repainted BR green
20-Jan-64	Withdrawn

Date applied or Ex-overhaul	SILURIAN
	Doncaster Works No.2038
22-Dec-48	Completed at Doncaster Works and entered traffic with 8 wh non-corridor tender No.739 in LNER apple green livery. Numbered BR No. 60121
19-May-50	Named and repainted BR blue
20-Dec-51	Repainted BR green
4-Oct-65	Withdrawn

Date applied or Ex-overhaul	CURLEW
	Doncaster Works No.2039.
3-Sep-48	Completed at Doncaster Works and entered traffic with 8 wh non-corridor tender No.745 in LNER apple green livery. Numbered BR No. 60122
5-May-50	Repainted BR blue
1-Jul-50	Named
2-Oct-52	Repainted BR green
17-Dec-62	Withdrawn

Date applied or Ex-overhaul	H A IVATT
	Doncaster Works No.2040
10-Feb-49	Completed at Doncaster Works and entered traffic with 8 wh non-corridor tender No.741 in LNER apple green livery. Numbered BR No. 60123
9-Dec-49	Repainted BR blue
13-Jul-50	Named
17-Dec-52	Repainted BR green
1-Oct-62	Withdrawn

Date applied or Ex-overhaul	KENILWORTH
	Doncaster Works No.2041
23-Mar-49	Completed at Doncaster Works and entered traffic with 8 wh non-corridor tender No.742 in LNER apple green livery. Numbered BR No.60124
16-Aug-50	Named and repainted BR blue
27-Dec-51	Repainted BR green
27-Mar-66	Withdrawn

Date applied or Ex-overhaul	SCOTTISH UNION
	Doncaster Works No.2043
22-Apr-49	Completed at Doncaster Works and entered traffic with 8 wh non-corridor tender No.743 in LNER apple green livery. Numbered BR No. 60125
25-Jan-51	Named and repainted BR blue
31-Oct-52	Repainted BR green
4-Jul-64	Withdrawn

Date applied or Ex-overhaul	SIR VINCENT RAVEN
	Doncaster Works No.2042
27-Apr-49	Completed at Doncaster Works and entered traffic with 8 wh non-corridor tender No.749 in LNER apple green livery. Numbered BR No.60126
28-Jul-50	Repainted BR blue
1-Aug-50	Named
17-Oct-51	Repainted BR green
18-Jan-65	Withdrawn

Date applied or Ex-overhaul	WILSON WORSDELL
	Doncaster Works No.2044
13-May-49	Completed at Doncaster Works and entered traffic with 8 wh non-corridor tender No.746 in BR blue livery with cylinders lined in red. Numbered BR No.60127
13-Sep-50	Named
26-Mar-52	Repainted BR green
14-Jun-65	Withdrawn

Date applied or Ex-overhaul	BONGRACE
	Doncaster Works No.2045
19-May-49	Completed at Doncaster Works and entered traffic with 8 wh non-corridor tender No.744 in BR blue livery. Numbered BR No.60128
29-Nov-50	Named
4-Feb-52	Repainted BR green
10-Jan-65	Withdrawn

Date applied or Ex-overhaul	GUY MANNERING
	Doncaster Works No.2046.
15-Jun-49	Completed at Doncaster Works and entered traffic with 8 wh non-corridor tender No.747 in BR blue livery. Numbered BR No.60129
10-Nov-50	Named
27-Feb-52	Repainted BR green
11-Oct-65	Withdrawn

Date applied or Ex-overhaul	KESTREL
	Darlington Works No.2049
28-Sep-48	Completed at Darlington Works and entered traffic with 8 wh non-corridor tender No.750 in LNER apple green livery. Numbered BR No. 60130
20-Jul-50	Named and repainted BR blue
22-Aug-52	Repainted BR green
4-Oct-65	Withdrawn

Date applied or Ex-overhaul	OSPREY
	Darlington Works No.2050
5-Oct-48	Completed at Darlington Works and entered traffic with 8 wh non-corridor tender No.751 in LNER apple green livery. Numbered BR No. 60131
16-Jun-50	Named and repainted BR blue
28-Sep-51	Repainted BR green
4-Oct-65	Withdrawn

Date applied or Ex-overhaul	MARMION
	Darlington Works No.2051
18-Oct-48	Completed at Darlington Works and entered traffic with 8 wh non-corridor tender No.752 in LNER apple green livery. Numbered BR No. 60132
3-Nov-49	Repainted BR blue
22-Dec-50	Named
6-Mar-52	Repainted BR green
14-Jun-65	Withdrawn

Date applied or Ex-overhaul	POMMERN
	Darlington Works No.2052
30-Oct-48	Completed at Darlington Works and entered traffic with 8 wh non-corridor tender No.753 in LNER apple green livery. Numbered BR No. 60133
12-Apr-50	Named and repainted BR blue
19-Jun-52	Repainted BR green
21-Jun-65	Withdrawn from Copley Hill (not Ardsley)

Date applied or Ex-overhaul	FOXHUNTER
	Darlington Works No.2053
10-Dec-48	Completed at Darlington Works and entered traffic with deflectors and 8 wh non-corridor tender No.754 in LNER apple green livery. Numbered BR No. 60134
3-Mar-50	Repainted BR blue
13-Oct-50	Named
6-Feb-53	Repainted BR green
12-Nov-62	Withdrawn

Date applied or Ex-overhaul	MADGE WILDFIRE
	Darlington Works No.2054
18-Nov-48	Completed at Darlington Works and entered traffic with deflectors and 8 wh non-corridor tender No.755 in LNER apple green livery. Numbered BR No. 60135
6-Oct-50	Named and repainted BR blue
11-Dec-52	Repainted BR green
12-Nov-62	Withdrawn

Date applied or Ex-overhaul	ALCAZAR
	Darlington Works No.2055
26-Nov-48	Completed at Darlington Works and entered traffic with deflectors and 8 wh non-corridor tender No.756 in LNER apple green livery. Numbered BR No. 60136
8-Dec-50	Named and repainted BR blue
17-Jan-52	Repainted BR green
22-May-63	Withdrawn

Date applied or Ex-overhaul	REDGAUNTLET
	Darlington Works No.2056
3-Dec-48	Completed at Darlington Works and entered traffic with deflectors and 8 wh non-corridor tender No.757 in LNER apple green livery. Numbered BR No. 60137
9-Jun-50	Named and repainted BR blue
6-Mar-53	Repainted BR green
29-Oct-62	Withdrawn

Date applied or Ex-overhaul	BOSWELL
	Darlington Works No.2057
10-Dec-48	Completed at Darlington Works and entered traffic with deflectors and 8 wh non-corridor tender No.758 in LNER apple green livery. Numbered BR No. 60138
27-Sep-49	Repainted BR blue
21-Sep-50	Named
9-Apr-52	Repainted BR green
4-Oct-65	Withdrawn

Date applied or Ex-overhaul	SEA EAGLE
	Darlington Works No.2058
23-Dec-48	Completed at Darlington Works and entered traffic with deflectors and 8 wh non-corridor tender No.759 in LNER apple green livery. Numbered BR No. 60139
26-May-50	Named and repainted BR blue
25-Sep-51	Repainted BR green
7-Jun-64	Withdrawn

Date applied or Ex-overhaul	BALMORAL
	Darlington Works No.2059
24-Dec-48	Completed at Darlington Works and entered traffic with deflectors and 8 wh non-corridor tender No.760 in LNER apple green livery. Numbered BR No. 60140
5-Jul-50	Named and repainted BR blue
23-Nov-51	Repainted BR green
11-Jan-65	Withdrawn

Date applied or Ex-overhaul	ABBOTSFORD
	Darlington Works No.2060
31-Dec-48	Completed at Darlington Works and entered traffic with deflectors and 8 wh non-corridor tender No.761 in LNER apple green livery. Numbered BR No. 60141
3-May-50	Named and repainted BR blue
6-Feb-53	Repainted BR green
5-Oct-64	Withdrawn

Date applied or Ex-overhaul	EDWARD FLETCHER
	Darlington Works No.2061
2-Feb-49	Completed at Darlington Works and entered traffic with deflectors and 8 wh non-corridor tender No.762 in LNER apple green livery. Numbered BR No. 60142
18-Oct-50	Named and repainted BR blue
12-Dec-51	Repainted BR green
14-Jun-65	Withdrawn

Date applied or Ex-overhaul	SIR WALTER SCOTT
	Darlington Works No.2062
22-Feb-49	Completed at Darlington Works and entered traffic with 8 wh non-corridor tender No.763 in LNER apple green livery. Numbered BR No. 60143
15-Sep-50	Named and repainted BR blue
18-Oct-51	Repainted BR green
6-May-64	Withdrawn

Date applied or Ex-overhaul	KINGS COURIER
	Darlington Works No.2063
2-Mar-49	Completed at Darlington Works and entered traffic with 8 wh non-corridor tender No.764 in LNER apple green livery. Numbered BR No. 60144
9-Jan-51	Named and repainted BR blue
31-Oct-51	Repainted BR green
30-Apr-63	Withdrawn

Date applied or Ex-overhaul	ST. MUNGO
	Darlington Works No.2064
23-Mar-49	Completed at Darlington Works and entered traffic with 8 wh non-corridor tender No.765 in LNER apple green livery. Numbered BR No. 60145
23-Aug-50	Named and repainted BR blue
1-Jan-52	Repainted BR green
19-Jun-66	Withdrawn

Date applied or Ex-overhaul	PEREGRINE
	Darlington Works No.2065
11-Apr-49	Completed at Darlington Works and entered traffic with 8 wh non-corridor tender No.766 in LNER apple green livery. Numbered BR No. 60146
15-Dec-50	Named and repainted BR blue
4-Dec-51	Repainted BR green
4-Oct-65	Withdrawn

Date applied or Ex-overhaul	NORTH EASTERN
	Darlington Works No.2066
13-Apr-49	Completed at Darlington Works and entered traffic with 8 wh non-corridor tender No.767 in LNER apple green livery. Numbered BR No. 60147
29-Nov-50	Repainted BR blue
29-Aug-51	Repainted BR green
10-Mar-52	Named
7-Jun-64	Withdrawn

Date applied or Ex-overhaul	ABOYEUR
	Darlington Works No.2067
25-May-49	Completed at Darlington Works and entered traffic with 8 wh non-corridor tender No.768 in LNER apple green livery. Numbered BR No. 60148
4-Jan-51	Named and repainted BR blue
11-Jul-52	Repainted BR green
21-Jun-65	Withdrawn

Date applied or Ex-overhaul	AMADIS
	Darlington Works No.2068
31-May-49	Completed at Darlington Works and entered traffic with 8 wh non-corridor tender No.769 in LNER apple green livery. Numbered BR No. 60149
20-Oct-50	Repainted BR blue
1-Dec-50	Named
16-Aug-51	Repainted BR green
7-Jun-64	Withdrawn

Date applied or Ex-overhaul	WILLBROOK
	Darlington Works No.2069
15-Jun-49	Completed at Darlington Works and entered traffic with 8 wh non-corridor tender No.770 in LNER apple green livery. Numbered BR No. 60150
12-Jan-51	Named and repainted BR blue
26-Mar-52	Repainted BR green
5-Oct-64	Withdrawn

Date applied or Ex-overhaul	MIDLOTHIAN
	Darlington Works No.2070
30-Jun-49	Completed at Darlington Works and entered traffic with 8 wh non-corridor tender No.771 in LNER apple green livery. Numbered BR No. 60151
2-Mar-51	Named and repainted BR blue
11-Jun-52	Repainted BR green
24-Nov-65	Withdrawn

Date applied or Ex-overhaul	HOLYROOD
	Darlington Works No.2071
8-Jul-49	Completed at Darlington Works and entered traffic with 8 wh non-corridor tender No.772 in LNER apple green livery. Numbered BR No. 60152
1-Jun-51	Named and repainted BR blue
21-Nov-52	Repainted BR green
21-Jun-65	Withdrawn

Date applied or Ex-overhaul	FLAMBOYANT
	Doncaster Works No.2047
26-Aug-49	Completed at Doncaster Works with roller bearings throughout and entered traffic with 8 wh non-corridor tender No.773 in BR blue livery. Numbered BR No.60153
21-Aug-50	Named
4-Dec-51	Repainted BR green
2-Nov-62	Withdrawn

Date applied or Ex-overhaul	BON ACCORD
	Doncaster Works No.2048
15-Jun-49	Completed at Doncaster Works with roller bearings throughout and entered traffic with 8 wh non-corridor tender No.777 in BR blue livery. Numbered BR No.60154
18-Apr-51	Named
15-Aug-52	Repainted BR green
4-Oct-65	Withdrawn

Date applied or Ex-overhaul	BORDERER
	Doncaster Works No.2049
29-Sep-49	Completed at Doncaster Works with roller bearings throughout and entered traffic with 8 wh non-corridor tender No.775 in BR blue livery. Numbered BR No.60155
1-Mar-51	Named
20-May-52	Repainted BR green
4-Oct-65	Withdrawn

Date applied or Ex-overhaul	GREAT CENTRAL
19-Oct-49	Doncaster Works No.2050 Completed at Doncaster Works with roller bearings throughout and entered traffic with 8 wh non-corridor tender No.776 in BR blue livery. Numbered BR No.60156
17-Jul-52	Named and repainted BR green
10-May-65	Withdrawn

Date applied or Ex-overhaul	GREAT EASTERN
3-Nov-49	Doncaster Works No.2051 Completed at Doncaster Works with roller bearings throughout and entered traffic with 8 wh non-corridor tender No.774 in BR blue livery. Numbered BR No.60157
12-Nov-51	Named and repainted BR green
10-Jan-65	Withdrawn

Date applied or Ex-overhaul	ABERDONIAN
17-Nov-49	Doncaster Works No.2052 Completed at Doncaster Works and entered traffic with 8 wh non-corridor tender No.778 in BR blue livery. Numbered BR No.60158
9-Mar-51	Named
4-Nov-52	Repainted BR green
26-Dec-64	Withdrawn

Date applied or Ex-overhaul	BONNIE DUNDEE
24-Nov-49	Doncaster Works No.2053 Completed at Doncaster Works and entered traffic with 8 wh non-corridor tender No.779 in BR blue livery. Numbered BR No.60159
13-Jul-51	Named
19-Dec-52	Repainted BR green
14-Oct-63	Withdrawn

Date applied or Ex-overhaul	AULD REEKIE
2-Dec-49	Doncaster Works No.2054 Completed at Doncaster Works and entered traffic with 8 wh non-corridor tender No.780 in BR blue livery. Numbered BR No.60160
1-Mar-51	Named
24-Mar-53	Repainted BR green
12-Dec-63	Withdrawn

Date applied or Ex-overhaul	NORTH BRITISH
19-Dec-49	Doncaster Works No.2055 Completed at Doncaster Works and entered traffic with 8 wh non-corridor tender No.781 in BR blue livery. Numbered BR No.60161
15-Jun-51	Named
6-Nov-52	Repainted BR green
14-Oct-63	Withdrawn

Date applied or Ex-overhaul	ST.JOHNSTOUN
19-Dec-49	Doncaster Works No.2056 Completed at Doncaster Works and entered traffic with 8 wh non-corridor tender No.781 in BR blue livery. Numbered BR No.60162. (Actually completed ahead of No.60161 but entered traffic on the same date.
21-Aug-51	Named and repainted BR green
28-Oct-63	Withdrawn

Date applied or Ex-overhaul	TORNADO
2008 (Prov)	Darlington North Road Works No.1 Completed at Darlington with roller bearings throughout and will enter preservation in BR green livery Numbered BR No.60163

APPENDIX B LEADING DIMENSIONS CLASSES A1, A2, P2s

	P2/1	P2/2	P26/3	A2/2	A2/2	A2/1	A2/3	A2	A2	A1/1	A1	A1(RB)
Introduced	1934	1935/6	1936	Jan-43	Jun-44	May-44	May-46	Dec-47	Aug-48	Sep-45	Aug-48	Aug-49
Boiler:-												
Boiler Diagram no.	106	106	108	106A	108A	109	117	118	118	107	118	118
Boiler Pressure	220	220	220	225	225	220	250	250	250	250	250	250
Grate Area	50	50	50	50	50	41.25	50	50	50	41.25	50	50
Max Outside Diameter	6ft5ins	6ft5ins	6ft5ins	6ft5ins	6ft5ins	6ft5ins	6ft5ins	6ft5ins	6ft5ins	6ft5ins	6ft5ins	6ft5ins
Min Outside Diameter	5ft9ins	5ft9ins	5ft9ins	5ft9ins	5ft9ins	5ft9ins	5ft9ins	5ft9ins	5ft9ins	5ft9ins	5ft9ins	5ft9ins
Tube length	18ft 11.75	18ft 11.75	17ft 11.75	16ft 11.625	16ft	16ft 11.625	16ft 11.625	16ft 11.625	16ft 11.625	17ft 11.625	16ft 11.625	16ft 11.625
No. tubes	121	121	121	121	121	121	121	121	121	121	121	121
No. superheater flues	43	43	43	43	43	43	43	43	43	43	43	43
Boiler Heating Surface Area:-												
Firebox	237	237	252	237.00	252.50	215.00	245.30	245.30	245.30	231.20	245.30	245.30
Tubes	1354.2	1354.2	1281.4	1211.57	1138.70	1211.57	1211.57	1211.57	1211.57	1281.40	1211.57	1211.57
Flues	1122.8	1122.8	1063.7	1004.50	945.40	1004.50	1004.50	1004.50	1004.50	1063.70	1004.50	1004.50
Subtotal (Evaporative)	2714	2714	2597.6	2453.07	2336.60	2431.07	2461.37	2461.37	2461.37	2576.30	2461.37	2461.37
Superheater	776.5	776.5	748.9	679.67	652.07	679.67	679.67	679.67	679.67	748.90	679.67	679.67
Total	3490.5	3490.5	3346.5	3132.74	2988.67	3110.74	3141.04	3141.04	3141.04	3325.20	3141.04	3141.04
Wheel Diameter:-												
Bogie	3ft 2ins	3ft 2ins	3ft 2ins	3ft 2ins	3ft 2ins	3ft 2ins	3ft 2ins	3ft 2ins	3ft 2ins	3ft 2ins	3ft 2ins	3ft 2ins
Coupled	6ft 2ins	6ft 2ins	6ft 2ins	6ft 2ins	6ft 2ins	6ft 2ins	6ft 2ins	6ft 2ins	6ft 2ins	6ft 8ins	6ft 8ins	6ft 8ins
Trailing	3ft 8ins	3ft 8ins	3ft 8ins	3ft 8ins	3ft 8ins	3ft 8ins	3ft 8ins	3ft 8ins	3ft 8ins	3ft 8ins	3ft 8ins	3ft 8ins
Cylinders (3)	21x26ins	21x26ins	21x26ins	20x26ins	20x26ins	19x26ins	19x26ins	19x26ins	19x26ins	19x26ins	19x26ins	19x26ins
Valves:-												
Piston Valve Diameter (all variations)	Poppet-valves	9ins	9ins	10ins	10ins	10ins	10ins	10ins	10ins	10ins	10ins	10ins
Travel (ins)	5.75	5.75	5.75	5.75	5.75	5.75	5.75	5.75	5.75	5.75	5.75	
Lap (ins). Steam/Exhaust	1.625/0	1.625/0	1.625/0	1.625/0	1.625/0	1.625/0	1.625/0	1.625/0	1.625/0	1.625/0	1.625/0	
Lead (ins)	0.125	0.125	0.125	0.125	0.125	0.125	0.125	0.125	0.125	0.125	0.125	
Clearance volume as % swept volume	11.78-16.10%	7.7% approx	7.7% approx	7.70% approx	7.70%	7.70%	7.70%	7.70%	7.70%	7.70%	7.70%	7.70%
Tractive Effort (85% boiler pressure)	43,462	43,462	43,462	40,318	40,318	36,387	40,430	40,430	40,430	37,397	37,397	37,397
Single Blastpipe orifice (ins)	28.27(2005)						23.76					
Double Blastpipe orifice (ins)	50 approx	44.2 approx	44.2 approx	39.27	39.27	39.27	39.27	39.27	39.27	39.27	39.27	39.27
Wheelbase length (6 wh.tender)	(2001/2)	(2002)				59ft2.125ins						
Wheelbase length (8 wh.tender)	64ft 0.875	64ft 0.875	64ft 0.875	63ft0.875	63ft0.875	61ft9.625	63ft1.375	60ft5.875	60ft5.875	63ft6.625	62ft5.25	62ft5.25
Total length, (8 wh.tender)	73ft 8.375	74ft 5.375	74ft 5.375	72ft8.375	72ft8.375	71ft5.125	72ft10.875	71ft0.375	71ft0.375	73ft2.125	72ft11.75	72ft11.75
Adhesive weight (tons)	80.6	80.5	78.95	66	66	66	66	66	66	66	66	66.55
Adhesive factor	4.15	4.15	4.07	3.67	3.67	4.06	3.66	3.66	3.66	3.95	3.95	3.99
Engine weight (tons)	110.25	109.4	107.15 (2003-6)	101.5	101.5	98	101.50	101.00	101.00	101.50	104.10	105.20

Tender details

Attached to	No.60501	No.60502	Nos.60503-60506	No.60507	Nos.60508-510	No.60500/511-524	No.60525-539	No.60113	No.60114-162	No.60153-157
Type	Expt 8 wh.	Std 8 wh	A4 non corr	A4 non corr	Gp Std 6wh	Std 8 wh	Std 8 wh	Std 8 wh	Std 8 wh	Std 8 wh RB
Built	1934	1934	1936	1944	1944-5					
Coal (tons)	9	9	9	9	7.1	9	9	8	9	9
Water (gallons, nominal)	5,000	5,000	5,000	5,000	4,200	5,000	5,000	5,000	5,000	5,000
Weight	56.3	57.9	60.35	60.35	52	60.35	60.35	57.9	60.35	60.9

APPENDIX C: Some Detail and Drawings
Kylchap Exhaust Design

The illustration of the double Kylchap exhaust is as used on MONS MEG. It is very similar to that used on the A4s. Although larger than on the Pacific, it is unique in the inclusion of the experimental by-pass behind the chimney.

The blastpipe top was a separate casting, fitted with carefully fashioned wedge-shaped knife edges at right angles, positioned so as to cut the exhaust jet into four parts. These were referred to at Doncaster as 'vee bars', or in the French design, *barrettes*, and they existed in four sets numbered 0 to 3, from the smallest to the largest. Immediately above was located the shaped Kyläla exhaust splitter or *ajutage*, registering with the barrettes below, splitting the exhaust steam flow into four separate jets. These were recombined in the cylindrical petticoat suspended above the *ajutage*, and further above, the chimney liner. The whole vertical assembly was held between two robust vertical bars, and had three openings at which the smokebox gases were entrained with the exhausting steam. In France, the surfaces in contact with exhausting steam were polished smooth.

If calculations showed that for a powerful locomotive the exhaust assembly required exceeded the limits of the loading gauge, the exhaust flow was simply halved and a double chimney assembly used. In such cases the double blastpipe, or 'breeches' pipe, was fitted with a dividing vane or mid-feather in each leg to smooth the passage of the exhausting steam. The exhaust orifice could be changed to give a different diameter, and likewise the set of barrettes could be changed to give a reduction in orificial area of roundly 5, 10, 15 and 25%. The 1K/T version was simpler design that used an extended chimney liner in place of the intermediate petticoat. In summary, the Kylchap exhaust made far more effective use of the exhausting steam, considerably increasing the draughting and forcing a far higher rate of combustion on the grate.

The rocking grate and hopper ashpan arrangements are illustrated, as used by both Thompson and Peppercorn. I have also included a diagram of the roller bearing arrangements first used on the tender of SILVER LINK, but then on the outside axleboxes of the five A2s, 60153-60157. The inside axleboxes of the coupled wheels and front bogie will have been of differing design but utilised the same principles.

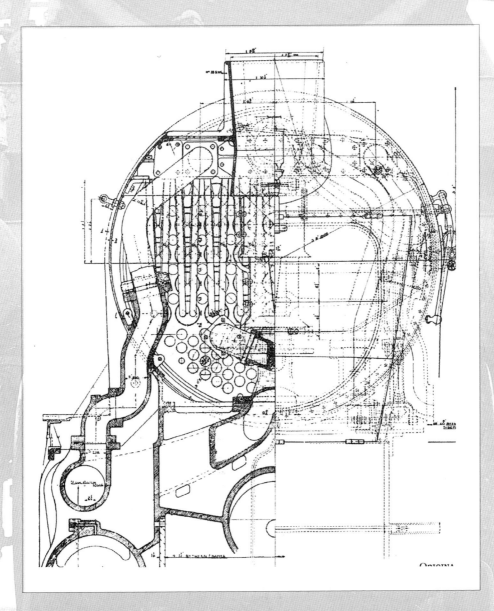

215

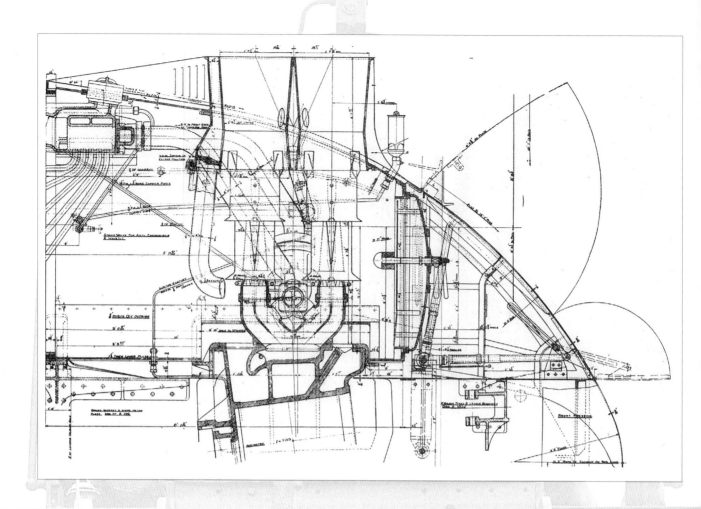

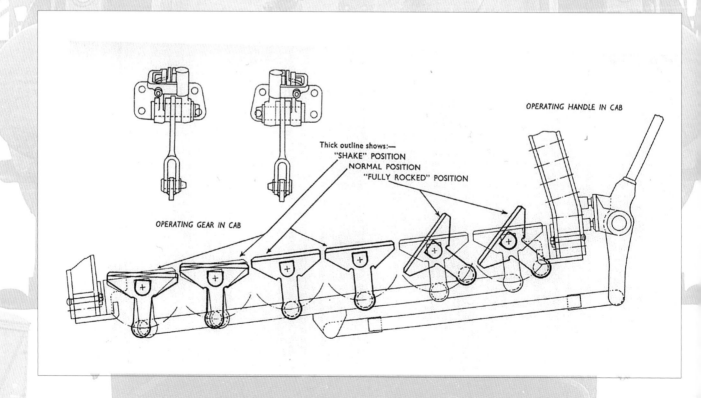

OPERATING HANDLE IN CAB

Thick outline shows:—
"SHAKE" POSITION
NORMAL POSITION
"FULLY ROCKED" POSITION

OPERATING GEAR IN CAB

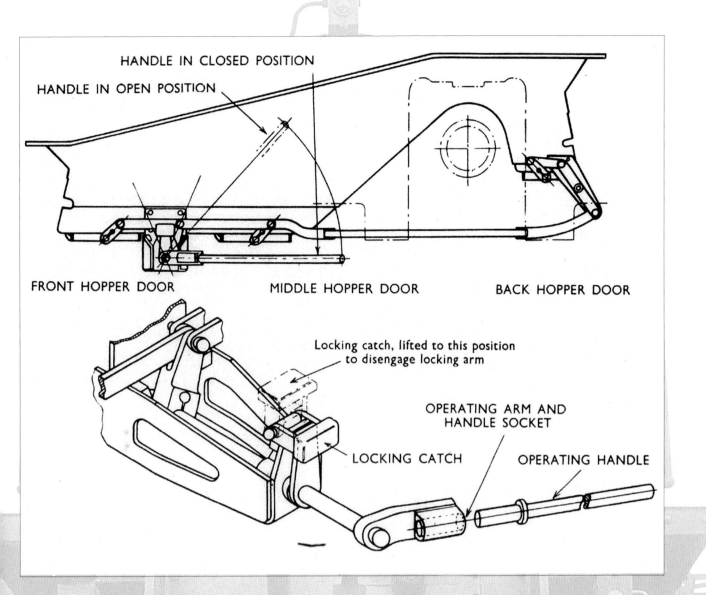

HANDLE IN CLOSED POSITION

HANDLE IN OPEN POSITION

FRONT HOPPER DOOR   MIDDLE HOPPER DOOR   BACK HOPPER DOOR

Locking catch, lifted to this position
to disengage locking arm

OPERATING ARM AND
HANDLE SOCKET

LOCKING CATCH

OPERATING HANDLE

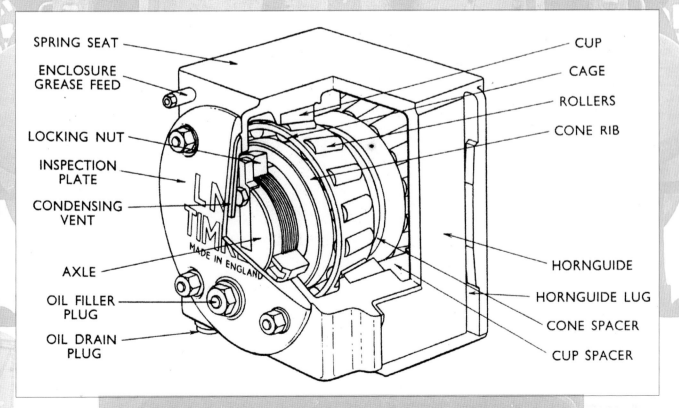

SPRING SEAT

ENCLOSURE
GREASE FEED

LOCKING NUT

INSPECTION
PLATE

CONDENSING
VENT

AXLE

OIL FILLER
PLUG

OIL DRAIN
PLUG

CUP

CAGE

ROLLERS

CONE RIB

HORNGUIDE

HORNGUIDE LUG

CONE SPACER

CUP SPACER

APPENDIX D

A Diary of the tests with engine No.2001 at the Locomotive Testing Plant, Vitry-sur-Seine covering the period between December 5th 1934, when the engine left Calais and February 21st 1935, when the engine returned from Calais. Produced for Nigel Gresley if not by O V S Bulleid, then certainly with his approval. There were a number of tables setting out the working of the engine with the diary, but they add little to the narrative and have been omitted.

Wednesday, December 5th 1934

The locomotive, together with three 40 ton wagons loaded with Yorkshire Main coal, a covered goods van containing spares for the locomotive, and a 20 ton brake van were placed on the train ferry at 6.15pm. The voyage over to Calais commenced at 8.30pm.

Thursday, December 6th

The train ferry was berthed at Calais at 8.20am, but owing to Customs formalities it was not until 12.30pm that the train was disembarked. There was some difficulty with the Customs authorities over the spare parts, and if in future any rolling stock or spares are sent over, it must be arranged that they stand at least 24 hours at Calais for Customs purposes. The engine was lit up and proceeded to Calais Locomotive Depot at 5.45pm and remained there throughout the night.

Friday, December 7th

The engine left Calais Maritime for Vitry at 7.36am, and travelled via Amiens, Montdidier, Le Bourget, Villeneuve St.Georges, Juvisy, and Ivry. It arrived at the Testing Plant at Vitry at 6.30pm.

Saturday, December 8th

The brakes of the Testing Plant were set to suit our wheelbase, and the engine was run on the testing plant for the first time at 5pm. It ran on to the test bed under its own steam.

Sunday December 9th

During the whole of the morning the engine was at the disposal of the representatives of the publication L'Illustration for photographic purposes.

Monday, December 9th to Wednesday, December 11th

The engine was being fitted up with the necessary pyrometers and water meters. The connections provided in the smokebox sides proved to be unsuitable for the OCEM pyrometers, and they put on new fittings of their own make. Additional fittings were also required in the manifold under the LH footstep for the smokebox vacuum, the firebox vacuum, and the back pressure in the exhaust passage.

Thursday, December 13th

The engine ran on the test bed for the first time. In the morning it was run lightly to see everything was in order, but in the afternoon it was run up to a speed of 76 mph to enable the cinematograph trade to obtain films of the engine in motion.

The engine was not riding evenly on the rollers, and while the frame remained central, the wheels, particularly the driving wheels, moved over towards the right, the inside of the RH tyre binding hard on the rail of the plant.

Towards the end of the afternoon the RH driving axlebox was observed to be running warm. On inspecting the axlebox tray it was found that a considerable amount of metal was melted out, and arrangements were made for the engine to be taken into the electric locomotive shops of the P-O Railway at Vitry where a suitable wheel drop is installed.

An examination of the plant after the engine had been removed showed, by the marks on the LH rail, that similar difficulty regarding the moving over had been experienced with other engines.

Friday, December 14th

At 6.30am the engine was taken to the P-O Works about a mile from the testing plant. The driving wheels were dropped and the axleboxes dismantled. Both RH and LH boxes were badly pounded on the back on the face of the horn, the LH box being rather the worse of the two. Two new boxes brought out from Doncaster were therefore fitted. The journals were in indifferent condition. Whilst the driving wheels were dismantled, opportunity was taken to grind off the corner on the inside of the tyre where the change of width from 4ft 5⁵/₈ins to 4ft 5⁷/₈ins takes place.

Saturday, December 15th and Sunday December 16th

The work of refitting the boxes and re-erecting the wheels, rods, etc, was completed in the early afternoon of Sunday, and the engine arrived at the plant at about 5.30pm. It was put on the test plant and run lightly for about 2½ hours.

Monday, December 17th

The engine was run light throughout the morning. Since fitting the new boxes to the driving wheels the effect of the side movement has transferred to the leading and trailing wheels, the root of the flange of the RH trailing wheel in particular binding hard on the RH roller of the plant.

In the afternoon a series of tests were carried out at 60 kmph at 12½, 18, 25 and 35% cut-off with the blastpipe as when the engine left Doncaster, i.e. 6ins diameter with the No.0, the smallest vee bars. There was considerable smoke at 12½ and 18% cut-offs, and the fire is somewhat sluggish.

At these cut-offs there was no exhaust pressure registered on the gauge. The pipe was coupled to the front on the blastpipe immediately under the blastpipe top joint. The position of this coupling was now altered to the exhaust passage in the cylinder casting immediately above the exhaust valve.

The beat at the chimney top was irregular, especially at low speeds. The engine returned to the sheds in good order.

Tuesday, December 18th

The engine was put on the plant at 9.00am with the object of carrying out tests at 60 kmph at 45% cut-off. After 20 minutes running, however, in order to bring the conditions up to test requirements, it was apparent that the LH crank pin was running hot. The engine returned to the shed at midday, and the remainder of the day was occupied in fitting a new bush which had been brought out from Doncaster.

Wednesday, December 19th

In order to run in the new coupling rod bush, the morning's work commenced with a run of 15 minutes duration, with little resistance on the brakes and a speed of about 25 mph. A second run of 20 minutes with a horsepower at the drawbar of 500 was made, and no further sign of overheating was apparent.

Tests were then commenced, but after running for only 20 minutes the RH coupling rod bush was again hot. As we had no further new bushes, the rod was sent to the P-O works to be remetalled and rebored. The question arose as to the disturbances of the wheel centres by the fitting of new driving boxes. Trammels were obtained from the works and the centres were checked both by our own people and by the works and testing plant staff.

The rod was returned to the engine at 4.30pm, but owing to the large number of blowholes in the metal it was rejected.

Thursday, December 20th

The rod was taken back to the P-O works at 7.0am, but they had difficulty in producing a bush in which the white metal was free from blowholes, and it was 7.0pm before a commencement was made in refitting it to the engine.

Friday, December 21st

The engine was placed on the test plant and ran light throughout the morning. During the afternoon a series of tests at 80, 100, and 120 kmph at 12½% cut-off were made. Between each test the engine was run light for 20 minutes. All the bearings both in the rods and in the boxes appeared to be bedding down well.

Saturday, December 22nd

The test was discontinued and the men returned to England for Christmas.

Monday, December 31st

Staff returned to France.

Tuesday, January 1st

In view of the uneven beat, the Paris representatives of the Dabeg company visited the engine to see the valve chests opened up. They suggested that the valves should be set to the crank angles rather than to the valve openings. At the request of the Dabeg people also two of the valves were reground. All the valve seatings were in good condition and secure within the cylinder castings. All the spring cams on both steam and exhaust were fitted when the valve covers were replaced.

Wednesday, January 2nd

The engine was ready to go on the plant at 8.0am, but as the French Est engine had been on test during our absence for Christmas, it was necessary to reset the brakes and the rollers of the plant to suit our wheelbase, and it was 10.0am before we were able to commence. A preliminary run was made for 15 minutes, after which the engine was put on test at 18% cut-off and at a speed of 100 kmph. The engine ran for about 20 minutes to bring the conditions constant when the vertical shaft rotated by our trailing crank pin, carrying the motion of our engine to the dynamometer table, twisted off and the test had to be stopped. The engine returned to the shed at mid-day.

During the Christmas break the back plate of the ashpan had been removed. It made no difference, however, to the amount of smoke emitted from the chimney top. The opportunity was now taken, while the plant was under repair, to change the blastpipe tops to 5½ins diameter with largest set of vee bars.

Thursday, January 3rd

The engine went on to the plant at 8.30am and commenced the first test at 9.25am. The first series of tests carried out were at 60 kmph and at 12½, 18, 25 and 35% cut-offs. The second series of tests were at 12½% cut-off and at speeds of 80, 100 and 120 kmph.

With the much smaller blastpipe the amount of smoke was much reduced, but the amount of coal thrown out at the chimney was excessive. At the conclusion of the tests there were signs of heating up at the LH leading axlebox, and on removal of the tray there was a considerable amount of white metal round the pad. A pilot driver was obtained and the engine was taken into the P-O works.

Friday, January 4th

While the leading wheels were being dropped and the boxes dismantled, the cam boxes were dismantled and opened up for examination. Considerable wear had taken place on the exhaust cam of the RH cylinder and on the roller of the front exhaust valve of the RH cylinder. The remaining cams and rollers were all in good condition.

Saturday, January 5th

The work at the P-O works progressed satisfactorily throughout the day and at 9.0pm the wheels had been replaced under the engine and the running gear, etc refitted. The roller of the RH exhaust valve proved to be so badly worn that it was necessary to grind off 2mm in diameter in order to regain its concentricity. The pin of this roller was also worn, and before refitting this cam box it was decided to await the arrival of spare pins and rollers from England. The Dabeg people recommended the use of bronze pins in line with Continental practice, and they put in hand a full set of bronze pins for future fitting, if necessary. The LH cam box was replaced and the valve setting again checked by the Dabeg representatives. The valve spindles were also ground to give them an extra 0.001 clearance in their housings.

Sunday January 6th

The spare rollers and pins were not immediately released by the Customs officials and were therefore not available. The RH cam box was reassembled and the necessary adjustment made to the valve spindles to accommodate the reground roller.

The blastpipe tops were changed to 5¾ins with the smallest of the vee bars. The engine was lighted up in the shop and was able to leave the works at 1.0pm. It was placed on the plant at 2.30pm and ran throughout the afternoon at 400 horsepower and from 25 to 30 mph. The beat at the chimney top is still imperfect and is being further investigated by the Dabeg people.

Monday, January 7th

The engine was placed on the plant, and after a period of running at 400 horsepower, testing was commenced at 12½ and 18% cut-off at 60 kmph. At the end of the tests the LH leading box again showed signs of heating up. The pad was withdrawn and there was a slight trace of metal on the pad. The pad was thoroughly cleaned and the engine run light for the remainder of the day. The engine was run light on the plant, but as the LH box was running rather warm, the engine was taken to the shed for examination.

Tuesday, January 8th

The whole of the pads, with the exception of those in the driving boxes, were withdrawn. The LH intermediate pad and tray contained a considerable deposit of white metal, and it was decided to take the engine into the P-O works to fit a remetalled box. There was some delay in the arrival of a pilot driver, and the work of stripping down did not start until 4.40pm.

The wheels were dropped the same evening, and the remetalled box set up on the machine for boring. The box had been remetalled by Messrs Corpet Louvet & Co with a new standard French metal known as AE1. Mr Gresley gave orders for the lubrication oil as used on the Est and P-O to be used in the axleboxes, and this was done.

Wednesday, January 9th

The wheels were replaced under the engine and it was returned to the testing plant at 7.30pm. It was the intention to run the engine on the plant the same evening, but owing to a failure on one of the roller bearings of the plant we had to wait until the morning.

Thursday, January 10th

The engine was on the plant at 8.0am and commenced running in half hourly periods at 18% cut-off and at 25 mph. During the morning it was inspected by a number of visitors, Members of the Committee of Scientific and Industrial Research, and it was kept running until midday, the maximum speed being 60 kmph. This was the first occasion on which the French oil had been used, and there appeared to be no sign of overheating. The engine came off the plant at 2.30pm to enable the brakes to be reset for the French Est engine which is being put on the plant tomorrow for comparison and for the benefit of the visitors.

Friday, January 11th

Engine No.2001 was standing aside while the Est engine was under test, and the opportunity was taken to make a small number of adjustments. The firebars were lifted to enable the ashpan wing plates to be freed from ashes, and the element ends were cleaned.

Saturday, January 12th

During the morning we commenced tests at 12½% cut-off and at 60, 80 and 100 kmph. At the end of the 80 kmph test everything appeared to be in order and running well, but after 12 minutes at 100 kmph the leading box was again hot.

It was now suggested by the P-O engineers that the principal cause of the heating was found in the brass bars, containing our oil grooves, bearing hard on the journal and thus setting up local heating. It was now decided that the remetalled box which we should fit on the LH leading wheel should have a complete white metal bearing in accordance with French practice. The Est engineers also gave us the adjustment they had found necessary to make to their wedges when running on the plant, and our wedges were set to give these clearances.

Sunday January 13th

The work of fitting the remetalled box to the leading LH wheel and the re-erection of the running gear was completed and the engine was returned to the plant at 7.30 pm. The blastpipe tops were again altered to 6 ins diameter with the No.1 vee bars.

Monday, January 14th

In order to give the remetalled boxes as good a chance as possible the engine was run with little load (up to 500 horsepower) throughout the day. There were no signs of heating.

Tuesday, January 15st

Tests were now made with the new blastpipe at a speed of 60 kmph and 12½, 18 and 25% cut-off. Everything was in order and the engine returned to the shed at 4.30 pm.

Wednesday, January 16th

In the morning tests were carried out at 80 kmph and 12½% cut-off, but before the test was completed the LH intermediate box failed. It was now decided to take out all the coupled wheels and to remetal the boxes with a complete white metal bearing. It was also decided to burnish up the journals.

The engine was taken into the Vitry shops at 6.0pm ready to commence dismantling the wheels early the following morning.

Thursday, January 17th

The first pair of wheels to be dropped was the intermediate wheels. Mr J Murphy of Messrs J Stone & Co arrived in the evening and went out to the works of Messrs Corpet Louvet to examine the methods employed in metalling the boxes.

Friday, January 18th

The wheel lathe in the P-O shops was quite unsuitable for burnishing up our journals. The nearest suitable lathe was that in the wheel shop of the Nord railway at Ermont, and arrangements were made for each pair of wheels to be taken there by motor lorry for the journals to be turned and burnished.

Saturday, January 19th

The first pair of wheels was returned to Vitry from Ermont, and the first pair of boxes from Corpet Louvet, but the metalling was not good, especially of the LH box, and they were rejected.

Sunday January 20th

The P-O works were closed down for Sunday. The metalling was proceeding at Corpet's works, who were now pouring with 2 ins head above the box. This appeared to be giving good results, and two boxes were sent over to Vitry to commence bedding on the journal the following morning.

Monday, January 21st to Friday, January 25th

The work of taking down the wheels and boxes and of reerecting progressed. The outstanding detail was the development of a flake in the RH side driving journal during the process of burnishing. This flake was equilateral triangle in shape, with a ¼ inch base and ³⁄₈ inch high). It was necessary to turn 0.8mm off the journal before the effect of this flake was totally eliminated.

The driving journals were finished turned, polished and lapped; the other journals were turned and burnished with a Krupp three roller burnisher.

Messrs Wakefield's Paris office staff thoroughly inspected and tested the lubrication system and went into the question of an oil guaranteed to maintain its viscosity at higher temperatures than LNER express engine oil. The following table gives the characteristics of the oil they supplied, and for comparison the same figures for LNER, Est and P-O oils. The superiority of Castrol oil at 140°F is very marked without being too viscous at 70°F to siphon freely through a pad. This oil was used for the remainder of the tests. The engine returned to the plant on Friday evening January 25th.

Saturday, January 26th

The engine left the shed at the Vitry testing plant for a run on the P-O line. We left Vitry at 7.30 am and except for slacks at stations and curves, maintained a fairly constant speed of 25 mph. We stopped at Juvisy and Bretigny to examine the boxes and arrived at Etampes at 9.25 am, a distance of about 60 kilometres. There was neither turntable large enough to accommodate the engine at Etampes, nor a triangle, and it was therefore necessary to return to Vitry tender first.

This was a good test for the engine as we had eliminated the front oil grooves on the boxes, so the principal source of lubrication when running backwards would be the pad. We stopped at Bretigny and Ivry, and arrived back at Vitry at midday. The whole of the boxes were cool. It was intended that the engine should go on to the plant in the afternoon, but owing to the failure of a brake roller bearing on the plant, we were unable to do so.

Sunday January 27th

The boiler was washed out, tubes blown out, side firebars lifted, and elements ends cleaned in preparation for starting consumption tests on Monday.

Monday, January 28th

Owing to resetting the changed rollers of the plant it was not possible to start until 10.50 am, when a hour's run was made with little load for the purpose of further running in the boxes. They appeared to be bedding down well and everything was cold. It was also noticed that with the changed rollers the engine rode on the plant much better and the moving over of the wheels was not nearly so pronounced.

In the afternoon the first consumption tests were commenced at 60 kmph and at 12½% cut-off. Excessive movement of the RH driving box in the horns was noticed when the engine was running and it was therefore kept under observation. After 10 minutes or so it appeared to settle down to normal movement, but after 20 minutes it bound in the horn and the test was stopped. There was considerable metal in the tray, and the engine went into the P-O shops at 5.15 pm.

Tuesday, January 29th and Wednesday, January 30th

A remetalled box was fitted to the RH driving wheel, and arrangements were made for the engine to go to Tours where it could be lifted and checked over, and could be thoroughly run in over the P-O line.

Thursday, January 31st

The engine was worked down to Tours, arriving at 5.30 pm where it was taken into the shops. All the bearings were entirely cold, and in view of this and the way the engine had run, it was felt undesirable to lift it. Arrangements were made for a fast run up to Orlèans next day to see if any heating took place under fast running conditions. French coal was to be used whilst running over the P-O railway.

Friday, February 1st

The engine ran two double trips between Tours and Orlèans, a distance of 72 miles in each direction. Each single journey was carried out non-stop, the average speeds being as follows:-

Morning, Tours to Orlèans: 53.328 mph
Orlèans to Tours: 61.68 mph
Afternoon, Tours to Orlèans: 64.44 mph
Orlèans to Tours: 63.48 mph

The maximum speed was 82.8 mph. All the bearings were cold and the engine was in good condition.

Saturday, February 2nd

One similar run to those carried out the previous day was made between Tours and Orlèans and back. The bearings were cold, and arrangements were made to carry out a series of brake engine trials the following week. As the engine had been so long in France a revised and shortened programme of tests to be carried out at Vitry were submitted to and approved by Mr. Gresley.

Sunday February 3rd

The boiler was washed out at Tours and the engine generally prepared for the brake engine tests.

Monday, February 4th

The engine was weighed and the necessary adjustment made. The engine then ran a brake engine test from St.Pierre des Corps to Orlèans with the P-O dynamometer car and three P-O brake engines. The booked average speed was 70 kmph, the cut-off 18% and the regulator was fully opened. The average speed was 65.9 kmph, and the average power was 1253 HP. All bearings were cold.

Tuesday, February 5th

A similar brake engine trial to the previous day was carried out from Orlèans to St.Pierre des Corps at an average speed of 90 kmph and at 25% cut-off. The average HP was 1640 and the average speed was 82 kmph. The engine again ran cold.

Wednesday, February 6th

A third brake engine trial was made between St.Pierre des Corps and Orlèans at a booked speed of 110 kmph, and at 35% cut-off. The average speed was 80.7 kmph and the average HP was 1910. The engine again ran cold.

These three trials were successful as regards the way the engine behaved. It was impossible, however, to maintain the boiler pressure. The French enginemen considered our firehole door too small, especially for high rates of combustion. They also thought our fire shovel too small, involving the fireman in unnecessary labour.

Thursday, February 7th

The engine worked back to Vitry leaving St.Pierre at 10.15 am, and arrived back at the test plant at 2.30 pm, again cold in all bearings.

Friday, February 8th

The engine was brought to the plant at 9.0 am, and the whole of the morning was occupied in resetting the rollers to our wheelbase. The revised programme of tests was taken in hand. The first test was commenced at 2.30 pm at 90 kmph with an HP of 750. The cut-off and steam chest pressure selected by the driver to maintain these conditions were 18% and 125psi respectively. The engine ran the full two hours test satisfactorily in every way. At the end of the test the regulator was fully opened for a short time, when it was found that at 90 kmph, 1600HP was developed.

Saturday, February 9th

A test at 90 kmph and at 1600HP was commenced, but the steam pressure could not be maintained. Various methods of firing were tried without any better results. There was much clinker in the fire, and the test was stopped and the engine returned to shed at 1.30 pm.

Sunday February 10th

The boiler, which was rather dirty, was washed out, the tubes blown through, firebars lifted for cleaning out, ashpan wing plates and element ends cleaned. There was a considerable accumulation of birdnesting on the small tubes at the firebox end and several of the large tubes were badly blocked at the element ends, explaining the failure of the engine to steam properly.

The blastpipe was changed to 6 ins in diameter with the No.3 vee bars, as too much smoke was being made and a sharper blast was required for the higher horsepowers.

Monday, February 11th

The 1600 HP tests were again commenced at 90kmph. The ACFI installation was not working satisfactorily, and was losing too much water out of the heater through the de-oiler valve. Full steam pressure could not be maintained despite the larger vee bars, and although the test lasted 1 hour and 51 minutes, the average HP was only 1180 instead of 1600.

There was also considerable trouble with the slipping of the wheel on the rollers, especially at the leading coupled wheels, the rollers under which, at intervals, ceased to revolve. The effect of this slipping appeared to make the leading wheels oscillate laterally, as the thrust of the coupling rods moved over from side to side. The RH driving box ran slightly warm and the engine was stopped to allow it to cool down. After the midday break the RH driving box ran cold, and it was decided to repeat the 90 kmph and 1600HP test. The engine, however, again developed a tendency for the wheel to move over towards the right, and excessive vibration, especially at the leading and driving wheels, was set up. After the test had run for 27 minutes the LH leading axlebox again ran hot.

It was decided that this should be the last test, and the engine went into the P-O shops in preparation for its return to England.

Tuesday, February 12th & Wednesday, February 13th

The work of refitting the remetalled box proceeded at the P-O shops, while the whole of our material was being collected together and packed into the LNER box wagon. The engine returned to the test plant to be coaled and prepared for its journey to La Chapelle.

Thursday, February 14th

Final arrangements were being made for the engine to be exhibited at Gare du Nord at Paris, and it left Vitry together with the three coal wagons, box wagon and brake van for the Nord shops at La Chapelle at 10.30 am. On arrival at Villeneuve St.Georges, two coal wagons containing about 80 tons of coal were detached as M.Vallentin had agreed to take over this coal in order to carry out a trial on the PLM railway. The engine and the remaining wagons left Villeneuve for La Chapelle via Le Bourget, arriving in the Nord shops at 4.30 pm.

Friday, February 15th & Saturday, February 16th

The engine was thoroughly cleaned and prepared for exhibition in the Nord works at La Chapelle.

Sunday February 17th

At 8.30 am Engine No.2001, together with M.Besnerais' saloon and one of the Nord Super Pacifics, were placed for exhibition in No.1 platform of the Nord station. The exhibition was opened to the public at 11.30 am and until 7.0 pm there was a continual stream of visitors. During the afternoon one of the Maybach diesel-electric streamlined trains arrived on No.2 platform, and this remained on exhibition for the afternoon. The engine was taken back to the shops at La Chapelle.

Wednesday, February 20th

The engine left La Chapelle at 9.01 am for Calais with its train of three empty 40 ton wagons, a 10 ton covered goods wagon, and brake van, via Montdidier, Amiens and Etaples, arriving at 4.10 pm.

Thursday, February 21st

The Customs formalities were completed and the engine and stock loaded on to the train ferry in the early afternoon. The ferry left for Harwich that evening.

THE END

APPENDIX E. COMPARATIVE PACIFIC FRONT END DIMENSIONS, A1 and A2 classes compared with the A4 class.
The relevant drawings are too old and far too large to reproduce for comparison. In this Appendix I have included the analysis of the power developed in the three cylinders of ALCAZAR to show how the developed power can vary.
Dimensions taken from prints of the original elevations.

Dimensions (ins)	A4 SB	A4 DB	A2/2 &c DB	A2 SB	A2 DB	A1 DB
Buffer to smokebox door	76.75	76.75	63	57	57	59.75
Buffer to front tubeplate	154.00	154.00	173.75	151.50	151.50	175.00
Buffer to C/L leading bogie axle	58	58	51	60	60	60
Buffer to leading coupled axle	199.00	199.00	224.00	202.00	202.00	204.00
Front tubeplate to C/L blastpipe	41.75	48.00	71.25	62.25	62.25	83.50
Smokebox door to C/L blastpipe	35.50	29.25	39.50	32.25	32.25	32.50
Smokebox length	77.25	77.25	110.75	94.50	94.50	116.00
Smokebox saddle width	56.00	56.00	44.25	47.50	47.50	47.50
Smokebox saddle length	68.00	68.00	38.50	37.00	37.00	37.00
Front tubeplate to C/L outside cylinders	51.75	51.75	12.25	50.25	50.25	71.00
Front tubeplate to C/L inside cylinder	15.59	15.59	89.50	90.25	90.25	111.00
C/L outside to C/L inside cylinder	36.16	36.16	77.25	40.00	40.00	40.00
C/L outside cylinders to C/L blastpipe	10.00	16.25	59.00	12.00	12.00	12.00
C/L inside cylinder to C/L blastpipe (-ve: to the rear)	-26.16	-32.41	18.25	28.00	28.00	28.00
C/L inside cylinder to buffer face	138.41	138.41	84.25	61.25	61.25	64.00
Position of smokebox front relative to leading bogie axle	18.75	18.75	12.00	-3.00	-3.00	-1.00
Leading coupled axle to leading bogie axle	141.00	141.00	173.00	142.00	142.00	144.00

APPENDIX F: ENGINE DIAGRAMS FOR CLASSES A1 & A2 CIRCA 1955

The locomotive diagrams for the 1953-55 period have been set out to illustrate how the various locomotives were deployed. Kings Cross is omitted for the sound reason that they had neither A1s nor A2s allocated there at that time. I need to make the point that this is not an exhaustive list, and it is not based on an individual year. For example, at one time Heaton worked the first 'Tees-Tyne Pullman' services both ways, and Kings Cross A4s worked the first 'Bradford Flyers', but both duties were changed after a while. The railway varies from day to day with reliefs, trains cancelled, light engine running, troop trains etc, and it is intended to be illustrative rather than exact.

NEW ENGLAND (153 miles except where stated)
5.23 Aberdonian, Peterborough to Kings Cross
10.5 Kings Cross – Glasgow as far as Peterborough

6.01 ex-Aberdeen, Peterborough to Kings Cross
Return working varied, usually 10.40 semifast to Grantham, which was later terminated at P'boro.

7.25 Parley to Kings Cross
12.35 842dn, Kings Cross to York parcels as far as P'boro.

9.25 Parley to Kings Cross
14.35 262dn class C freight to P'boro.

11.47 ex Newcastle, P'boro to Kings Cross
16.15 Parley to Peterborough

17.05 Parley to Kings Cross (Usually a V2)
23.00 122dn, Kings Cross to York parcels as far as P'boro.

19.01 Parley to Kings Cross
00.55 Kings Cross-Edinburgh as far as Peterborough

02.28 (time at Peterborough)
00.55 Kings Cross-Edinburgh from Peterborough to York (224 miles)
14.40 Ex Glasgow, York-Peterborough.

GRANTHAM
4.13 Grantham to Kings Cross (first portion of the 'Night Scotsman')
10.00 'Flying Scotsman' Kings Cross to Grantham (later 9.40 Newcastle)
19.50 'Heart of Midlothian' from Grantham to Kings Cross
22.45 'Tynesider' Kings Cross to Grantham (422 miles)

12.03 'Flying Scotsman' Grantham to Newcastle returning on an overnight sleeper or Parcels (328 miles)

1.24 Grantham to Kings Cross (Sleeper)
5.45 'Parley' Kings Cross to Grantham
11.28 Grantham to Kings Cross

15.10 Kings Cross to Grantham. (422 miles)

13.52 Grantham to Kings Cross
19.00 'Aberdonian' Kings Cross to York
       Parcels to Grantham. (376 miles)

17.10 Grantham to Newcastle, returning on an overnight sleeper/parcels (328 miles)

 2.22 Grantham to Kings Cross (Sleeper)
6.45   'Parley' Kings Cross to Grantham
13.26 'Northumbrian' Grantham to Kings Cross
17.35 Kings Cross to Grantham. (422 miles)

In winter months the Gateshead A1 worked the first portion of the 'Night Scotsman', and so the Grantham engine worked the main train. Also as Kings Cross took over the summer working of the 'Flying Scotsman', the Grantham A1 dropped back on to the 9.40 Kings Cross to Newcastle.

COPLEY HILL (371 miles except where stated)
7.50   Leeds to Kings Cross 'West Riding'
15.45 Kings Cross to Leeds 'West Riding'

10.7   Harrogate to Kings Cross 'Yorkshire Pullman'
18.18 Kings Cross to Leeds

7.28   Leeds to Grantham (160 miles)
12.34 Grantham to Leeds

10.50 Glasgow, from Leeds to Kings Cross 'Queen of Scots' Pullman.
7.50   Kings Cross to Leeds SX, 9.18 'White Rose' SO
(Two A1s)

18.17 Bradford, from Leeds to Kings Cross.
12.05 Kings Cross to Leeds 'Queen of Scots' Pullman
(Two A1s)

ARDSLEY (371 miles)
19.30 Wakefield to Kings Cross (Parcels)
13.18 Kings Cross to Leeds

YORK
21.56 York to Kings Cross (Sleeper)
8.00   Kings Cross to York. (377 miles)

9.15   York to Kings Cross (Worked by a Doncaster A3 in some years)
15.50 Kings Cross to York (377 miles)

19.37 Cross-country from York to Newcastle
7.35   ex Aberdeen, from Newcastle to York (160 miles)

(A2)
10.5 York to Newcastle
15.57 Newcastle to York cross country (160 miles)

11.10 York Dringhouses to Newcastle (Goods)
3.15 Heaton Up Yd to York Up Yd (Goods) (164 miles)

(A2)
17.10 York to Darlington
19.17 Darlington to York (Parcels)
00.03 York to Grantham (Parcels)
7.33 Grantham to York (Parcels) (254 miles)

(A2)
1.09 York to Newcastle (Mail)
5.35 Heaton Up Yd to York Dringhouses (Goods)
13.40 York to Newcastle
17.30 Newcastle Park Lane to York Dringhouses (Goods) (324 miles)

GATESHEAD
(Two A1s)
1.20 Newcastle to Kings Cross ('Night Scotsman')
22.15 Kings Cross to Newcastle ('Night Scotsman') (536 miles)
(See above note for Grantham ref 'Night Scotsman'

11.21 Newcastle to Edinburgh ('North Briton')
17.14 Edinburgh to Newcastle ('North Briton') (249 miles)

4.16 Newcastle to Edinburgh (Sleeper)
10.00 Edinburgh to Newcastle ('Flying Scotsman')
19.05 Newcastle to York
23.00 York to Newcastle ('Aberdonian') (329 miles)

2.20 Newcastle to Edinburgh (Parcels)
10.27 Edinburgh to Newcastle (249 miles)

23.20 Newcastle to York
6.40 York to Edinburgh (Parcels)
16.35 Edinburgh to Newcastle (Fish) (410 miles)

(A2)
11.50 Newcastle to Edinburgh (Parcels)
17.35 Edinburgh to York (Fish)
1.35 York to Newcastle (Parcels) (410 miles)

(A2)
19.54 Newcastle to Grantham (Goods)
2.13 Grantham to Newcastle ('Tynesider') (328 miles)

(A2)
9.35 Delaval to York (ECS)
16.00 York to Doncaster (ECS)
17.45 Doncaster to Peterborough Westwood (ECS)
2.28 Peterborough to Newcastle (Sleeper) (384 miles)

(A4)
2.34 Newcastle to Peterborough (Sleeper)
11.40 Peterborough to Newcastle (384 miles)

(A4)
12.30 Newcastle to Grantham ('Flying Scotsman')
19.44 Grantham to Newcastle (328 miles)

(A4)
16.35 Newcastle to Grantham ('Heart of Midlothian')
1.14 Grantham to Newcastle (Sleeper) (328 miles)

HEATON
5.47 Heaton Carr Sidings to Sunderland (ECS)
7.53 Sunderland to Grantham
14.26 Grantham to Newcastle ('Northumbrian') (330 miles)

12.37 Newcastle to York
16.20 York to Newcastle via Sunderland
22.30 Newcastle to York
3.50 York to Newcastle via Sunderland (340 miles)

8.15 Newcastle to York
11.30 York Yd to Heaton (Goods)
17.40 Newcastle to Edinburgh ('Queen of Scots' Pullman)
22.40 Edinburgh to Newcastle ('Night Scotsman') (332 miles)

(A2)
6.58 Newcastle to York
11.30 York to Newcastle
16.18 Newcastle to Edinburgh
11.53 Edinburgh to Newcastle (Parcels) (410 miles)

7.35? Newcastle to Leeds City
15.20 Leeds Central to Newcastle (Queen of Scots) (170 miles)

HAYMARKET
10.10 Edinburgh to Newcastle
15.06 Newcastle to Edinburgh ('Flying Scotsman')
22.20 Edinburgh to Newcastle (Sleeper)
2.42 Newcastle to Edinburgh (498 miles)

12.00 Edinburgh to Newcastle ('Queen of Scots' Pullman)
15.36 Newcastle to Edinburgh

23.20 Edinburgh to Newcastle
3.35 Newcastle to Edinburgh ('Night Scotsman') (498 miles)

14.00 Edinburgh to Newcastle ('Heart of Midlothian')
19.23 Newcastle to Edinburgh ('Heart of Midlothian') (249 miles)

19.20 Edinburgh to Newcastle (Parcels)
00.38 Newcastle to Edinburgh ('Aberdonian') (249 miles)

23.00 Edinburgh to Newcastle ('Aberdonian') (249 miles)
3.04 Newcastle to Edinburgh (Mail)

20.00 Edinburgh to Newcastle (Sleeper) (249 miles)
00.53 Newcastle to Edinburgh (Sleeper)

APPENDIX G.
LOGS OF RUNS WITH CLASSES A1, A2 variants and P2s
Published runs from the principal sources, 'Trains Illustrated' and 'Railway Magazine'.

BR No LOCO	Tons LOAD	MILES	Mins SCH.	Mins ACT.	Mins NET	MPH ACTUAL	MPH NET	D/U	MAG	DATE
60151	350	76.35	83.0	78.00	75.00	58.73	61.08	D		
60154	405	76.35	79.0	69.17	69.17	66.23	66.23	D	T	5808
60156	385	76.35	78.0	83.25	73.00	55.03	62.75	D	T	5904
60156	385	76.35	78.0	81.25	76.00	56.38	60.28	D		
60157	400	76.35	80.0	74.47	71.50	61.52	64.07	D	T	6002
60500	470	76.35	78.0	83.25	79.00	55.03	57.99	D		
60128	470	105.45	123.0	119.00	111.00	53.17	57.00	U		
60148	460	105.45	123.0	109.92	103.00	57.56	61.43	D	R	5307
60149	430	105.45	112.0	110.05	109.00	57.49	58.05	D	T	5512
60156	490	105.45	122.0	118.52	113.00	53.38	55.99	D	R	5201
60157	340	105.45	104.5	101.87	101.87	62.11	62.11	D	T	5807
60158	515	105.45	122.0	115.38	108.00	54.83	58.58	U	R	5706
60114	330	29.10	31.0	26.78	26.78	65.19	65.19	U	T	6109
60125	285	29.10	30.0	27.63	26.00	63.18	67.15	U	T	6002
60125	320	29.10	31.0	25.93	25.93	67.33	67.33	U		6302
60126	470	29.10	34.0	27.77	27.77	62.88	62.88	D	T	5509
60128	500	29.10	33.0	35.17	32.00	49.64	54.56	U	R	5307
60148	450	29.10	33.0	27.50	27.50	63.49	63.49	U	R	5508
60151	350	29.10	33.0	28.98	28.50	60.24	61.26	U	R	5307
60155	360	29.10	33.0	27.67	27.67	63.10	63.10	U	R	5307
60157	470	29.10	34.0	32.58	32.58	53.59	53.59	D	RW	5902
60117	355	106.70	96.5	95.25	93.00	67.21	68.84	D	R	5611
60117	360	106.70	89.0	99.28	92.50	64.48	69.21	D		6201
60117	355	106.70	96.5	91.75	91.75	69.78	69.78	D	R	5611
60117	360	106.70	96.5	107.00	90.50	59.83	70.74	D	R	5611
60117	370	106.70	89.0	104.43	89.50	61.30	71.53	D	T	6110
60119	355	106.70	96.5	99.47	92.00	64.36	69.59	D	R	5410
60120	350	106.70	96.5	94.07	90.25	68.06	70.94	D	R	5410
60123	360	106.70	89.0	92.52	90.50	69.20	70.74	D	T	6307
60130	355	106.70	96.5	104.53	92.50	61.24	69.21	D	R	5410
60130	360	106.70	96.5	107.10	90.50	59.78	70.74	D	R	5611
60134	360	106.70	96.5	96.50	93.50	66.34	68.47	D	R	5410
60141	350	106.70	96.5	94.00	94.00	68.11	68.11	D	R	5410
60148	365	106.70	96.5	96.00	93.00	66.69	68.84	D	R	
60119	250	124.05	113.0	115.72	106.50	64.32	69.89	D	R	5311
60131	250	124.05	113.0	114.88	108.00	64.79	68.92	D	R	5311
60139	255	124.05	113.0	113.02	109.50	65.86	67.97	D	R	5311
60141	255	124.05	113.0	113.72	108.00	65.45	68.92	D	R	5311
60133	380	155.95	160.0	154.83	151.00	60.43	61.97	D		
60148	400	155.95	170.0	159.80	159.80	58.55	58.55	D	R	5806
60156	385	155.95	170.0	164.95	144.50	56.73	64.75	U	T	6110
60158	395	155.95	170.0	165.62	155.75	56.50	60.08	D		6209
60526	335	155.95	169.0	172.67	133.00	54.19	70.35	U	R	6103
60118	380	185.80	199.0	203.53	176.00	54.77	63.34	U	R	5405
60123	450	185.80	195.0	192.88	176.50	57.80	63.16	D	R	5311
60133	380	185.80	195.0	192.33	177.00	57.96	62.98	D	R	5503
60133	425	185.80	215.0	236.00	191.00	47.24	58.37	U		
60139	380	185.80	195.0	193.63	180.50	57.57	61.76	D	R	5503
60140	325	188.15	193.0	169.20	158.00	66.72	71.45	U	R	5903
60126	470	111.80	122.0	117.98	105.75	56.86	63.43	D	T	5509
60155	515	82.70	91.0	89.48	85.00	55.45	58.38	U	R	5706
60157	430	82.70	87.0	97.57	84.00	50.86	59.07	D	T	5512
60503	440	82.70	93.0	89.02	85.00	55.74	58.38	D	R	
60122	490	162.90	186.0	182.18	175.00	53.65	55.85	D	R	5201
60113	485	44.15	41.0	42.17	42.17	62.82	62.82	D	R	5407
60156	295	44.15	41.0	38.13	38.13	69.47	69.47	U	R	5811
60501	355	44.15	41.0	39.57	39.57	66.95	66.95	D	R	5407
60502	220	44.15	40.5	37.22	37.22	71.18	71.18	U		
60502	220	44.15	38.0	36.42	35.75	72.74	74.10	U	R	5502
60512	365	44.15	43.0	39.50	39.50	67.06	67.06	U	R	5407
60513	455	44.15	41.0	42.30	42.30	62.62	62.62	D	R	5407
60515	480	44.15	44.0	42.37	40.00	62.53	66.23	D		
60521	375	44.15	41.0	41.18	41.18	64.32	64.32	D	R	5407
60524	370	44.15	45.0	40.10	40.10	66.06	66.06	D	R	5312
60524	380	44.15	41.0	36.48	36.48	72.61	72.61	U	R	5811
60513	395	80.20	88.0	80.15	79.00	60.04	60.91	D	R	5607
60149	320	268.25	278.0	266.00	247.00	60.51	65.16	U		
60156	435	268.25	285.0	293.00	266.00	54.93	60.51	D	RW	5907
60124	495	124.45	147.0	144.73	129.75	51.59	57.55	U	R	5405
60127	355	124.45	136.0	129.67	125.00	57.58	59.74	D	T	5210
60127	355	124.45	136.0	141.43	120.00	52.80	62.23	D	T	5210
60159	320	124.45	126.0	130.32	112.75	57.30	66.23	D		6209
60511	355	124.45	135.0	124.28	120.50	60.08	61.97	D	R	5201
60511	355	124.45	137.0	124.28	120.00	60.08	62.23	D	T	5210
60519	325	124.45	128.0	121.62	120.00	61.40	62.23	U		
60538	330	124.45	150.0	142.75	140.00	52.31	53.34	D	R	5607
60137	370	57.50	65.0	62.58	62.58	55.13	55.13	U	R	5607
60507	410	57.50	62.0	59.82	59.82	57.68	57.68	D	R	5607
60509	375	57.50	62.0	64.38	59.50	53.59	57.98	D	R	5607
60154	280	95.20	115.0	99.60	95.00	57.35	60.13	U	R	5201
60161	420	66.90	80.0	81.33	75.00	49.35	53.52	D	R	5201
2001	510	59.20	85.0	86.28	86.28	41.17	41.17	U	R	1/36
2001	530	59.20	85.0	84.95	84.95	41.81	41.81	U	R	1/36
2001	540	59.20	85.0	86.37	86.37	41.13	41.13	U	R	1/36
2001	550	71.30	103.0	92.52	92.52	46.24	46.24	U		
2002	510	16.20	25.0	22.42	22.42	43.36	43.36	U	R	6005
2002	510	54.40	79.00	77.63	77.63	42.05	42.05	U	R	1/36
2002	515	54.40	80.0	76.20	76.20	42.83	42.83	U	R	1/36
2002	530	54.40	80.0	75.98	75.98	42.96	42.96	U	R	1/36
2002	515	54.40	82.0	75.30	75.30	43.34	43.34	U	R	1/36
60527	400	71.30	100.0	92.42	83.50	46.29	51.23	U	T	5904
60529	400	71.30	101.0	95.80	94.00	44.66	45.51	U	R	5607

Note: The date column has the year followed by the month so that 5307 indicates July 1953.
The mileages (third column) indicate where the runs took place:
76.35: Kings Cross-Peterborough
105.45: to Grantham
29.10: Peterboro-Grantham
106.7: Hitchin-Retford
124.05: Hitchin-Doncaster
155.95: Kings Cross-Doncaster
185.8: Kings Cross-Leeds Central
111.80: Peterboro-York
82.70: Grantham-York
162.90: Grantham-Newcastle
44.15: York-Darlington
80.2: York-Newcastle
268.25: Kings Cross-Newcastle
124.45: Newcastle-Edinburgh
57.5:Berwick-Edinburgh
66.9: Symington-Carlisle
59.2: Edinburgh-Dundee
71.3: Dundee-Aberdeen
16.2 and 54.4: parts of the Dundee-Aberdeen divided at Stonehaven
95.2: Newcastle-Dunbar

Appendix H Performance
(a) Mikado High Power

APPENDIX H. These are some estimated performances on Stoke Bank by COCK O'THE NORTH and a number of A1s. Again, these are intended to be illustrative rather than precise. At high rates of working a difference of 1mph on a heavy train can throw the calculation out by 50-100 HP, so although exact figures are shown, they may be up to at least 100 HP out if not more. The record of No.2001 is based in the speeds known with the times estimated. Likewise SIR VINCENT RAVEN, where the speeds were known but not the passing times. The four records showing the best of Copley Hill's work are based on the published times and speeds. The record of BONGRACE is based on speeds read from the dynamometer car roll, but the calculated and measured DBHP and EDBHPs differ by large amounts, as I indicated above. Therefore I have shown the estimated horsepowers, then the *measured* EDBHP, and the IHP calculated from the measured EDBHP plus the power consumed in moving the locomotive. It may be that 2,900-3,000 IHP was developed briefly but without firmer information we cannot tell.

I would take it kindly if nobody writes to tell me or Irwell Press that my arithmetic is unreliable or inaccurate. We both know that. As I have stated before, a considerable effort has gone into making this record reasonably accurate otherwise. If it is not, I must apologise. Otherwise, enjoy reading about some remarkable locomotives. We have BLUE PETER to remind us of the A2s, but when TORNADO is running, those who never saw the A1s in action will be able to see and experience how good they were and how impressive they looked. Fitting heirs to the Gresley tradition.

P2 2001 COCK O' THE NORTH Test Train 649 tons

Miles	Location	Mins	Secs	Speed mph	Av. Sp mph	DBHP	EDBHP	IHP
76.35	PETERBOROUGH. NTH	0	0	0.0	0	0	0	0
79.5	Werrington Jct	6	0	63.0	31.5	1905	2141	2625
81.95	Helpston	8	20	65.0	63.0	1222	1267	1776
84.85	Tallington	11	5	65.0	63.3	1240	1290	1797
88.65	Essendine	14	40	60.0	63.6	1313	1422	1863
92.25	Little Bytham	18	16	60.0	60.0	1394	1522	1962
97.1	Corby Glen	23	7	60.0	60.0	1697	1900	2337
100.1	Stoke	26	12	56.5	58.4	1913	2194	2589
102.1	Gt. Ponton	28	12	65.0	60.0	280	92	587
105.45	GRANTHAM	34	0	0.0	34.7	0	0	0

Mileage ex-Kings Cross

(b) Notable A1 Performance

Miles	Location	60126 480 tons			60148 460 tons			60117 360 tons			60130 360 tons				60134 360 tons		
		Mins	Secs	mph	Mins	Secs	mph	Mins	Secs	mph	mph	Mins	Secs	mph	Mins	Secs	mph
0	PETERBOROUGH. NTH	0	0	0.0	0	0	0	0	0	0	Pass	0	0	Pass	0	0	Pass
3.15	Werrington Jct	5	59	56.0	6	7	60	4	24	62		4	58	60	4	11	63
5.6	Helpston	8	11	69.0	8	17	69.5	6	27	68		7	15	68	6	23	70
8.5	Tallington	10	39	76.5	10	46	75	9	0	73		9	48	72	8	51	75
12.3	Essendine	13	39	78.0	13	47	75	12	8	72		13	0	72	11	59	72
15.9	Little Bytham	16	30	74.0	16	38	72	15	7	68		16	2	68	15	1	70
20.75	Corby Glen	20	39	73.0	20	42	73	19	23	69		20	20	70.5	19	26	67
23.75	Stoke	23	18	67.0	23	17	67.5	22	7	65		22	53	70.5	22	9	66.5
25.75	Gt. Ponton	24	56	72.0	24	55	74				15 tsr	24	24	80.5			
29.1	GRANTHAM	27	46	60.0	28	44	0	29	4	68		27	5	72	26	47	69

60126 SIR VINCENT RAVEN
Loco wt 165.55 tons
Train gross wt 470 tons

Ht	Miles	Location	Mins	Secs	Speed mph	Av. Sp mph	DBHP	EDBHP	IHP
92	76.35	PETERBOROUGH. NTH	0	0	0.0	0	0	0	0
89	79.5	Werrington Jct	5	59	56.0	31.6	1083	1268	1665
94	81.95	Helpston	8	20	69.0	62.6	1341	1508	2069
106	84.85	Tallington	10	44	76.5	72.5	1503	1649	2323
154	88.65	Essendine	13	40	78.0	77.7	1694	1889	2585
196	92.25	Little Bytham	16	30	74.0	76.2	1350	1469	2096
286	97.1	Corby Glen	20	30	70.0	72.7	1502	1712	2276
375	100.1	Stoke	23	8	67.0	68.4	1781	2112	2632
326	102.1	Gt. Ponton	24	50	72.0	70.6	231	-10	579
247	105.45	GRANTHAM	27	46	60.0	68.5	-377	-719	-290

60130 KESTREL
Loco wt 165.55 tons
Train gross wt 360 tons

Ht	Miles	Location	Mins	Secs	Speed mph	Av. Sp mph	DBHP	EDBHP	IHP
92	76.35	PETERBOROUGH. NTH	0	0	15.0	0	0	0	0
89	79.5	Werrington Jct	5	59	60.0	31.6	833	991	1438
94	81.95	Helpston	8	18	65.0	63.5	747	824	1332
106	84.85	Tallington	10	49	72.0	69.1	1007	1137	1743
154	88.65	Essendine	14	1	72.0	71.3	1093	1260	1864
196	92.25	Little Bytham	17	3	68.0	71.2	887	1000	1542
286	97.1	Corby Glen	21	21	70.5	67.7	1256	1509	2084
375	100.1	Stoke	23	54	70.5	70.6	1541	1921	2494
326	102.1	Gt. Ponton	25	25	80.5	79.1	558	394	1124
247	105.45	GRANTHAM	28	6	72.0	74.9	-156	-544	46

60128 BONGRACE AN ALL-OUT EFFORT (Loco wt 165.55 tons, Train gross wt 465 tons)										
Miles	Location	Est'd Mins	Est'd Secs	Speed mph	Av. Sp mph	Est'd DBHP	Est'd EDBHP	Est'd IHP	EDBHP actual	IHP calc'd
0	GRANTHAM	0	0	0.0		0	0	0	0	0
					33.5					
3.35	Gt. Ponton	6	0	52.0		2153	2563	2916	2350	2703
					54.5					
5.35	Stoke	8	12	57.0		1579	1886	2292	2150	2556
					71.1					
8.35	Corby Glen	10	44	82.0		1678	1529	2297	2000	2768
					87.3					
9.95	MP 95.5	11	50	90.0		1867	1737	2658	1900	2821

(c) fast Running by A1s

Three notable runs by A1s on the fastest East Coast main line up expresses of the late 1950s are summarised here. Two are Guard's journal extracts of runs by Bill Hoole on the up Tees-Tyne Pullman and the down Talisman, and for comparison, Dick Turner's remarkable run on the up Talisman is set alongside in similar fashion. The latter exists in a far more detailed form of course. From the times recorded it is clear that some notable work was done, but a sequence of accurately recorded passing times and speeds would be essential for the performances to be analysed properly. The first run was with 60149 AMADIS hauling 8 Pullmans, 340 tons gross, and the second was with 60140 BALMORAL hauling 325 tons, the A1 having deputised for a failed diesel locomotive. In the down run, SIR NIGEL GRESLEY failed, alas, and coincidentally, BALMORAL was on hand to take over, spectacularly so north of York.

NB. RT is right time, BT is before time.

LOCOMOTIVE	60149			60140		
TRAIN	9.25 dep N'cle			16.00 dep Edinboro		
LOAD	325/340			308/325		
DATE	14/05/1957			Nov-58		
LOCATION	TIME	+/-		TIME	+/-	
Newcastle dep	9.25	RT				
Durham	9.42	RT				
Ferryhill	9.54	2-	TSR			
Darlington arr	10.11	5-				
dep	10.13	5-				
Northallerton	10.27	5-		(Loco change York)		
York	10.49	2-		19.51	26-	dep
Shaftholme Jct	11.14	4BT		20.17.5	21.5-	
Doncaster	11.18	4BT		20.21	20-	
Retford	11.36	3BT	TSR	20.38.5	21.5-	Sigs 20
Newark	11.55	1BT		20.52.5	19.5	
Grantham	12.12	3-	TSR	21.04	14-	
Peterborough	12.39	1BT		21.26.5	10.5-	Sigs 10
Huntingdon	12.56	1BT		21.45	12-	TSR 20
Hitchin	13.18	1BT		22.07	13-	TSR 30
Hatfield	13.32	1BT		22.18	7-	
Finsbury Park	13.46	12BT		22.33	2-	
Kings Cross	13.51	12BT		22.4	2-	

The running time for the first run is 266 minutes, but the net running time is difficult to estimate. The guard booked 12 minutes lost, but in reality it would be nearer 16-18. A 20 mph TSR normally cost about four minutes with a moderate load, and the length of TSRs was increasing to over 1,000 yards and more. My estimate is 248 minutes. With the second run the gross time was just over 169 mins, and the net time, allowing for the stop at York instead of passing through, is 158 mins, four minutes less than the Coronation, although once again it would depend very much on the length and nature of the TSRs and signal checks.

The third run has emerged from records of Passenger Train Journals, and once again BALMORAL gave an impressive demonstration of the A1's capacity for speed when put to it. The times from York northwards are quite possibly as fast as any with steam, even with a light train such as this. Allowing for the light train and the Cowton TSR, a 33 min pass to pass time from York to Darlington would indicate a likely maximum of over 90mph maintained for some way, while further north I have no doubt that the speed limits were observed in the breach rather than the rule! Clearly Bill was not inhibited by any deficiencies in the A1's riding!

LOCOMOTIVE	60007		
CHANGED TO	60140		
TRAIN	16.00 dep Edinboro		
LOAD	240/260		
DATE	14/05/1957		
LOCATION	TIME	+/-	
Kings Cross	16.00	RT	
Hatfield	16.22.5	RT	
Hitchin	16.35.5	2.5BT	
Huntingdon	16.54.5	2.5BT	
Peterborough	17.15	3BT	Sigs Werr'n
Grantham arr	17.57.5	12-	TSR & Sigs
Change Loco dep	18.10.5	25-	
Newark	18.27	27-	TSR Trent 20mph
Retford	18.41	26-	
Doncaster	18.55.5	18-	
Shaftholme Jct	18.59	17-	
York	19.24	15-	
Northallerton	19.44	14-	TSR Cowton 20mph
Darlington	20.00	13-	
Newcastle arr	20.31	3-	
No.60140			
Grantham-Newcastle			
Booked pass to stop	154.5		
Gross	140.5		
Net	132		
York -Darlington			
Booked pass to stop	38		
Gross	36		
Net	33		
Net Average	80mph approx		

229

(d) Comparative Performance between A1, A2 and A4 Pacifics

TABLE I TESTING OF A1 and A2 COMPARED WITH A4	A4	A1	%	A2	%	A1	%	A2	%
Miles	2845.90	743.00		743.00		843.60		843.60	
Load (tons)	486.96	497.63	2.19	486.00	-0.20	608.16	24.89	612.00	25.68
Time booked	4339.00	934.00		934.00		992.00		992.00	
Actual time	4414.30	936.02		935.50		988.57		996.06	
Average speed booked	39.35	47.73	21.29	47.73	21.29	51.02	29.66	51.02	29.66
Average speed actual	38.68	47.63	23.12	47.65	23.19	51.20	32.36	50.82	31.37
Average DBHP under power	750.00	803.00	7.07	776.00	3.47	1031.00	37.47	996.00	32.80
Av.coal consumption (lbs/mile)	41.00	40.20	-1.95	40.65	-0.85	47.50	15.86	44.50	8.54
Av.coal consumption (lbs/DBHP.Hr)	3.08	2.97	-3.51	3.03	-1.56	2.87	-6.79	2.81	-8.71
Av.water consumption (galls/mile)	32.46	31.98	-1.48	31.45	-3.11	35.80	10.29	34.78	7.15
Av.water consumption (lbs/DBHP.Hr)	24.35	23.64	-2.92	23.38	-3.99	21.32	-12.45	21.65	-11.09

CLASS P2/1

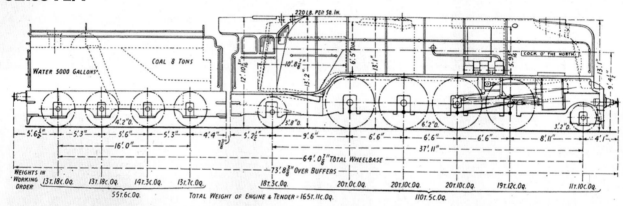

CLASS P2/2 and P2/3

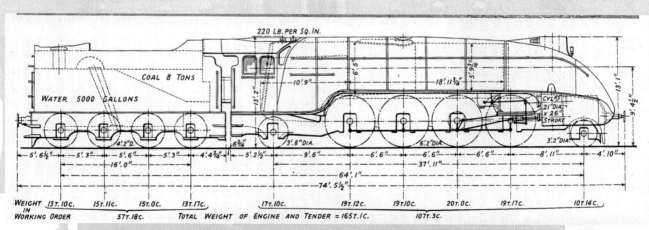

CLASS A1

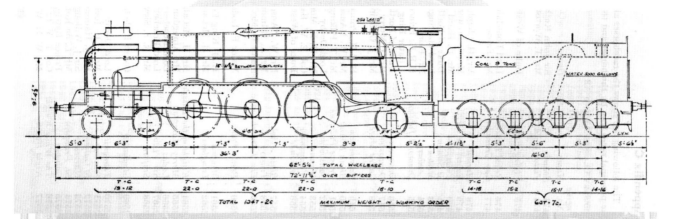

CLASS A2

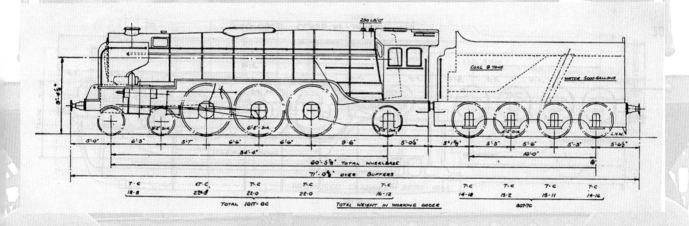

CLASS A2/1

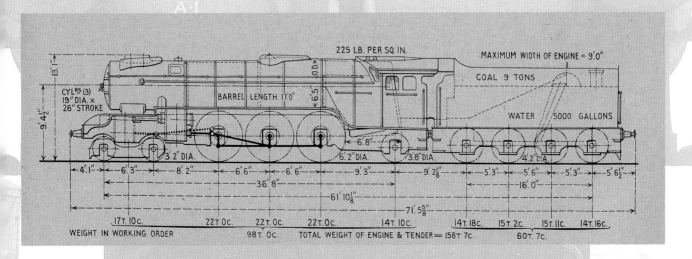

CLASS A2/2

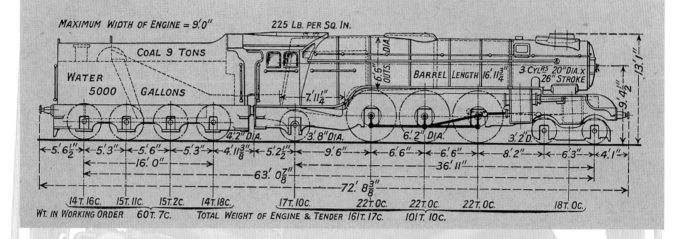

MAXIMUM WIDTH OF ENGINE = 9'.0"   225 LB. PER SQ. IN.

COAL 9 TONS

WATER 5000 GALLONS

3 CYL^{RS} 20" DIA. x 26" STROKE

BARREL LENGTH 16'.11¾"

6.5" OUTS DIA.

13'.1"

9'.4½"

7'.11¼"

4.2" DIA.   3'.8" DIA.   6'.2" DIA.   3'.2" D.

5'.6½"   5'.3"   5'.6"   5'.3"   4'.11⅜"   5'.2½"   9'.6"   6'.6"   6'.6"   8'.2"   6'.3"   4'.1"

16'.0"   36'.11"

63'.0⅞"

72'.8¾"

14 T. 16 C.   15 T. 11 C.   15 T. 2 C.   14 T. 18 C.   17 T. 10 C.   22 T. 0 C.   22 T. 0 C.   22 T. 0 C.   18 T. 0 C.

WT. IN WORKING ORDER 60 T. 7 C.   TOTAL WEIGHT OF ENGINE & TENDER 161 T. 17 C.   101 T. 10 C.

CLASS A2/3

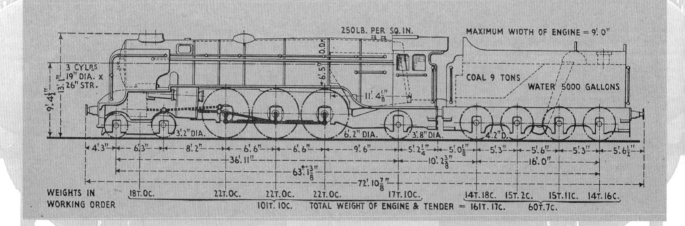

250 LB. PER SQ. IN.   MAXIMUM WIDTH OF ENGINE = 9'.0"

3 CYL^{RS} 19" DIA. x 26" STR.

6.5" .0.D

11'.4⅛"

13'.1"

9'.4½"

COAL 9 TONS   WATER 5000 GALLONS

3.2" DIA.   6'.2" DIA.   3'.8" DIA.   4.2" D.

4'.3"   6'.3"   8'.2"   6'.6"   6'.6"   9'.6"   5'.2¼"   5'.0⅛"   5'.3"   5'.6"   5'.3"   5'.6½"

36'.11"   10'.2⅜"   16'.0"

63'.1³⁄₈"

72'.10⅞"

18 T. 0 C.   22 T. 0 C.   22 T. 0 C.   22 T. 0 C.   17 T. 10 C.   14 T. 18 C.   15 T. 2 C.   15 T. 11 C.   14 T. 16 C.

WEIGHTS IN WORKING ORDER   101 T. 10 C.   TOTAL WEIGHT OF ENGINE & TENDER = 161 T. 17 C.   60 T. 7 C.